Law and Economics of International Telecommunications

Under the Auspices of the
Max Planck Institute for Foreign and International Private Law
edited by Ernst-Joachim Mestmäcker

Volume 4

Prof. Stephen R. Barnett
Prof. Michael Botein
Prof. Eli M. Noam

Law of International Telecommunications in the United States

Nomos Verlagsgesellschaft
Baden-Baden

CIP-Titelaufnahme der Deutschen Bibliothek

Barnett, Stephen R.:
Law of International Telecommunications in the United States / Stephen R. Barnett; Michael Botein; Eli M. Noam. – 1. Aufl. – Baden-Baden: Nomos Verl.-Ges., 1988
(Law and Economics of International Telecommunications; Vol. 4)
ISBN 3-7890-1308-0
NE: Botein, Michael; Noam, Eli M.; GT

1. Auflage 1988

Editor's Preface

This book on the »Law of International Telecommunications in the United States« is part of an ongoing research project on the international communications system undertaken at the Max Planck Institute for Foreign and International Private Law in Hamburg. Like similar reports on other countries, this report is based upon questionnaires prepared at the Institute and reproduced at the end of the volume. The questionnaires are identical for all countries in order to facilitate comparative evaluations of the national reports. They serve as guidelines without, however, interfering with the authors' individual judgment in adapting their presentation to the special national situation. The project will include comparative analyses of key problem areas and the examination of the role of international organizations, the task of which is the facilitation of international communications.

The Max Planck Institute is most grateful for the cooperation of Professors Stephen R. Barnett, Michael Botein and Eli M. Noam. Professor Barnett, A.B., 1957, LL.B., 1962, Harvard University, is a professor of law at the University of California, Berkeley. Professor Botein, B.A., 1966, Wesleyan University; J.D., 1969, Cornell University; LL.M., 1972, J.S.D., 1979, Columbia University, is a professor of law at the New York Law School. Professor Noam, A.B., 1970, A.M., 1970, J.D., 1975, Ph.D., 1975, Harvard University, is director of the Center for Telecommunications and Information Studies at the Columbia University Graduate School of Business.

We gratefully acknowledge a grant from the Volkswagen Foundation, which made this Report possible. We also extend thanks to Paul Aliferis, J.D. for his editorial assistance.

Table of Contents

PART II: REGULATION OF MASS MEDIA

PART I: REGULATION OF COMMON CARRIERS

by *Michael Botein and Eli M. Noam**

* The authors gratefully acknowledge the contributions of Leslie Taylor, Esq. in preparing Chapter II, and of Mr. W. Edward Singletary in preparing Chapter III.

Introduction

Inspired by Lockean principles of natural law, classic American ideology seeks individualism, fragmentation of private power, limitation of government (with the notable exception of guaranteeing physical security) and protection of property rights and contracts. As applied to communications policy, this philosophy has justified a governmental role that is far narrower than in most other countries and has based government's residual role largely on the grounds of market failure and national security.

Market failure exists when the traditional competitive mechanisms for limiting economic power cannot operate, due to the peculiarities of an industry. In the case of telecommunications, these pecularities include: the absence of property rights in the electromagnetic spectrum; the natural-monopoly characteristics often found in telecommunications networks; and the public-good externalities of universal service.

Until the mid-1970s, these were the fundamental goals of U.S. telecommunications policy. More recent trends, however, have shifted them in two contradictory directions. On the one hand, many of the market-failure arguments have been discarded as either inherently flawed or obsolete through technological change and entrepreneurial initiative. On the other hand, national-security arguments have become more important to U.S. policy makers.

For many other Western countries, however, the trends have been the opposite. National security concerns now have a lower priority, while a government's role in telecommunications often has become the foundation for industrial policy in the electronics field.[1]

There have been other divergences. U.S. efforts to protect individual privacy have been applied vigorously against the state but not as against private parties. The U.S. Constitution only occasionally applies.[2] Protections are mostly by adaptation of the common law or by heterogeneous state legislation dealing with specific abuses.[3] Many other Western countries reverse these priorities; they are vigilant about private power and often more tolerant of government authority.

The United States thus has diverged from European countries recently in

1 *E.g.*, S. NORA & A. MINC, L'INFORMATISATION DE LA SOCIÉTÉ (1978).
2 *E.g.*, Griswold v. Connecticut, 381 U.S. 479 (1965).
3 *E.g.*, A. WESTIN, PRIVACY AND FREEDOM (1967).

its general outlook on basic telecommunications policy, as it has moved from a somewhat social-democratic New Deal to a marketplace ideology. Since no country is an ideological island, this has led to problems of adjustment and coordination. An excellent example of this is the international flow of electronic information, at present subject to several multilateral harmonization efforts.

To shed light on this area, it is necessary to understand the rules governing information flows in the United States. This survey describes U.S. regulatory policies for those information flows using telephone, telegraph and other point-to-point communications, excluding the mass media. It begins with a survey of the basic regulatory scheme and is followed by a discussion of regulations in areas such as national security, privacy, common law and statutory restrictions. A host of other U.S. domestic laws – such as stock-trading regulations and the Uniform Commercial Code as to sales of goods – potentially impact on international information flows. But coverage of all these topics would require a multi-volume treatise. This survey thus focuses upon the domestic U.S. legal and regulatory structures and some of their aspects that impact on international telecommunications – export licensing, national security and privacy statutes.

This piece distinguishes between conduit and content – i.e., between medium and message – in examining U.S. restrictions on international telecommunications. It begins by reviewing U.S. regulatory and economic restrictions on the methods of point-to-point transmission into or out of the United States. It then considers a wide variety of piecemeal limitations on the content of these information flows.

The survey concludes that U.S. governmental control over the channels of communication is rapidly disappearing, that various common-law and regulatory restrictions also are declining and that national-security concerns apply more strictly than before.

Chapter I: The U.S. Carrier System

A. *Overview*

The basic framework of government involvement in U.S. telecommunications is simple in theory and complex in reality. The public sector does not own or operate civilian telecommunications services, except for a few small municipally-owned cable television operations, rural telephone systems and educational television broadcasting stations.

Although almost all civilian telecommunications facilities are privately owned, their use is often – but not always – subject to licensing and regulatory oversight. These regulations are set on the federal, state and, occasionally, local levels.

Federal policy emanates mainly from the Federal Communications Commission (FCC), a body of five commissioners appointed by the president but independent of that office. It operates as a hybrid within the American constitutional order, with some legislative powers (adoption of regulations), some executive authority (enforcement of its rules) and some judicial powers (adjudication of cases). The Commission allocates frequencies and regulates all broadcasting, satellite and other civilian uses of the electromagnetic spectrum.[4] The FCC is also in charge of *inter*state telephony – that is, transmissions from one state to another – and everything affecting interstate communications. The FCC has some jurisdiction over cable television.[5]

State regulatory commissions, which also are usually independent in status, play an important role in regulating *intra*state telephone and, in some instances, also cable television.[6] Municipal authorities regulate cable television through their powers to grant franchises to lay cable in their streets.[7]

On the executive level, the Commerce Department's National Telecommunications and Information Agency (NTIA) helps to coordinate the presi-

4 47 U.S.C. §§ 214, 301 (1982).
5 *E.g.*, FCC v. Midwest Cable Co., 440 U.S. 369 (1979).
6 *E.g.*, N.Y. Exec. Law § 811 *et seq.* (1979).
7 *E.g.*, New York City Charter § 362 (1985).

dent's – that is, the executive branch's – overall telecommunications policy. It plays a role in international communications, together with the Office of the U.S. Trade Representative and the State Department, which is the lead agency in international negotiations.[8] Despite its international visibility, the NTIA cannot match the FCC's domestic regulatory powers.

In addition, the executive branch's Department of Justice plays a major role through its Antitrust Division, which oversees much of the telephone industry by way of enforcing the 1982 court order that broke up AT&T.[9] The primary authority in that case is federal district court Judge Harold Greene, who frequently decides whether telephone companies and other parties are complying with the AT&T divestiture decree and who has thus become a major presence in telecommunications matters.[10]

Conforming to a broader policy trend in the U.S. governmental decision-making process, federal courts – particularly the U.S. Court of Appeals for the District of Columbia Circuit – have become a significant locus of telecommunications policy making. (The circuit courts hear appeals from trial courts and administrative agencies; their decisions can be reviewed only by the Supreme Court, which hears only a few percent of circuit court decisions.)[11] For example, the D.C. Circuit forced the FCC to allow non-AT&T equipment manufacturers to sell terminal units for connection into the local AT&T exchanges, making competition in the equipment market possible.[12] The Justice Department and the Federal Trade Commission also play a role in regulating industry competitive behavior and structural changes – primarily mergers and acquisitions – and in forcing divestitures, as with AT&T.[13]

Most important for telecommunications policy, at least in theory, is the U.S. Congress. The primary legislation for U.S. telecommunications is the Communications Act of 1934.[14] This Magna Charta of U.S. telecommunications has rarely been amended, despite many attempts. Policy making in light of changed circumstances has been left largely to the FCC's and the courts' discretion. Congress often wields its power indirectly, however, by

8 *See* GOVERNMENT SERVICES ADMINISTRATION, GOVERNMENT ORGANIZATION MANUAL (1985)
9 *See* discussion in text at note 27 *et seq. infra*.
10 *See* S. SIMON, AFTER DIVESTITURE 31 et seq. (1985).
11 *See* discussion in text at note 52 *infra*.
12 Hush-a-Phone v. FCC, 238 F.2d 266 (D.C. Cir. 1956).
13 *See* L. SULLIVAN, HANDBOOK OF THE LAW OF ANTITRUST 751 *et seq.* (1977).
14 47 U.S.C. § 151 *et seq.* (1982).

giving signals to the FCC through bills, resolutions, hearings and the budgetary process. Congress can reduce an agency's budget unless it adopts certain policies, a power that obviously can have a strong influence on an agency.[15]

This multiplicity of decision-making governmental bodies frustrates coordinated and comprehensive policy making. But this process also accommodates decentralized and ad hoc decisions, many of which are responses to specific problems rather than part of a grand design. This has permitted a fairly rapid reorientation of U.S. telecommunications policy, without major upheavals – except perhaps for the AT&T divestiture.

B. *Regulatory Authorities*

Most telephone service in the United States is provided by firms regulated as »common carriers.« This concept requires some explanation. The Communications Act of 1934 defines a »common carrier« merely as a »common carrier for hire, in interstate or foreign communication by wire or radio or in interstate or foreign radio transmission of energy.«[16] In less circular terms, a common carrier is a firm that either holds itself out or is required by law to provide transmission services to any financially qualified customer.[17]

A common carrier offers to lease transmission facilities to the public on a nondiscriminatory basis, usually under a tariff of rates and services approved by the Federal Communications Commission and/or a state regulatory agency. A common carrier does not control the content of the information transmitted over its facilities. Local-exchange telephone operators, domestic as well as international long-distance networks and communications satellites are common carriers, despite the widely divergent services they offer.

Because of traditionally federalist U.S. policies, carriers are regulated by several levels of government – federal, state and local. Local-exchange operators – primarily, of course, the divested AT&T companies, called

15 *E.g.*, E. KRASNOW, L. LONGLEY, & H. TERRY, THE POLITICS OF BROADCAST REGULATION (3d ed. 1982).

16 47 U.S.C. § 153(h) (1982).

17 National Ass'n of Regulatory Util. Comm'rs v. FCC, 525 F.2d 630 (D.C. Cir.), *cert. denied*, 425 U.S. 992 (1976).

Bell Operating Companies (BOCs) – must secure state and occasionally even local approval of their operations. (Whether local approval is necessary depends upon whether a state has authorized cities to grant authorizations – generally termed »franchises« or »consents.« Although local franchising was quite common during the early days of telephony, virtually all states today have prohibited local regulation of telephony.)[18]
The states in turn have created specialized administrative agencies – usually called »public utilities commissions« or »public service commissions« – to regulate telephone companies' rates and practices. State agencies may regulate only *intra*state activities – that is, activities occurring wholly within one state – such as charges for calls within or between exchange service areas in a state.[19] Both local-exchange and long-distance service providers must apply to the state agencies for approval of their tariffs and for »certificates of public convenience and necessity.«[20]
Rate setting is a complex matter. Rates usually are designed to generate enough aggregate revenues to cover costs and depreciation, plus a reasonable profit on invested capital. Rate cases often involve protracted battles to define and measure costs, depreciation and investments and to define a reasonable profit, given the risk characteristics of the business. Furthermore, the allocation of costs and profits to some services and not to others can have major implications as to whether some customers subsidize others and whether a competitive communications offering receives a subsidy by shifting some of its costs to a securely monopolistic service.
The FCC must approve any interstate carrier's rates and practices.[21] Although the Commission largely has abandoned its strict rate-of-return regulation, tariff filings and »section 214 certificates« still are necessary.
This »content-neutral« or »conduit« status of common carriers often creates a set of public-policy problems totally unrelated to a carrier's basic-service obligations. For example, the last few years have witnessed a variety of disputes over local telephone companies' provision of »dial-it« recorded messages – that is, local numbers that a customer can call, at a charge, to hear a recorded message provided by a third party. Some of these services contain sexually oriented or »dial-a-porn« material.[22]

18 W.K. Jones, Cases and Materials on Regulated Industries 30–35, 74–76 (2d ed. 1976).
19 *E.g.*, 47 U.S.C. § 152(a) (1982).
20 *E.g.*, N.Y. Public Service Law art. 8 (1979).
21 47 U.S.C. § 214 (1982).
22 *E.g.*, 47 U.S.C. § 223 (Supp. 1985).

Because of its passive nature as a conduit, however, a telephone company cannot censor such material.
Regulation of the telephone industry historically has been justified by the existence of economies of scale – i.e., the view that some services are most inexpensively delivered by a single firm or monopoly since it can achieve the lowest average costs.[23] Interstate telephone service traditionally has been regulated by the FCC, while local or intrastate service is subject to regulation by state public utilities commissions.[24] To the extent that a call involves both interstate and intrastate facilities, the FCC and state authorities collaborate in setting the rate for the call.[25] Regulators must publish rate applications and conduct public hearings prior to rendering decisions. In theory, tariffs are designed to give a common carrier a fair rate of return on its capital investment.[26]

C. *AT&T*

The U.S. telecommunications industry was a simple affair for a very long time. There was one telephone company, the American Telephone and Telegraph Company (AT&T). Despite its name, it was barred from telegraphy, which was the domain of Western Union; internationally, Western Union was excluded from the telegraph market in favor of a handful of so-called international record carriers.
This was a structure of stability, in which companies were carefully excluded from each other's markets. Instead of competition, federal and state regulation kept the various companies – most particularly, AT&T – from exploiting their market power. Over the past two decades, however, this traditional arrangement increasingly has exploded in a mutually reinforcing process of competitive entry and government liberalization and has given way to a highly dynamic structure of overlapping markets, which also has affected United States international telecommunications.
American Telephone and Telegraph had operated for twenty-five years pursuant to a 1956 Consent Decree, which terminated an antitrust suit

23 *E.g.*, Handler, *Regulation vs. Competition*, 44 U. CIN. L. REV. 191, 206 (1975).
24 47 U.S.C. § 152(a) (1982).
25 W. BOLTER, TELECOMMUNICATIONS POLICY FOR THE 1980's 181 (1984).
26 FPC v. Hope Natural Gas Co., 320 U.S. 591 (1944).

brought by the Justice Department in 1949.[27] The pre-divestiture AT&T was substantially different than today's often confusing mixture of entities. AT&T was perhaps the most vertically integrated telecommunications corporation in the world, since it provided almost everything from equipment service to long-distance transmission and local service. Western Electric (now AT&T Technologies) produced both terminal and switching equipment; Long Lines Division (now AT&T Communications) provided ninety percent of the nation's long-distance traffic; Bell Labs (the only AT&T entity to survive without a name change) did basic research through a complex set of contracts with the other AT&T components; and twenty-two wholly or majority-owned local telephone companies – such as New York Telephone Company or Southern Bell – provided local-exchange service to one or more states.[28]

The divestiture ended the most significant portion of AT&T's vertical integration – namely, the common ownership of the local-exchange companies and equipment as well as long-distance service providers. At least in theory, this removed a number of perceived conflicts of interest, such as local-exchange companies' paying inflated prices for Western Electric equipment.[29] Put in a simplisticly graphic way, the diagram below shows the major separation created by the of divestiture of AT&T:

AT&T Technologies (Western Electric)	AT&T Communications (Long Lines Division)	Bell Labs	AT&T Information Services	RETAINED BY AT&T
	7 Bell Regional Holding Companies 22 Bell Operating Companies			DIVESTED

The divestiture came about in a relatively complicated procedural fashion. In 1982, AT&T settled a 1974 antitrust case, under a Modification of Final Judgment (MFJ).[30] This technically was an amendment to the 1956 Consent Decree. The MFJ required AT&T to divest its twenty-two local-exchange Bell Operating Companies, which now are owned by seven Bell Regional Holding Companies (RHCs). (It is not yet clear whether an RHC is a common

27 *See* discussion in text at note 30 *et seq. infra.*
28 W. BOLTER, *supra* note 25, at 174 *et seq.*
29 *See* discussion in text at note 54 *et seq. infra.*
30 United States v. AT&T, Civ. No. 74–1698 (D.D.C. 1984), *modifying* United States v. Western Electric Co., Civ. No. 17–49 (D.C.N.J. 1956).

carrier.)[31] AT&T also kept several key entities: its research-and-development arm, Bell Labs; its manufacturing arm, Western Electric; its regulated long-distance operation, Long Lines Division; and a new entity for providing enhanced services (AT&T Information Services), which was later combined with AT&T Communications. The FCC supported the settlement but urged that the BOCs also be permitted to enter unregulated fields – a position for which there is increasing support.

While the Justice Department was pursuing its case, the FCC was imposing structural restraints on AT&T. The FCC found it necessary during the 1970s to decide how AT&T could provide data-processing and other »enhanced« services; under the 1956 Consent Decree, AT&T could provide only telecommunications transmission service. Because of the capabilities of electronic switching and of customer demand for new services, AT&T increasingly felt pressure to offer enhanced services. These services were provided at first through AT&T's common-carrier offerings – over the objections of the data-processing industry – and were considered communications services. The FCC addressed this dilemma in three so-called *Computer Inquires (Computer I, Computer II* and *Computer III*). In *Computer II*, the Commission developed a distinction between »basic« or communications services and »enhanced« or software-driven services. AT&T could provide only basic services through its regulated offerings. Enhanced services had to be provided by an unregulated and »fully separated« subsidiary.[32]

Despite strenuous objections by U.S. service providers, the FCC in 1983 changed the effect of the *Computer II* »basic« and »enhanced« classifications. If a carrier provided »enhanced« rather than »basic« service, it no longer needed – and, indeed, no longer could obtain – an authorization pursuant to the certification processes of section 214. Since most new value-added carriers in fact were providing »enhanced« services by utilizing both data processing and telecommunications, they thus fell within this category. Because of this decision, providers of international enhanced services no longer could obtain FCC section 214 authorizations for their services. The service providers argued that lack of section 214 authority would impede their ability to obtain operating agreements with overseas PTTs since they would not be treated as common carriers under domestic U.S. law.

In August of 1985, the Commission initiated yet another rule-making pro-

31 U.S. West, Inc. v. FCC, Civ. No. 84–1448 (D.C. Cir. 1985).

32 *See* Amendment of Section 64.702 of the Commission's Rules and Regulations (Computer II), 77 F.C.C.2d 384 (1980); 84 F.C.C.2d 50 (1980); 88 F.C.C.2d 512 (1981); *aff'd sub nom.* CCIA v. FCC, 693 F.2d 198 (D.C. Cir. 1982).

ceeding, *Computer III*, to re-examine restrictions on both AT&T's and the BOCs' activities.[33] In general, the FCC's initial proposals would have allowed both AT&T and the BOCs not only to offer enhanced services jointly but also to operate without any requirement of a separate subsidiary in some circumstances. In addition, the Commission at least suggested abolishing the separate-subsidiary requirement and replacing it with detailed regulatory requirements.[34]

In the summer of 1986, the Commission did away with *Computer II's* separate-subsidiary requirement in the *Computer III* proceeding.[35] The FCC's view was that AT&T's market power was declining in the interexchange service market and that the separate-subsidiary requirement imposed unnecessary regulatory burdens. One result of the Commission's decision was the merger of AT&T Information Services into AT&T Communications, with the aim of reducing some duplication. Side effects included the intensification of efforts to repeal the separate-subsidiary limitations on the BOCs and to transfer jurisdiction over enforcement of the MFJ from Judge Green to the FCC, which had come to be viewed as more sympathetic to AT&T.[36]

D. *The FCC's Jurisdiction*

There are telecommunications common carriers other than telephone companies. They take different forms and are not restricted to point-to-point transmissions. For example, a totally different type of common carrier is the Multipoint Distribution Service (MDS), which transmits omnidirectional microwave signals to multiple receivers with directional antennae. MDS operates on a small portion of the electromagnetic spectrum – 2150-2162 MHz – far above the frequencies that conventional television sets can receive. Authorized in 1962 for a variety of uses, MDS has been used until recently for »pay«-television programming and high-speed data transmission. An MDS licensee leases its facilities on a nondiscriminatory

33 Computer III, Docket No. 85–229, FCC 85–397 (Aug. 16, 1985).

34 *See* Marks & Casserly, *An Introduction to the FCC's Third Computer Inquiry*, THE COMPUTER LAWYER, Oct. 1985 at 1 *et seq.*; Wiley & Polsky, *Understanding the Computer III Inquiry*, TELEMATICS, Nov. 1985 at 3 *et seq.*

35 Report and Order, 102 F.C.C.2d 655 (1985); Memorandum, Opinion and Order on Reconsideration, Common Carrier Docket No. 85-229 (May 22, 1987).

36 S. 2565, 99th Cong., 2 Sess. (1986).

basis in accordance with FCC tariffs, although it usually has a pay-television service as its primary customer. The Commission prohibits an MDS operator from leasing more than half of its transmission time to any affiliated company.[37]

The MDS example shows how technological developments and their applications have created strains on the FCC's traditional definition and treatment of communications services. Under the Communications Act of 1934, the FCC has at least five different types of regulatory jurisdiction. These distinctions, although technical in nature, can be important in determining what types of FCC regulations – e.g., common-carrier or broadcasting – apply to a particular communications service. This can make a great difference in the nature of regulation. In simplistic terms, broadcast status imposes content regulation but no economic restrictions or access requirements. On the other hand, common-carrier status often requires approval of rates and service conditions but does not restrict content.[38]

In addition, the Commission has jurisdiction under title III of the Act over use of »any apparatus for the transmission of energy or communications or signals by radio,« – that is, any over-the-air use of the radio-frequency spectrum.[39] This jurisdiction in turn breaks down into three distinct subcategories. The most visible type of title III jurisdiction is regulation of broadcast stations, and title III contains special provisions applicable only to broadcasters, such as the requirement of reply time under the fairness doctrine.[40] In addition, a license is necessary under title III for any title II common-carrier spectrum use – from a mobile telephone to an international satellite. Moreover, title III gives the Commission jurisdiction over spectrum uses that are neither broadcasting nor common carriage, under the general classification of »private radio.«[41]

Finally, the FCC has a very vague type of implied jurisdiction over activities that are not clearly within either title II or title III. The most significant example of this type of jurisdiction is the Commission's »reasonably ancillary« jurisdiction over cable television. As defined by case law, this jurisdiction appears to allow the FCC to regulate cable in order to prevent any adverse impact on broadcast television.[42] Although the extent of this jurisdiction is unclear, it appears to be totally separate from – but implied

37 47 C.F.R § 21.900 (1986).
38 *See* discussion in text at note 22 *supra*.
39 47 U.S.C. § 301 (1982)
40 47 U.S.C. § 315 (1982)
41 47 U.S.C. § 301 (1982); *e.g.*, 47 C.F.R. § 95.401 *et seq.* (1986) (Citizens Band radios).
42 FCC v. Midwest Video Corp., 440 U.S. 689, 696 (1979).

by – the Commission's other jurisdictions.[43] The scope of this jurisdiction may have been somewhat cast in doubt by the passage of the Cable Communications Policy Act of 1984, which enumerates certain limited powers for the FCC in the regulation of cable television.[44]

The FCC's choice of a jurisdictional basis has a significant impact upon the legal status of a medium. If a medium is classified as broadcasting, it becomes subject to the wide variety of statutory requirements, such as the fairness doctrine, the political »equal time« reply requirements, the sponsorship-identification rules and the like.[45] On the other hand, classification as a common carrier requires an operator to file tariffs for its rates, subjecting it at least potentially to rate-of-return regulation.[46]

The D.C. Circuit recently limited the FCC's discretion in choosing jurisdictional bases for the media. In *National Association of Broadcasters v. FCC* (*NAB* decision),[47] the court held that the Commission was required to regulate either direct-broadcast satellite (DBS) operators or their channel lessees as broadcasters, thus subjecting them to the full panoply of fairness, equal-time and other traditional broadcast regulations. The court reasoned that since »DBS systems transmit signals directly to homes with the intent that those signals be received by the public, such transmissions rather clearly fit the definition of broadcasting.«[48] Moreover, it noted that the Act »does not give the Commission a blank check to regulate DBS in any way it deems fit.«[49] At the same time, the court rejected analogies to regulation of MDS as a common carrier, suggesting that the Commission's initial classification of MDS may have been misconceived.

As a result, the *NAB* decision casts considerable doubt on the FCC's classification of the electronic media, in terms of common-carrier or other status. In the fall of 1985, the FCC initiated a rule-making proceeding in response to the *NAB* decision. The Commission recently proposed regulating both DBS and subscription television (STV) along the same lines as MDS, thus relieving them of any broadcast-style responsibilities.[50] Whether the FCC's proposal would withstand judicial review under the *NAB* decision is, of course, open to question.

Judical review of FCC actions is quite simple in nature. In order to chal-

43 *E.g.*, United States v. Southwestern Cable Co., 392 U.S. 157, 167 *et seq.* (1968).
44 47 U.S.C. § 601 *et seq.* (Supp. 1986).
45 *E.g.*, 47 U.S.C. § 315 (1982).
46 47 U.S.C. § 214 (1982).
47 740 F.2d 1190 (D.C. Cir. 1984).
48 *Id.* at 1194.
49 *Id.* at 1207.
50 Notice of Proposed Rulemaking, Gen. Dkt. No. 85–305 (Oct. 4, 1985).

lenge the Commission's adoption of a rule, a party need only file a »petition for review.«[51] Review of a licensing decision under Title III of the Act, on the other hand, is by an »appeal.«[52] Under section 402(a), a challenger may file its petition with any court of appeals in whose circuit it has a principal place of business. Under section 402(b), however, all appeals go to the District of Columbia Circuit Court, in order to allow one court to make national licensing policies. Both section 402(a) and section 402(b) proceedings are appellate in nature and thus involve merely the submission of briefs and the presentation of short oral arguments – rather than the introduction of evidence as in a trial court.[53]

E. *Types of Networks*

1. *Public Networks*

Operation of the various types of telephone networks in the United States is highly decentralized.[54] Following the AT&T divestiture, the structure of networks is as follows:

a. *Local service*

(i) There are twenty-two Bell Operating Companies, such as the New England Telephone Company. They are organized into seven Bell Regional Holding Companies, such as NYNEX. The BOCs provide the bulk of local service, with more than 1000 small independent companies serving approximately 10% of the nation's geographic area and 20% of its population. The largest independent company is General Telephone & Electronics (GTE). Local companies are restricted to service within their Local Access and Transport Areas (LATAs) and may not enter long-distance or international communications. They are regulated by various bodies, primarily state commissions and the FCC.

(ii) Various private »bypassers« compete with the BOCs in providing local

51 47 U.S.C. § 402(a) (1982).
52 47 U.S.C. § 402(b) (1982).
53 47 U.S.C. § 402 (1982).
54 For a general description, see W. BOLTER, *supra* note 25.

service through a number of technologies.[55] These technologies include:

a. Cable television;
b. Point-to-point microwave;
c. Digital Termination Service (DTS), a two-way point-to-point switched microwave service;[56]
d. Fiber-optic links;
e. Infrared transmission, which does not require an FCC license; and
f. Cellular radio, primarily in the form of mobile car telephones.[57]

(iii) Shared tenant services (STS) is a hybrid new form of local transmission in which landlords resell local service using a private branch exchange (PBX) and lines leased from telephone companies or other carriers.

b. *Long-distance service*

(i) AT&T controls more than 80% of the »interexchange« or »inter-LATA« service.[58]

(ii) Other common carriers (OCCs), such as MCI and Sprint, provide the rest.

(iii) »Resellers« of long-distance service (including in part the OCCs, which often lease lines from AT&T) and many others buy long-distance service at low bulk rates and resell it to smaller users.

(iv) Lessors of long-distance links include a growing number of railroads or highway authorities, which install fiber-optic lines on their routes.

(v) Domestic record carriers, primarily Western Union and RCA, provide mostly telegraph services and, increasingly, data transmission.

(vi) Specialized companies – including data networks and value-added networks such as Telenet and Tymnet – provide packet switching and other high-technology services over leased circuits.

(vii) Satellite carriers (such as RCA), often operating as common carriers, lease transponder capacity to other common carriers and private users.

55 Noam, *The »New« Local Communications*, 6 COMPUTER L.J. 247 (1986).
56 *E.g.*, D. IRWIN, TELECOMMUNICATIONS REGULATORY MONITOR II–29 *et seq.* (1985).
57 Davis, *Making Sense of the Telecommunications Circus*, HIGH TECHNOLOGY Sept. 1985, at 22–25.
58 *Id.* at 22.

c. *International carriers*

(i) AT&T provides the bulk of international voice service and now also provides record service.

(ii) Other common carriers, such as MCI International and Sprint, provide service to countries with whose postal, telegraph and telephone (PTT) authorities they have agreements. In the Pacific, the Hawaiian Telephone Co. handles much of the traffic.

(iii) Comsat, the U.S. signatory to INTELSAT and INMARSAT, originally operated solely as a »carrier's carrier« and is now able to access users directly. For international civilian satellite communications (as distinguished from cable or microwave), INTELSAT was the sole link. U.S. carriers may go through either Comsat or a private carrier to access INTELSAT for international satellite service. As noted below, INTELSAT also now faces »bypass« from private satellite operators.[59]

(iv) International record carriers (IRCs), such as RCA, ITT, TRT and MCI International (formerly Western Union International), also offer telegraph and telex service. The IRCs originally were restricted to international record service. These restrictions now have been abolished.

(v) Specialized carriers and value-added carriers such as Telenet use leased circuits to provide data-base and related services.

(vi) Applications have been approved for new international satellite carrier systems; similarly, approvals have been granted for new transatlantic cable ventures.[60]

None of these new carriers can function without a link to a foreign carrier. Hence, U.S. approval is not sufficient for actual service. These networks – local, long-distance and international – are substantially free to offer all types of telecommunications services, under restrictions that include the following:

1. Although AT&T can *carry* other companies' electronic publishing or videotex communications, it may not provide its *own* information service until 1989.[61]
2. The BOCs may provide such services as their own information services only through fully separated subsidiaries.[62]

59 *See* discussion in text at note 172 *et seq. infra*.
60 *See* discussion in text at note 174 *infra*.
61 W. BOLTER, *supra* note 25, at 178 *et seq.*
62 Davis, *supra* note 57, at 22.

3. Under the Cable Communications Policy Act of 1984, local telephone companies may provide cable television service only in »rural« areas, which a cable company would find too unprofitable to enter. They are however free to construct and lease back cable facilities to cable companies, as long as the local telephone companies do not control the systems' programming in any way.[63]
4. Since local telephone companies' rates are regulated, an expansion of their service offerings is subject to regulatory scrutiny if it affects rates.
5. For local transmission, the situation is very much in flux. Some states have instituted rules to restrict local »bypass« in favor of the local-exchange telephone companies. Bypass occurs when an unregulated company uses any of the means discussed previously to provide services within a LATA without using the local public switched exchange.)[64] In several instances, *intra*state long-distance service entry – that is, service between LATAs – is also restricted to entry by additional carriers under state rules. Many of these regulations are now subject to litigation.

In addition, certain geographical service restrictions apply. BOCs and other local telephone companies have exclusive franchises for public switched service in their geographic areas, though this exclusivity is being undermined de facto by various forms of bypass and shared tenant services. BOCs cannot offer long-distance or international service, while AT&T cannot provide local service. GTE has provided both local and long-distance services but must do so through separate entities.
Common carriage provides access rights to all users, including resellers that compete with a carrier. Local-exchange companies must grant access to all long-distance carriers, as long as they pay for access. By the middle of 1986, equal-quality access – i.e., equal availability of all long-distance carriers to all telephone users – was required to have been provided to all long-distance carriers;[65] in fact, equal access was still being implemented in late 1986. Customers indicate their »primary« carrier, to which domestic and international long-distance calls automatically are routed by a local exchange. A customer thus is connected directly to the long-distance carrier of its choice without having first to enter elaborate access codes, as was necessary in the past. Customers also can utilize private branch

63 47 U.S.C. § 613(b) Supp. (1985).
64 *See* discussion in text at note 55 *supra*.
65 *E.g.*, S. SIMON, *supra* note 10.

exchanges to select a different long-distant carrier for each call according to a »least-cost-routing« computer, which chooses the least expensive carrier for each route.

A form of universal-service obligation requires common carriers to accept all customers who pay their bills. Local telephone companies also must serve customers in undesirable locations. State rules vary on the extent of this requirement.[66] A typical arrangement is for customers to get a certain connection distance (e.g., up to three utility poles or their equivalent) as part of the basic installation charge, with additional distance requiring an extra fee.

As a matter of law, the FCC and state agencies do not currently impose any absolute universal-service obligations. As a matter of practice, however, both AT&T and local-exchange companies effectively must serve all customers. Over the last century, their networks have expanded to cover virtually the entire country, and, under both federal and state law, they may not withdraw service without the prior approval of the FCC or the relevant state authority.[67] Since the FCC requires a carrier to make a relatively difficult showing of economic necessity before discontinuing service, carriers effectively are locked into serving their present areas – which for AT&T includes interstate service for virtually the whole country.

Reselling of domestic local and long-distance transmission is allowed and extensive. Indeed, carriers must sell even to carriers that compete with them. Recent trends include the sharing of bandwidth on satellite transponders, the reselling of local transmission by shared tenant services and competing coin and credit-card public telephones.[68]

Resellers do not require an authorization from the FCC. They merely need to file a notification with the FCC if they hold themselves out to the public generally.[69] Where there is no such general offering – e.g., one bank reselling its surplus transmission capacity to another – no FCC filing at all is necessary.

Of particular importance are the rates for access to local-exchange networks by long-distance carriers. In the past, complex financial accounting rules (»separations and settlements«) arguably provided an internal subsidy from AT&T's long-distance service to the BOCs. Complicated FCC tariffs also governed the access charges paid by the OCCs. After divestiture, this system was revamped, with equal access charges for carriers to be phased in

66 *E.g.*, N.Y. Pub. Serv. Law § 92 (1979).
67 *E.g.*, 47 U.S.C. § 214(a) (1982).
68 *E.g.*, Universal Payphone, 58 P&F RR2d 76 (1985).
69 D. IRWIN, *supra* note 56, at II–38 *et seq.*

as equal access to the BOCs for non-Bell long-distance carriers was introduced.[70] Furthermore, a new system of customer access charges partially replaces carrier-paid access fees for the use of local-exchange networks.

At least in theory, introduction of customer access fees forces all long-distance carriers to compete on an equal footing, since they are not subject to different charges for use of local-exchange facilities. (The FCC has allowed state commissions to waive consumer access charges, however, for low-income users.)[71] Because of the extremely large amounts of money at issuc to the carriers and because of redistributional impact of access fees, these fees have become a very controversial subject. For example, the OCCs fear that by being forced to pay the same as AT&T – compared to roughly half as much in the past – they will lose their price advantage with consumers and thus suffer market erosion. The OCCs contend that the BOCs' provision of better technical facilities to them does not justify equalization of access costs – particularly since implementation of equal access has been behind schedule.

Various other telecommunications charges are regulated. The BOCs' rates and terms are regulated by state commissions on the principle of rate-of-return regulation. Due to the dominance of the local-exchange companies in local residential distribution, deregulation of these charges is unlikely in the near future.

The principle of rate setting is to permit a »fair« return on invested capital at a rate comparable to investments of similar risk. Rates thus include revenues that – after allowance for operating expenses, depreciation and taxes – result in a fair profit.[72] Because this return is aggregated, not every service or customer category need pay its share of costs and return on capital. Internal subsidies are common. For example, rates often are lower for rural than for urban users and for residential than for business users. Since rate setting is meaningless without a definition of the product, federal and state agencies also set service-quality requirements.[73]

Where local exchanges face competition from bypassers, their rates will probably be deregulated as well. In domestic and international long-distance service, rate regulation is already on its way out. The OCCs need only file tariffs with the FCC stating their rates. Internationally, only AT&T (and the Hawaiian Telephone Company on some Pacific routes) are subject to rate regulation. Only »dominant carriers,« i.e., those with monopoly

70 *Id.* at II–13 *et seq.*
71 Report and Order, 97 F.C.C.2d 834 (1985).
72 C.F. PHILIPPS, THE REGULATION OF PUBLIC UTILITIES, 331 *et seq.* (1984).
73 *E.g.*, 47 C.F.R. Part 68 (1985).

power, must secure prior approval of their rates.[74] In practice, rate regulation is handled quite laxly. Domestically, the goal of regulating AT&T's rates has shifted from protecting users against monopolistic price increases to protecting competitors from predatory price reductions. Long-distance rate regulation is likely to disappear as the OCCs establish themselves.

At least at present, the Communications Act requires all charges for interstate common-carrier services to be just and reasonable.[75] Under the statute, the reasonableness of charges is subject to review by the FCC, which has the authority to prescribe just and reasonable charges and to order rebates and refunds of overcharges.[76] In order to establish the reasonableness of their rates, carriers must submit to the Commission schedules of their rates. In the past, these filings were voluminous in nature, containing complex technological and economic showings prepared by experts. In today's deregulated environment, they tend to be much less formal. Changes in rates must be submitted to the Commission and do not become effective until the FCC approves a proposed rate change or until ninety days after filing of the proposed change.[77] In practice, only AT&T must file tariffs with the Commission.[78]

2. *Private Networks*

Over the last few years, large-volume users of data- and voice-transmission services increasingly have utilized private-line telephone facilities. These operations often totally bypass the BOC or other local-exchange facility by direct connections to the uplink and downlink satellite installations of interexchange carriers. For example major brokers in New York use private lines to connect Manhattan offices directly with satellite transmission facilities in New Jersey. The local BOC plays no role in linking the terminal equipment to the satellite facility and consequently derives no revenue from the transmission.

The OCCs' uplink and downlink facilities are regulated by the FCC as interstate common carriers. State agencies may regulate them only to the limited extent that they provide intrastate long-distance services. (The FCC's power to preempt state regulation was recently slightly reduced by

74 D. IRWIN, *supra* note 56, at II–38 *et seq.*
75 47 U.S.C. §§ 201, 202 (1982).
76 47 U.S.C. §§ 203, 204, 205 (1982).
77 47 U.S.C. § 203 (1982).
78 D. IRWIN, *supra* note 56, at II–38 *et seq.*

a Supreme Court decision.[79]) A non-carrier uplink or downlink, however, is subject to no federal regulation beyond the requirement of securing a license under the Communications Act to use the radio-frequency spectrum. As yet, satellite transmission services have not been used for private-line purposes because of these systems' high construction and maintenance costs. (This does not include the use of satellites by cable television programmers, however, which might be considered a type of private-line activity.) These private systems would not be subject to state or federal regulation as common carriers since they do not hold themselves out to the public; they thus would be unregulated in every sense except for needing FCC licenses under title III of the Act.[80]

3. *Closed User Groups*

Closed user groups are located conceptually somewhere between a single user's private network on the one hand and a reseller's public services on the other. Since both are almost totally deregulated (except for a few restrictions in several states concerning local service), closed user groups are unregulated in terms of charges, access and content. No licensing is necessary, except to the extent that over-the-air transmissions are involved. Liability is based on contractual provisions or general commercial law.

There is no right of access to join a closed user group. If a group restrained trade by refusing to allow a competitor to join a group deemed to be an »essential facility,« however, traditional antitrust principles would require it to grant access.[81] Some closed user groups' provision of value-added services might turn out to be natural monopolies, that is, single-firm production will prove to be substantially less expensive than multi-firm production, and no segment of users will be exposed to lower-priced and loss-free entry. In those cases, antitrust prohibitions on discrimination against competitors may apply.[82] For example, the Supreme Court prohibited the Associated Press from refusing to sell news to its members' competitors, because no practicable substitute for its news service existed.[83]

Defining a closed user group is extremely slippery; no legal definition

79 Louisiana Pub. Serv. Comm'n v FCC, 106 S.Ct. 1890 (1986).
80 47 U.S.C. § 301 (1982).
81 United States v. St. Louis Terminal Ass'n, 224 U.S. 383 (1912).
82 L. SULLIVAN, *supra* note 13, at 125.
83 United States v. Associated Press, 326 U.S. 1 (1945).

exists. There are literally thousands of electronic bulletin boards and specialized data bases through which private and commercial users communicate with each other via computers. Users range from major banks to antique traders to baseball fans. Some operate with leased lines, while others use conventional local and long-distance telephone services.

4. *Domestic Carriers and International Communications*

The U.S. experience has been that pro-competitive forces are expansionary. Once competition is permitted, pent-up user demand and entrepreneurial suppliers provide new services.[84]

The federal government has been more deregulatory than the states and has continuously expanded the scope of its primacy over the states by invoking the doctrine of federal preemption, that is, invalidation of state laws inconsistent with federal laws, even where the federal policy is abstention from regulation.[85] Perhaps the most significant case establishing federal primacy was *North Carolina Utilities Commission v. FCC*,[86] which authorized the FCC to preempt most state telephone regulation.

Although it lacks similar preemption powers in the international sphere and cannot act unilaterally, the FCC has not been highly flexible and has not striven for international harmonization. The Commission has rather sought deregulation of U.S. firms where unilateral action was at all practical and has hoped that market forces would take care of the details.

There is no statutory distinction under the Communications Act between domestic common carriers that provide transborder transmission services and carriers that do not. No special regulatory requirements apply to carriers with transborder as well as domestic transmission capabilities. Any communications common carrier operating within the United States is subject to state and/or federal regulation.

Because they are common carriers, if U.S. carriers provide international service, they must grant access to domestic customers, including resellers.[87] Under most foreign administrations' current policies, however, resellers would not be able to link up at the other end; the carrier rather

84 *E.g.*, Henry, *The Economics of Pay-TV Media*, in VIDEO MEDIA COMPETITION 19 *et seq.* (E. Noam ed. 1985).

85 Noam, *Federal and State Roles in Telecommunications: The Effects of Deregulation*, 36 VAND. L. REV. 949 (1983).

86 537 F.2d 787 (4th Cir.), *cert. denied*, 429 U.S. 1027 (1976). *See also supra* note 79.

87 *See* discussion in text at note 58 *supra*.

than the reseller would be viewed as the authorized user. But since neither a U.S. carrier nor a foreign administration would necessarily know whether a reseller were using a leased line, unsanctioned resale might be impossible to detect and thus to prohibit.

A U.S. carrier obviously needs a foreign carrier counterpart. Although a variety of U.S. carriers may want to operate internationally, they cannot provide service without foreign local and long-distance distribution. Foreign administrations are wary of introducing competitive complexity into their international service; furthermore, transactions with multiple U.S. carriers may impose extra costs. For example, European arrangements with MCI appear to involve primarily traffic inbound from the United States. A minimum amount of inbound traffic must be generated by MCI before a PTT will install outbound transmission equipment.[88]

Access of foreign carriers to the United States is affected by several restrictions:

1. Foreign entities may not own more than 25% of U.S. local telephone companies and long-distance carriers.[89] There do not appear to be any restrictions against foreign companies owning a U.S. value-added network or reseller, unless it functioned as a common carrier. Through such resale, foreign carriers could distribute their service within the United States.
2. In order to serve U.S. customers, foreign carriers have to link up with a U.S. carrier for long-distance service – such as AT&T and the IRCs (the traditional partners) or the OCCs (newer partners). They presumably also would need to deal with a BOC or a bypass operator for local distribution, unless a customer had its own satellite downlink. From the U.S. perspective, the only restrictions (except for those discussed below) are on direct links to the BOCs, due to the prohibition against their providing long-distance service.[90]
3. The nature of foreign carriers' communications links to the United States is governed by the Cable Landing License Act of 1921, which goes back to 19th-century agreements concerning telegraphic cable.[91] That Act requires bilateral reciprocity for carrier access. In practice, this has led to an FCC policy of approving only half-circuit access for foreign carriers in order to guarantee the other half circuit for a U.S. carrier in

88 Remarks of Mr. William McGowan, president, MCI, before IDATE, Montpellier, France, Oct. 23, 1984.

89 47 U.S.C. § 310(a) (1985).

90 *See* discussion in text at note 54 *supra*.

91 47 U.S.C. § 234 (1982).

the reverse direction.[92] Beyond trade reciprocity, the half-circuit policy also has technical reasons, since control of a full circuit by a foreign carrier from a country with a congested telephone system might create burdens on domestic U.S. networks. Conversely, the half-circuit arrangement gives foreign carriers an economic incentive to upgrade their domestic network capacity. Capacity differentials might not be at issue if U.S. carriers had full landing rights in a foreign country. The United States might treat this as adequate reciprocity and give a foreign carrier similar rights in the United States.

The development of overcapacity in international circuits is likely to affect U.S. international carriers' activities in the future. U.S. international communications needs are rising by about 15% annually. But TAT-8, the new INTELSAT satellites, private satellites, private oceanic cable and regional satellite projects will add more capacity than is demanded; they thus may create a glut. The existence of excess capacity and of marginal costs substantially below average costs may lead to price wars. In that situation, some form of U.S. rate regulation or other restraint on pricing might reemerge.

5. *The Equipment Market*

The connection of terminal equipment to the interstate network is regulated by the Communications Act[93] and FCC regulations.[94] Part 68 of the FCC's rules sets minimum technical standards that equipment must meet in order to be connected to any public switched network.[95] The FCC's objective is to provide uniform interconnection standards to protect the telephone network from improper terminal equipment and wiring.

Because interconnection standards are uniform, terminal-equipment users have nondiscriminatory access to the telephone network. Equipment sellers must register their products, however, with the FCC before marketing them.[96] Registration requires the disclosure of a unit's technical specifications, allowing the FCC staff to identify any possible system degradation prior to installation of the equipment; there is no approval process to go through. Moreover, there is a national-security exception to the registra-

92 *E.g.*, Report and Order, 93 F.C.C.2d 701 (1983).
93 47 U.S.C. § 201 *et seq.* (1982).
94 47 C.F.R. Part 68 (1986).
95 47 C.F.R. § 68.2(a)(1), (2), (3), (4) (1986).
96 47 C.F.R. § 68.200 (1986).

tion requirement. If a federal agency certifies that compliance with registration procedures would jeopardize national-security interests, equipment may be connected to the network without publication of technical data.

Part 68's objectives and the registration requirements are relatively recent developments in U.S. common-carrier policy. Prior to *Carterphone*,[97] AT&T and the OCCs developed their own interconnection standards and manufactured or procured equipment compatible with those standards. Competitive terminal-equipment suppliers had no access to the telephone network since users could connect only equipment leased from AT&T.

The U.S. market for central-office (i.e., local-exchange) equipment was characterized in the past by a fairly competitive situation only in the procurement of equipment for independent telephone exchange companies and independent telephone companies – that is, non-AT&T companies. AT&T was precluded from that market, but – perhaps as a result – many other companies were active in it, including such foreign suppliers as Ericsson and Northern Telecom. On the other hand, the vast Bell system and all of its customers – comprising 80% of the total market – were foreclosed to other suppliers by the former's ties to the AT&T manufacturing subsidiary, Western Electric. The *Carterphone* case and subsequent liberal equipment-approval policies opened up customer terminal equipment to a large variety of suppliers.[98] Today, one can buy a telephone for as little as four dollars on a New York City street corner.

The AT&T divestiture radically changed the market for local-exchange equipment. By severing the link between the BOCs and AT&T, it freed the former from having to buy from Western Electric (now AT&T Technologies). (Until recently, AT&T also marketed equipment through its fully separated subsidiary, AT&T Information Systems, a relic from prior FCC attempts to deal with AT&T's market power through internal restructuring.[99])

Although most analysts expected the BOCs to cling to AT&T as their equipment supplier, they in fact have embraced a wide variety of non-AT&T equipment quite rapidly.[100] They are responsible to their state regulatory commissions to use the least expensive qualified supplier. In one instance involving equipment allegedly affecting defense communications, the Defense Department reportedly used pressure to influence a carrier not to buy non-U.S. equipment. Nevertheless, the opening of the U.S. market to

97 Carterphone, 13 F.C.C.2d 420, *recon. denied*, 14 F.C.C.2d 571 (1968).
98 *E.g.*, Universal Payphone, 58 P&F RR2d 76 (1985).
99 *E.g.*, CCIA v. FCC, 693 F.2d 198 (D.C. Cir. 1982).
100 Computer World, Mar. 14, 1984, at 63.

non-AT&T and foreign network equipment generally has been rapid.
Network standards are coordinated for the BOCs by Bell Communications Research (Bellcor). There appears to be no sign that Bellcor is using this role to favor AT&T or other U.S. manufacturers. Neither the executive branch, the FCC nor the state commissions have shown a desire to set standards beyond those already in place.
Procurement of network equipment by local telephone companies is governed by their obligation to state regulators to pay the lowest possible prices. Pressure is on them to keep rates low because of the loss of subsidies from long-distance service.[101] The ability to compare cost trends for the twenty-two companies also forces them to seek low-cost equipment. The »gold plating« (overcapitalization) of the past is unlikely to persist in today's environment.[102] Because of the divestiture, the BOCs no longer have any incentive to increase Western Electric's profits, since none of those profits are returned to the BOCs.
The opening of the U.S. telecommunications equipment market to foreign suppliers has not been matched by a reciprocal opening of foreign markets to U.S. producers. The U.S. balance of trade in telecommunications equipment thus has become increasingly negative, even though U.S. manufacturers have begun to sell equipment in countries such as Japan.[103] One response to these developments has been the introduction of proposed federal legislation to require reciprocity; several bills slowly moved through the Congress.[104] The United States also has exerted pressure on Japan to lower its non-tariff barriers in equipment procurement. For example, the U.S. International Trade Commission ruled that a number of Japanese manufacturers had »dumped,« i.e., sold below cost, cellular car telephones in the United States.[105] The decision allows the U.S. Customs Service to increase duties on these manufacturers' products. Similar stresses are likely to develop with European countries as they increase their U.S. market share. As has been the case in the automotive industry, one response to this problem may be for foreign manufacturers to open plants in the United States. Apparently a number of major Japanese firms are considering this option.[106]

101 *See* discussion in text at note 70 *supra*.
102 C.F. PHILLIPS, *supra* note 72, at 633 f.
103 Communications Week, Dec. 30, 1985, at 1, 18; Communications Week, Dec. 23, 1985, at 1.
104 Communications Week, Dec. 2, 1985, at 8.
105 Communications Week, Dec. 9, 1985, at 10.
106 Interview with Mr. Michael Lactorin, analyst, DAIWA Securities, Inc., in New York City, June 18, 1985.

On the software side, both AT&T and the BOCs are subject to a number of significant restrictions under both the MFJ and the FCC's *Computer III* decision.[107] AT&T may not offer »electronic publishing« on its own until 1989.[108] Although the reason behind choosing this particular period of time is less than clear, the Department of Justice and Judge Greene, after extensive argumentation by the publishing industry, were concerned that AT&T would drive burgeoning new companies out of the software business. Furthermore, the FCC required AT&T under *Computer II* from 1983 to 1986 to offer all »enhanced« telecommunications services – such as data processing or value-added networks – only through a structurally fully separated subsidiary. This restriction was later deleted, as discussed above.[109] Similarly, BOCs may not offer enhanced services at all, except through a »fully separated subsidiary,« that is, a corporation outside of the BOCs' legal control, and only with the prior approval of Judge Greene under the MFJ.[110]

This new competition on both ends of the equipment supply market is fully consistent with the traditional U.S. emphasis on enhancing competition through the antitrust laws. Section 2 of the Sherman Act imposes both civil and criminal liability on any type of monopoly activity, including monopsony.[111] Precisely for this reason, the 1956 Consent Decree was necessary to immunize AT&T from liability because of the »captive consumer« relationship between Western Electric and the BOCs – a relationship with both monopoly and monopsony characteristics. Although the Antitrust Division of the Department of Justice and the Federal Trade Commission have primary responsibility for enforcement of the U.S. antitrust laws, the FCC and the state commissions must give at least some consideration to the antitrust aspects of regulated firms' conduct.

The effect of the antitrust laws has changed substantially with the advent of deregulation. In the past, the existence of a regulatory scheme often was held by the courts to protect a firm from antitrust liability under the general rubric of »primary jurisdiction.« As will be discussed, this doctrine has a variety of different aspects. Its central rationale, however, is simply that

107 *See* discussion in text at note 33 *infra*.
108 United States v. AT&T, 1982–2 Trade Cas. (CCH) para. 73,116.
109 *See* discussion in text at note 33 *infra*.
110 1982–2 Trade Cas. (CCH) para. 73,118.
111 15 U.S.C. § 2 (1982).

a court should not hold a firm liable for engaging in governmentally sanctioned activities.

»Primary jurisdiction« includes at least four major doctrines: primary exclusive jurisdiction, true primary jurisdiction, statutory exemptions and agency immunizations.[112] Under primary exclusive jurisdiction, a court loses all power over a case, except the very limited ability to review any ensuing agency action. On the other hand, true primary jurisdiction gives an agency the initial opportunity to consider a legal issue or to find facts but reserves for the court the ultimate power to render a judgment. A statutory exemption is simply a congressional act that bars antitrust claims against particular industries. An agency immunization has virtually the same effect of removing potential liability but is not self-executing and must be secured from an agency. Statutory exemptions and agency immunizations thus are quite similar in terms of both policy and impact. On the state level, legislation often also creates antitrust immunity under the »state action« doctrine.[113]

The original statement of primary exclusive jurisdiction came in the context of protecting Interstate Commerce Commission tariffs from collateral attacks in state courts. The putative parent of the doctrine is *Texas & Pacific Railway v. Abilene Cotton Oil Co.*[114] In fact, the Court there held only that an aggrieved shipper could not challenge the validity of a railroad's tariff filing with the Interstate Commerce Commission in state court but instead had to commence a proceeding before the Commission.

Statutory exemptions and agency immunizations create inherent problems with regulated industries since the theories behind regulation and antitrust are naturally antithetical. Although the basic regulatory and antitrust schemes evolved at roughly the same time toward the end of the nineteenth century, the Supreme Court has recognized very properly that they represent »two regimes.«[115] Since administrative agencies often apply anticompetitive standards, statutory exemptions and agency immunizations may result in approval of anticompetitive conduct.[116] Every such decision is thus at least potentially anticompetitive.

The easiest cases naturally are those in which the status of an agency's immunization power or of an industry's statutory exemption is clear. When

112 McGovern, *Types of Questions over Which Administrative Agencies Do Not Have Primary Jurisdiction*, 13 ABA ANTITRUST SECTION 57, 61 (1958).

113 Parker v. Brown, 317 U.S. 341 (1943).

114 204 U.S. 426 (1907).

115 Pan American World Airways, Inc. v. United States, 371 U.S. 296, 310 (1963).

116 Hughes Tool Co. v. Trans World Airlines, Inc., 409 U.S. 363 (1973).

a court finds that an agency could not conceivably immunize a violation of the antitrust laws, the court need not consider whether the agency must pass on the conduct.[117] Conversely, many industries operate under express statutory exemptions from the antitrust laws.[118]

The situation becomes infinitely more complicated, however, either where the scope of an exemption is unclear or where an implied exemption may exist. Congress is often deliberately or carelessly vague in its language. In this area of comparatively free decision, the courts have established virtually no standards at all. The Supreme Court occasionally has suggested that immunization power should turn on whether an agency's regulatory scheme is sufficiently »pervasive.« But the Supreme Court has vacillated in using even this general test, applying or ignoring it as it has wished in order to retain or relinquish judicial jurisdiction.[119] The cases indicate that the Supreme Court tends to look to an agency's effectiveness in protecting some public interest other than competition.

True »primary jurisdiction« exists only where there is concurrent jurisdiction between a court and an agency. In this situation, the question is which tribunal will proceed first, rather than which tribunal will proceed.[120] To be sure, primary jurisdiction has some impact upon the outcome of a case; after all, if an agency uses its »expertise« to find facts, review under the substantial evidence rule will restrict a court's role greatly. (The substantial evidence rule prevents a court from reversing an agency unless the court finds that the agency made a clear and material mistake.) A court may well be able to refer a case in such a way, however, as to preserve unlimited review powers.

One of the less visible but increasingly tangible effects of deregulation has been to remove the traditional protections of the primary jurisdiction doctrine. As federal administrative agencies – particularly the FCC – have removed regulatory requirements, they have opened the door to new antitrust suits. Although no definitive statistical data exists, the sheer volume of antitrust litigation has increased substantially during the last few years, particularly in the telecommunications field.[121] One factor naturally is the loss of many defenses or immunities. Another is the need for an alternative forum to resolve private disputes that deregulatory agencies refuse to handle.

117 *See* Maryland & Virginia Milk Producers Ass'n v. United States, 362 U.S. 458, 464–71 (1960); United States Alkali Export Ass'n v. United States, 325 U.S. 196, 204–06 (1945).

118 Walden, *Antitrust in the Positive State*, 41 TEXAS L. REV. 741, 767–88 (1963).

119 *E.g.*, United States v. Radio Corp. of Am., 358 U.S. 334, 348–51 (1959).

120 *See* Comment, *New Twists on Old Wrinkles: Primary Jurisdiction and Regulatory Accommodation with the Antitrust Laws*, 15 B.C. IND. & COMM. L. REV. 80, 93–94 (1971).

121 *See* C.F. PHILIPPS, *supra* note 72, at 670–83.

Also, there is the prospect of treble damages and attorneys' fees for a successful plaintiff in an antitrust case. Indeed, some executives at regulated firms have commented informally that they would prefer returning to the old regulatory rules rather than coping with the new antitrust regime.

Chapter II: Developments in U.S. Regulation of International Common Carriers

A. *Overview of Deregulatory Policies*

Almost by definition, all U.S. regulation of common carriers affects their ability to disseminate information to and receive information from entities in other countries. In some cases, U.S. authorities have made regulatory changes without regard to the international impact. In other cases, however, international effects were of central importance.

The past decade has seen dramatic changes in U.S. governmental policies as to provision of telecommunications facilities and services in the United States. The most dramatic single act, of course, was the breakup of AT&T.[122] But other significant actions include: the deregulation of subscriber terminal equipment; alternative long-distance companies; an »open-skies« policy allowing privately owned domestic satellites; the use of computer technology by telecommunications networks; the liberalization of international service restrictions; the opening of local-exchange service to competitive »bypassers« and the authorization of the resale of long-distance and local telephone service.[123]

Because of the size of the domestic U.S. carrier market and the recognition of the complexities in the international market, the United States – primarily through the FCC – has moved slowly to take actions relating to international telecommunications. In April 1985, FCC Chairman Mark Fowler announced that the FCC increasingly should turn its attention to the international arena, since the Commission's work in the area of fostering compe-

122 *See generally* TELECOMMUNICATIONS REGULATION TODAY AND TOMORROW 205–350 (E. Noam ed. 1983).

123 *E.g.*, Hush-a-Phone v. FCC, 238 F.2d 266 (D.C. Cir. 1956); Carterphone, 13 F.C.C.2d 420, *recon. denied*, 14 F.C.C.2d 571 (1968); Customer Interconnection, 61 F.C.C.2d 766 (1976); *see also* North Carolina Util's Comm'n v. FCC, 537 F.2d 787 (4th Cir.), *cert. denied*, 429 U.S. 1027 (1976); Specialized Common Carriers, 29 F.C.C.2d 870 (1971), *aff'd sub nom.* Washington Utils. & Transp. Comm'n v. FCC, 513 F.2d 1142 (9th Cir. 1975); Domestic Satellites, 335 F.C.C.2d 844 (1972), *aff'd sub nom.* Network Project; Shared Use of Common Carrier Services, 60 F.C.C.2d 261 (1976), *recon. denied*, 62 F.C.C.2d 588 (1977), *aff'd sub nom.* AT&T v. FCC, 572 F.2d 17 (2d Cir.), *cert. denied*, 439 U.S. 875 (1978).

tition in domestic telecommunications was winding down.[124] Several recent FCC actions confirm this view. The FCC has stated:

> We also seek comment on the extent to which differences in the international market should be reflected in the extension of our competitive carrier policies to that market. In particular, would competition among U.S. international carriers be sufficient to make the international telecommunications market competitive given the presence of foreign PTTs in the provision of all international telecommunications services?[125]

Since the Carter administration, the FCC's philosophy has been that a government agency has neither the resources nor the expertise to make judgments about economic developments.[126] This approach was a radical change from the more than forty years of making just such judgments under the Communications Act, which is viewed as almost a model statute in terms of giving flexibility to regulators. Indeed, even as the Commission was moving into uncharted deregulatory territory, the 1934 Act changed little – except perhaps for the recent cable television amendments and the Record Carrier Competition Act of 1981.[127] Instead of seeking new legislation, the Commission relied on the Act's broad mandates.

In moving forward on the international front, the Commission has recognized the increasingly global nature of U.S. firms' activities, the reliance on telecommunications as an integral part of both domestic and international business and the U.S. economy's increased focus on services rather than goods. In order to apply their policies internationally, U.S. regulators have had to deal with major differences between the domestic and international environments. Most importantly, the Commission has had to recognize and evaluate the role of the overseas PTT or correspondent carrier in every international telecommunications enterprise. In the United States, of course, U.S. government policies apply to both ends of the circuit. In international telecommunications, however, a foreign PTT is at the other end and generally has different regulatory goals than the FCC's – most significantly, the subsidization of domestic systems with revenues from international service.[128] Competition among international carriers obviously would reduce these subsidies.

124 Remarks of Hon. Mark Fowler, U.S. Global Telecommunications: The Popcorn Principle, in Washington, D.C., Feb. 26, 1985.

125 *See* International Competitive Carrier Policies, 100 F.C.C.2d 1270, 1271 (1985).

126 *E.g.*, Fowler, *The Public's Interest*, 4 COMMUNICATIONS AND THE LAW 51 (1982).

127 47 U.S.C. § 222 (1982); 95 Stat. 1687 (1981).

128 R. EWALD, THE DEREGULATION OF INTERNATIONAL COMMUNICATIONS 245 *et seq.* (1985).

The rigid structure of international telecommunications also creates hurdles for U.S. deregulatory objectives. International service providers previously were separated from each other by segmentation of the international telecommunications market.[129] The sub-markets included: the distinction between undersea cable and satellite facilities; a separation between the provision of voice and record services; and a differentiation between domestic and international service.[130]

A key FCC policy in the past was its restrictive approach to international facilities, particularly undersea cables. Although it subjected AT&T to overall rate regulation, the Commission rarely questioned any domestic facility proposal by AT&T. With regard to international facilities, however, the FCC closely scrutinized applications. Its policy was based on both AT&T's fairly large investment and pressure from Comsat to protect satellite traffic. In addition, the Commission limited the firms that could provide each type of service. It generally restricted AT&T to international message telephone service (IMTS) and limited the U.S. international record carriers – ITT World Communications, RCA Global Communications, TRT Telecommunications, Western Union International and FTC Communications – to non-voice service (e.g., telegram and telex). New entry into international telecommunications was virtually impossible for years, and even the FCC's efforts to permit Western Union to provide international service required an amendment to the Communications Act.[131]

Not surprisingly, as its liberal domestic policies took shape, the FCC's entry and service policies for international telecommunications appeared to make less and less sense, at least from the U.S. perspective. New carriers, such as Graphnet, Telenet and International Relay, sought to enter the market; users wanted new services and options; and observers increasingly recognized that the traditional market share for certain carriers maintained rates at a fairly high level.

129 Noam, *Telecommunications Policy on the Two Sides of the Atlantic: Divergence and Outlook*, in ECONOMIC POLICY TOWARDS TELECOMMUNICATIONS IN THE INDUSTRIALIZED COUNTRIES (M. Snow ed. 1986).

130 Goldberg, *One-Hundred and Twenty Years of International Communications*, 37 FED. COMM. L.J. 131 (1985).

131 47 U.S.C. § 222 (1982); 95 Stat. 1687 (1981).

B. *Providers of International Service*

Although foreign common carriers are free to interconnect and do business with both local and long-distance U.S. carriers, they may own only limited amounts of stock or other equity in U.S. carriers. Under the Communications Act,[132] a foreign individual or entity may own only 20% of a U.S. carrier or 25% of a holding company of a U.S. carrier. The FCC enforces the statute rather strictly and has looked beyond corporate structural devices – including voting trusts, preferred stock and management contracts – in order to find illegal alien ownership.[133]

This limitation obviously may be a bit anomalous, since it does not apply uniformly to all of the electronic media – most particularly, to cable television, which has many of the passive »conduit« aspects of a carrier.[134] The reason for this distinction seems to be solely the historical accident that the terms of section 301(a) apply only to broadcasting and common carriage.

AT&T continues to be the dominant provider of U.S. international message telephone service, with more than 98% of the market. This percentage is likely to drop, since the OCCs – e.g., MCI and Sprint – initiated international message telephone service. In the record-carrier, i.e., telegraph and telex, market, ITT World Communications, RCA Global Communications, TRT Telecommunications, MCI International (formerly Western Union International) and FTC Telecommunications continue to provide most telex services. With the authorization of the Record Carrier Competition Act (RCCA) of 1981, Western Union also provides international telex service.[135] Most of the data traffic and newer electronic mail services are carried by voice carriers, primarily AT&T.

The RCCA was enacted to permit Western Union to reenter the international record market and to eliminate the artificial barriers between domestic and international record service created by former section 222 of the Communications Act. This 1943 amendment barred Western Union from providing international record service because Congress feared that Western Union would use its domestic market power to monopolize international record service.

132 47 U.S.C. § 310(a) (1982).
133 *E.g.*, Airsignal Corp., 81 F.C.C.2d 472 (1980).
134 *E.g.*, Cable Television Citizenship Requirements, 56 F.C.C.2d 159 (1975).
135 47 U.S.C. § 222 (1982); 95 Stat. 1687 (1981).

Within the past ten years, additional firms – including International Relay, Telenet, Graphnet and Consortium Communications International – have entered the international record market. While these companies hold authorizations to provide international service, they actually use other carriers' facilities.

Regulation of facilities ownership and use still creates significant U.S. government involvement in international telecommunications. AT&T, the international record carriers and the OCCs hold ownership interests through »indefeasible rights of use« (IRUs) in submarine cables and participate in U.S.-mandated »facility-planning« exercises.[136] These are a prerequisite to FCC consideration of applications for authority to invest in and construct such facilities.[137] Rather than consider individual applications for international facilities, the FCC created the facilities-planning process to take a comprehensive view of plans by carriers and PTTs for submarine cables and satellite circuits. One commentator has pointed out somewhat ironically that when the FCC initiated this process, »the European administrations ... learned that, no matter what arrangements they made with the carriers, the FCC had the final say in their investment decisions, so they might as well deal directly with the FCC.«[138]

The FCC has authorized new transoceanic cables, despite their siphoning of traffic for international satellite facilities. It also has begun approving the cables of new ventures, such as Tel-Optik, a consortium led by Cable & Wireless, as well as E.F. Hutton.[139] Comsat continues in its role as U.S. signatory to INTELSAT. Comsat is still a »carrier's carrier,« in that it deals solely with U.S. carriers. Several new private satellite operators appear to be well on their way to »bypassing« it, however, by establishing their own satellites and earth stations.[140] Comsat has also established a corporate entity to provide end-user services.

C. *Changes in Regulation of International Telecommunications Services and International Service Providers*

As indicated above, over the past few years the FCC has removed many of

136 R. EWALD, *supra* note 128, at 145.
137 Third Notice of Inquiry, CC Docket 79–184, Aug. 3, 1984.
138 Goldberg, *supra* note 130, at 145.
139 Report and Order, 100 F.C.C.2d 1033 (1985).
140 *See* discussion in text at note 171 *infra*.

the historical restrictions on international telecommunications and the U.S. players. These FCC actions include the following:

1. *Elimination of the Voice/Record Dichotomy*

Until recently, there was a sharp distinction between voice and non-voice service. The FCC allowed AT&T to provide voice service but generally not to expand into the non-voice market. The dichotomy resulted partly from historical circumstances and partly from the FCC's interest in retaining a viable international record carrier industry. In 1982, however, the FCC ruled that any carrier could provide any service.[141] This followed a number of other decisions that had gradually allowed AT&T to enter the data market and the IRCs to enter the voice market.

2. *Entry of Western Union into International Telecommunications*

This was effected through the Record Carrier Competition Act of 1981, which repealed former section 222 of the Communications Act.[142] When section 222 was enacted, Western Union had a monopoly on U.S. domestic telegraph business and was required to divest its international operations in order to protect the other IRCs. Shortly before the RCCA's passage, the FCC determined that section 222 was not reciprocal – that is, that the IRCs were free to provide domestic record service even though Western Union could not offer international service.[143] The Justice Department had kept AT&T out of the domestic telegraphy since the famous »Kingsbury Commitment« of 1913, under which AT&T agreed to avoid that market.[144]

3. *Entry of Additional International Carriers*

In 1976 the FCC authorized Graphnet and Telenet to provide international record service, thereby allowing competitive entry into international tele-

141 Overseas Communications Services, 92 F.C.C.2d 641 (1982).
142 47 U.S.C. § 222 (1982); 95 Stat. 1687 (1981).
143 Western Union International, 76 F.C.C.2d 166 (1980).
144 W.J. Blyth & M.M. Blyth, Telecommunications: Concepts, Development and Management 39–41 (1985).

communications.[145] More recently, the FCC routinely granted applications by MCI and Sprint to provide international service.

4. *Extension of* Computer II *Rules to Provision of International Service*

As noted before, the FCC's *Computer II* and *Computer III* proceedings have increased substantially AT&T's ability to provide »enhanced services.«[146] This may have an impact on international telecommunications. Some U.S. carriers fear that deregulation of enhanced service providers would increase foreign PTTs' powers in dealing with U.S. entities and thus result in playing off U.S. companies against each other. Since service providers are not subject to FCC authorization, they could negotiate arrangements with PTTs that do not conform to the FCC's policies for allocating costs among common carriers and BOCs. At least theoretically, an enhanced service provider thus could divert traffic and revenue from certificated U.S. carriers and/or force them to reduce settlement rebates with the PTTs. A foreign company even could become a U.S. enhanced service provider; it would not own the transmission facilities, and it might be able to obtain preferential treatment on its home territory. Another issue is whether enhanced service providers would utilize private lines and divert revenues from the public switched networks. One response for the PTTs would be to eliminate flat-rate tariffs for private line service, as Germany already has done. Many U.S. users (such as IBM, Control Data and General Electric) utilize private lines not only to control costs for international data transmission but also to keep transmissions confidential.

5. *Applicability of Deregulation of Common Carriers to International Communications*

During the past few years, the FCC has eliminated rate-of-return regulation for most common carriers except AT&T. In the *Competive Carrier* proceeding, the Commission developed a doctrine of »forebearing« from

145 Graphnet Systems, Inc., 63 F.C.C.2d 402 (1977), *recon. denied*, 67 F.C.C.2d 1020 (1978), *remanded*, 595 F.2d 897 (1979). *See also* ITT World Communications Inc., 76 F.C.C.2d 15 (1979); International Relay, Inc., 77 F.C.C.2d 819 (1980).

146 *See* discussion in text at note 32 *supra*.

regulation, such as certification of carriers and their investments under section 214 of the Communications Act, as well as from rate regulation under sections 201 and 202 of the Act.[147] The FCC determined that only a dominant carrier needed to – or would be permitted to – file tariffs. This decision still required the filing of section 214 applications and tariffs, however, for international service.

The premise of the *Competitive Carrier* proceeding was that entry into and exit from the telecommunications services market need not be determined by the FCC and that users are adequately protected by competition as well as the FCC's complaint mechanisms. The FCC thus believes that tariffs no longer are necessary to protect the public. To this end, the FCC has increased the number of auditors in its Common Carrier Bureau from twenty-seven to eighty.[148] Whether this larger staff can monitor the practices of AT&T, the BOCs and the OCC, however, remains to be seen.[149] The effectiveness of *Computer III's* shift from structural restrictions – e.g., fully separate subsidiaries – to regulatory requirements thus may depend heavily upon the Commission's ability to implement an effective supervisory procedure.

On the international front, the FCC initiated a proceeding in 1985 to consider extending some of the deregulatory *Competitive Carrier* findings to international telecommunications service.[150] In the international proceeding, the FCC defined two separate product markets – international message telephone service (IMTS) and non-IMTS. The Commission also proposed to examine the question of dominance on a country-by-country basis. If only one carrier provided IMTS or non-IMTS to a certain country, it would be considered dominant and subject to rate regulation.

For example, the FCC found that AT&T and the Hawaiian Telephone Company were the only dominant IMTS providers and therefore subject to full rate regulation. The FCC tentatively concluded that no non-IMTS carriers were dominant and thus that they should be subject to »streamlined« regulation – much like the FCC's »regulatory forebearance« in the domestic *Competitive Carrier* proceeding. Thus, although the non-dominant carriers would need to file initial applications to serve new points, they would merely need to report their circuit activations twice a year. Tariffs would be presumed lawful if filed on fourteen days' notice and would not be required to include supporting data.

147 Telenet, 91 F.C.C.2d 232 (1982).
148 Remarks of Dr. Alan Pearce, in New York City, Dec. 12, 1985.
149 *Id.*
150 International Competitive Carrier Policies, CC Docket No. 85–107, FCC 85–177 (released Apr. 19, 1985).

6. Uniform Settlements Docket

The extent of U.S. government involvement in the settlement arrangements between U.S. carriers and their overseas correspondents is a critical issue for U.S. international carriers. When different entities provide international telecommunications service at each end of a circuit, they agree upon a division of the revenues between them. The entities create an »accounting rate« or »settlement rate« – that is, an amount to be paid by the carrier collecting from a customer to the other carrier – which may bear little or no relationship to the actual customer charge or »collection« rate. The FCC administers a Uniform Settlements Policy, which requires all U.S. carriers to have uniform settlement rates with all other carriers for the same routes.[151]

As a hypothetical example, the accounting rate for the first three minutes of a telephone call between New York and Paris might be $3.00, the charge for the call in the U.S., $4.50 and the charge in France, $6.00. When U.S. customers call, they pay $4.50 to AT&T, which credits $3.00 to the French PTT. When French customers call, they pay $6.00 to the French PTT, which in turn credits $3.00 to AT&T. The Uniform Settlements Policy does not regulate U.S. carriers' rates on the U.S. end; instead, it attempts to protect U.S. companies from »whip-sawing« by foreign PTTs by requiring all U.S. carriers to pay a uniform rate. So far, the FCC has been reluctant to deviate from this policy.

The FCC recently denied a request by FTC Communications (FTCC) for a waiver of the Uniform Settlements Policy to allow FTCC to reduce accounting rates for telex service with the United Kingdom and twenty-six European countries. In denying the request, the Commission stated that FTCC had not shown that collection rates would decrease or that other benefits to the public would result.[152] Although the FCC has indicated interest in reexamining the Uniform Settlements Policy, a 1984 staff background paper suggested that the FCC scrutinize international accounting rates more closely in order to protect U.S. consumers and to prevent U.S. firms from unfavorable terms.[153]

151 47 C.F.R. Part 31 (1985)

152 Report and Order, Gen. Docket No. 85–249 (1985).

153 E. KWEREL, PROMOTING COMPETITION PIECEMEAL IN INTERNATIONAL TELECOMMUNICATIONS (OPP Working Paper Series, Federal Communications Commission, December 1984).

D. *Facilities-Related Regulatory Decisions*

In addition to extending its pro-competitive and deregulatory policies to international services, the FCC also has sought to increase competition between types of transmission media and service providers. Prior to the advent of communications satellites, the Commission focused on authorization for and ownership of submarine cable facilities. The FCC scrutinized applications for these facilities to decide whether their need justified an increase in a carrier's rate base. Partly because investments in international submarine cables were visibly large in comparison to investments in most domestic facility applications, the Commission reviewed them closely.

AT&T, the IRCs and other carriers used these cables and were at least theoretically subject to rate-base regulation; they thus sought to obtain ownership interests in these facilities, in the form of the previously mentioned indefeasible rights of use (IRUs). The FCC concluded that it was impossible to audit the IRCs and that no benefits would flow from rate regulation of that industry.[154] The carriers sought ownership interests in order to expand their rate bases and realize certain benefits under the U.S. Tax Code. These IRUs still exist. This creation of new ownership interests in the cables (in addition to the PTTs' interests) added new parties to the negotiating process.

Further complexity resulted from the activities of INTELSAT, through Comsat. Anxious to implement the Communications Satellite Act of 1962, the FCC initially made Comsat a carrier's carrier in providing international satellite service.[155] The Commission also required carriers to use satellites as well as cables, in order to promote the international satellite system. The carriers preferred the submarine cables, however, because of their familiar technology and the carriers' ownership of the IRUs. Moreover, satellites were under leases, which could not be included in a carrier's rate base.

As new carriers entered the international market and new services were offered domestically, the FCC found that flexibility was not common in the use of international facilities. The »fifty-fifty« balanced loading principle, in force since 1979, was modified to permit AT&T to carry up to 60%

154 *See* Preliminary Audit and Study of the Rates of Return of the IRCs, 75 F.C.C.2d 726 (1979), *appeal docketed sub nom.* Western Union Telegraph Co. v. FCC, No. 79–2497 (D.C. Cir. Dec. 14, 1979).

155 47 U.S.C. § 701 *et seq.* (1982).

of its traffic on cables by 1990, with total freedom for the other carriers.[156] Even the remaining restriction seems fated for extinction.

Comsat's role in the use of international satellite services has come under intensive scrutiny. The mammoth *Comsat Study*[157] identified Comsat's possible conflicts of interest and suggested several changes in U.S. firms' procurement of international satellite service. These changes authorized entities to obtain service directly from Comsat, allowed private ownership of U.S. earth stations for accessing INTELSAT, permitted direct access to INTELSAT satellites and structured Comsat to avoid conflicts of interest in its role as U.S. signatory and monopolist.[158]

Perhaps somewhat ironically, one of the first issues was not the question of providing greater flexibility to carriers in accessing the international satellite system, but whether Comsat could serve end users directly. In the 1960s, the FCC implemented the *Authorized User*[159] decision, involving the question whether the U.S. government could purchase service from Comsat rather than an international service carrier. The Commission determined that only in »unique and exceptional« circumstances could Comsat serve end users directly. Users of international television service sought to overturn this policy.[160] In *Authorized User II*,[161] the Commission reaffirmed its position.

Ultimately, the Commission decided that INTELSAT users could be served directly and went on to consider a more liberal policy.[162] The D.C. Circuit remanded this decision to the Commission,[163] on the ground that the FCC had not fully considered questions of earth-station ownership and direct access to INTELSAT, which the U.S. international carriers viewed as a necessary prerequisite to any expansion of Comsat's ability to provide service. Comsat also recently completed a reorganization required to provide competitive end-user service.

Following enactment of the Comsat Act,[164] the FCC developed various policies to effectuate and protect Comsat's role as the U.S. signatory and monopoly U.S. provider of international satellite service. A key compo-

156 Report and Order, 98 F.C.C.2d 1166 (1985).

157 88 F.C.C.2d 564 (1980).

158 *See* Authorized User Policy, 90 F.C.C.2d 1394 (1982); Communications Satellite Corp., 81 F.C.C.2d 287 (1980); COMSAT, 90 F.C.C.2d 488 (1982).

159 Authorized Entities and Users – Comsat, 4 F.C.C.2d 421 (1966), 6 F.C.C.2d 593 (1967).

160 Spanish International Network, 70 F.C.C.2d 2127 (1978).

161 Report and Order, 50 Fed. Reg. 2552 (1985).

162 Authorized User Policy, 90 F.C.C.2d 1394 (1982).

163 ITT World Comm'ns Co. v. FCC, 725 F.2d 732 (D.C. Cir. 1984).

164 47 U.S.C. § 701 *et seq.* (1982).

nent of this role was the construction and operation of earth stations to uplink to INTELSAT satellites. In 1966 the FCC outlined an »Interim Policy« for the ownership and operation of these stations. Comsat and the U.S. international service carriers – AT&T and the IRCs – would own and operate the stations jointly through a cooperative Earth Station Ownership Committee (ESOC).[165] This approach gave Comsat the major role in earth-station management as well as investment decisions and allowed Comsat to bundle earth-station costs with space-segment costs in setting rates.

Following pressure from various carriers and users, in 1982 the FCC proposed a more liberal international earth-station policy.[166] Carriers and users wanted Comsat to separate its space-segment (satellite) from its earth-segment (earth-station) charges; they also wanted the option of building their own lower-cost earth stations at sites with efficient access to INTELSAT. In 1984 the FCC authorized international carriers to construct and operate international earth stations.[167] The Commission endorsed »competition by permitting carriers other than Comsat to own and operate earth stations.«[168]

The Commission's new policy on international earth-station ownership has some restrictions. Applicants may not receive routine action on their applications unless they propose specialized new services, such as the INTELSAT Business Service (IBS). The FCC indicated that it was unlikely to grant applications for general-purpose earth stations accessing the international satellite system. The Commission also required Comsat to separate its earth- and space-segment charges in order to further competition. Finally, the Commission imposed additional requirements on the phase-out of the ESOC arrangement.[169]

Not suprisingly, the competitive pressures that led to modifications of the earth-station-ownership and authorized-user policies necessitated an examination of whether Comsat should continue to be the sole U.S. source of access to INTELSAT.

Even though the Commission at times has acknowledged the difficulty of extending its pro-competitive policies internationally, it has attempted to inject as much competition as possible on the U.S. side. An opportunity for

165 Interim Earth Station Ownership Policy, 5 F.C.C.2d 812 (1966).

166 U.S. Earth Stations Ownership Inquiry, 90 F.C.C.2d 1458 (1982); 97 F.C.C.2d 444 (1984).

167 Frieden, *Getting Closer to the Source: New Policies for International Satellite Access*, 37 FED. COMM'NS L.J. 293, 320–23 (1985).

168 Modification of Policy on Ownership and Operation of U.S. Earth Stations that Operate with the INTELSAT Global Communications Satellite System, 49 Fed. Reg. 50,030 (1984).

169 *Id.*

furthering competition, a development perhaps unforeseen, resulted from both applications for satellite systems to compete with INTELSAT and, most recently, applications for private submarine cables.

The applications follow the same procedure as any request for authorization to operate a radio-frequency spectrum device under title III of the Communications Act.[170] This procedure essentially requires an applicant to show its financial and legal, as well as technical, qualifications and to establish that its operation would not cause electrical interference with any other service. The only difference between an application for an international satellite facility and any other title III application – whether for a television station or a mobile radio – is that a geosynchronous orbital position must be available for allocation by the FCC. The total number of available orbital slots is governed by the regulations of the International Telecommunication Union.[171]

In 1983 Orion Telecommunications applied for a license to build a private satellite system over the North Atlantic. Orion would launch its own satellites and not make use of any INTELSAT facilities.[172] Its application was followed by filings from other companies: International Satellite, Inc. (backed by TRT); Cygnus (backed by the earth-station manufacturers MA/COM); RCA Americom (for modification of a U.S. domestic satellite); and PanAmerican Satellite (for service to the Caribbean, Mexico and Latin America). These applications were opposed by foreign governments and touched off a debate within the U.S. government as to whether the U.S. should endorse or permit international systems to »bypass« INTELSAT. A large part of this concern emanated from provisions in the INTELSAT agreements concerning non-INTELSAT international satellite systems.[173]

The intragovernmental debate kept the applications pending at the FCC, culminating in the issuance of a *White Paper* intended to provide guidance to the FCC in its deliberations.[174] The executive branch's involvement in the debate probably was discretionary on its part and not legally required in any fashion.[175] Although the president has a statutory role under the Act,

170 *See* discussion in text at note 39 *supra*.

171 Rice, *Regulation of Direct Broadcast Satellites: International Constraints and Domestic Options*, 44 *et seq.*, in DEVELOPMENT AND REGULATION OF NEW COMMUNICATIONS TECHNOLOGIES 31–82 (D.M. Rice, M. Botein & E.B. Samuels eds. 1980).

172 R. EWALD, *supra* note 128, at 283 *et seq.*

173 Article XIV(d), INTELSAT Agreement, Aug. 20, 1971, 24 U.S.T. 564, T.I.A.S. No. 7532.

174 Senior Interagency Group on International Communication and Information Policy, A White Paper on New International Satellite Systems (Feb. 5, 1985).

175 *E.g.*, 47 U.S.C. § 701(a) (1982).

executive branch participation never has been held to be mandatory. The FCC thus presumably could have proceeded on its own, since it is a legally independent agency. The executive branch often uses its obvious influence, however, to break regulatory logjams – such as that involved in Orion's application.

The executive branch's *White Paper* cautiously approved the concept of separate systems, as long as they did not interconnect with public switched networks – thus restricting them to private line service. The FCC conducted a proceeding on the pending applications and eventually granted them, subject to limited conditions.[176] Not surprisingly, Comsat has vehemently opposed private satellite systems. Indeed, both Comsat and INTELSAT have sought legislation to preclude such systems or to restrict their operations. Moreover, INTELSAT dragged its feet in implementing »consultation« proceedings with the first private satellite system – Pan American – to secure an agreement with a foreign carrier.

Not to be outdone by the competitive satellite applicants, two companies – Tel-Optik Limited and Submarine Lightware Cable Company (SLCC) – applied for licenses to operate international submarine cables in the United States.[177] The submarine cable applications did not raise issues under the INTELSAT agreements. Moreover, the major U.S. owner of submarine cable systems, AT&T, did not file any substantial objections. The FCC thus moved expeditiously in granting the Tel-Optik application.[178] The Tel-Optik application proposed two cables to be operated in conjunction with Cable & Landing in the United Kingdom, with the first cable to be implemented in 1989, the second in 1992. Similar applications are pending for Pacific routes.[179] Apart from questions about the availability of capital, the competitive submarine cables generally face less regulatory opposition and will not be restricted as to the services they can provide.

176 In the Matter of Establishment of Satellite Systems Providing International Communications, CC Docket No. 84–1299, FCC 84–632 (Jan. 4, 1985).
177 R. EWALD, *supra* note 128, at 318 *et seq.*
178 Report and Order, 100 F.C.C.2d 1033 (1985).
179 R. EWALD, *supra* note 128, at 295 *et seq.*

Chapter III: The International Impact of Domestic U.S. Restrictions on the Availability of Data

A. *Limitations on the Export of Data*

As noted in Chapters I and II, U.S. regulatory agencies increasingly have deregulated both domestic and international facilities for data transmission. The conduits of communication thus are less restricted than ever before. Clearing the international channels, however, does not per se assure a free flow of information. Like other countries, the United States has many restrictions upon the availability of certain types of information – for reasons ranging from personal privacy to national security. Indeed, the trend towards both domestic and international deregulation makes these restrictions particularly significant. With the removal of substantial impediments to international transmissions, domestic restrictions on the availability of data may become the most significant burden on the free flow of information from the United States side.

Chapter Three thus gives a sampling of the major domestic U.S. restrictions on the availability of data – whether for domestic or international transmission. As noted in the Introduction, no overall scheme exists for this patchwork of laws. Nevertheless, an overview is useful.

In general, the U.S. regulatory regime does not impose restrictions upon the import or export of data and data processing or similar services. There are numerous restrictions, however, on the domestic use and transmission of security-related information. These regulations naturally affect international telecommunications.

Both cooperatively with several Western-bloc nations and on its own, the United States restricts the transfer of technology and technological information to hostile or non-aligned nations. This section briefly reviews the domestic and multilateral regulatory schemes for controlling the export of sensitive data. Current U.S. export controls fall into three categories:

- *Nuclear information* is regulated by the Nuclear Regulatory Commission (NRC) and the Department of Energy (DOE) under the Atomic Energy Act of 1954, as amended by the Nuclear Non-Proliferation Act of 1978;

- *Munitions and related information* is controlled by the State Department, under the Arms Export Control Act of 1976; and
- *»Dual use« information and technology* (e.g., information with both military and civilian applications) is regulated by the Commerce Department under the Export Administration Act of 1979.

1. *Atomic Energy Information*

The Atomic Energy Act imposes criminal sanctions for divulging »restricted data« to unauthorized recipients.[180] Restricted data is:

> all data concerning (1) design, manufacture, or utilization of atomic weapons; (2) the production of special nuclear material; or (3) the use of special nuclear material in the production of energy, but shall not include data declassified or removed from the Restricted Data category.[181]

A quirk in this law is that data remains restricted until declassified – even if it already is in the public domain. This led to the celebrated *Progressive* case,[182] in which a federal district court enjoined publication of a magazine article explaining how to build a hydrogen bomb. This appears to be the only case in U.S. history in which a lower court imposed a prior restraint on a print medium.

2. *Munitions Information*

Under the Arms Export Control Act, the State Department maintains a »Munitions List« and licenses the import as well as export of any items on the list.[183] The State Department's International Trade in Arms Regulations (ITAR) restrict the disclosure of technical data pertaining to weapons, including »any unclassified information that can be used or adapted for use in the design, production, operation, maintenance or reconstruction« of items on the Munitions List.[184] The ITAR also prohibit the export of technology or information that »advances the state-of-the-art or estab-

180 42 U.S.C. §§ 2011–2296 (1982).
181 *Id.* § 2014(y).
182 United States v. The Progressive, 467 F. Supp. 990 (D. Wisc. 1979).
183 22 U.S.C. § 2751 (1982).
184 22 C.F.R. § 125.01 (1986).

lishes a new art in an area of significant military applicability in the United States« without State Department authorization.[185]

3. *»Dual Use« Technology and Technical Information*

Under the Export Administration Act (EAA),[186] the Commerce Department controls the export of commodities, technologies and data on industrial processes that affect national security, foreign policy or limited domestic resources. Technical information about industrial processes is defined in the Department's Export Administration Regulations (EAR) as »information of any kind that can be used or adapted for use in the design, production, manufacture, utilization, or reconstruction of articles or materials.« This information is placed on a Commodities Control list – an approach similar in concept to the State Department's Munitions List.[187] The EAR define »export« not only as the transmission of technical data outside of the United States but also as the verbal or written release of such data to foreign nationals within the United States. Unlike nuclear-information restrictions, however, the EAR exempt public-domain information from export restrictions.[188] The reasoning of the *Progressive* case thus presumably would not justify a prohibition on the publication of such data.

Items on the Commodity Control List and information related to these items may be exported only with a license from the Commerce Department. »Validated licenses« are required for some exports, depending upon both the nature and the destination point of an item. »General licenses« cover exports not requireing a validated license.[189]

Both the ITAR and EAR definitions of technical data are broad enough to require export licenses for a wide range of information. These regulations require information providers to determine whether their information includes »technical data« and whether the information will be available to aliens. If so, an information provider must obtain a license from either the Commerce or the State Department prior to disclosure. (Exemptions for material in the public domain sometimes are applicable, as noted above.) The State Department may deny, revoke, suspend or amend licenses

185 *Id.* § 379.3
186 50 U.S.C. § 2401 (1982).
187 15 C.F.R. § 379.1 (1986).
188 *Id.* § 379.3.
189 50 U.S.C. § 2404(e)(2), (3) (1982).

without notice if it determines that such action is necessary in the interests of world peace, national security or U.S. foreign policy.[190] Similar provisions apply to the Commerce Department.[191]

4. *Multilateral Export Controls*

In 1950 the United States, Canada, the United Kingdom, France, West Germany, Italy and Japan created a multilateral consulting organization to coordinate export controls for mutual security – the Coordinating Committee (COCOM). This agency controls 150 items for export to the U.S.S.R., other Warsaw Pact nations, Albania, North Korea, Mongolia, Vietnam and the People's Republic of China. COCOM reviews this list approximately every three to four years. All member-nations must concur in additions to or deletions from the list. Exceptions may be obtained – and the United States has received more than any other nation – upon the approval of member-nations.[192]

B. *Privacy*

The United States has been active in protecting personal privacy against *governmental* intrusion. A number of laws prohibit the collection of personally identifiable data by both public and private entities in a comparatively narrow set of circumstances. A melange of federal, state and local statutes protects personal data on a piecemeal basis. In most cases, federal or state legislatures have acted upon highly particularized fears – e.g., governmental data processing for administration of welfare payments or use of interactive cable television for audience research.

Although these restrictions mainly inhibit domestic activities, they also might impact on a variety of international transactions. For example, credit

190 22 C.F.R. § 123.05(a)(1–3) (1986).

191 15 C.F.R. § 370.3(b) (1986).

192 *See, e.g.*, Maly, *Technology Transfer Controls*, 23 JURIMETRICS JOURNAL 33 (1982). Flow of information between signatory nations is also regulated by the Agreement for Facilitating the International Circulation of Visual and Auditory Materials of an Educational, Scientific and Cultural Character, 17 U.S.T. 1578, T.I.A.S. No. 6116 (1967). This Agreement curtails import duties, licenses and special taxes through the issuance of exemption certificates. For a detailed discussion, compare Barnett, *Part II: Mass Media, infra* at 232–35.

ratings on U.S. investors might not be available for overseas entities because of federal or state laws to protect personal privacy.

1. *Restrictions on the U.S. Government*

The Privacy Act of 1974 regulates the collection, maintenance, use and dissemination of information by federal agencies.[193] The Act defines a »record« as any piece, collection or grouping of information about an individual that is maintained by a federal agency. This includes data on an individual's education, medical history, financial transactions, criminal activities or employment history, if it contains his or her name, identifying number, symbol or other identification.[194]

Under the Act, no agency may disclose any record to another person or agency except pursuant to a written request by – or with the prior written consent of – the individual affected, unless the record falls within one of several exemptions. For example, exceptions exist if disclosure of a record would be pertinent to a civil or criminal law enforcement activity, which is authorized by law and carried out by any properly authorized U.S. law enforcement agency or pursuant to an appropriate court order.[195]

If an agency maintains records, an individual may gain access to any information about him or her. The agency must: (1) permit the individual to review the record and have a copy made; (2) allow the individual to request the agency to amend any such record; and (3) upon refusal to amend a record, grant an administrative review of such refusal within thirty days.[196] A final agency decision is reviewable, of course, in the federal courts.

An agency also may keep only such information about an individual as is relevant and necessary to accomplish the agency's goals. It must, to the extent possible, collect data from a person directly, if the information might result in adverse determinations about an individual's rights, benefits and privileges under federal programs.[197]

The Act does not create a central administrative or enforcement agency. The executive Office of Management and Budget, however, oversees agencies' compliance with the Act's procedural guidelines.[198]

193 5 U.S.C. § 552 *et seq.* (1982).
194 *Id.* § 552a(a)(4).
195 *Id.* § 552a(b).
196 *Id.* § 552a(d)(1), (2), (3).
197 *Id.* § 552a(e).
198 *Id.* § 552a(g), (i).

2. *Governmental Interception of Wire and Oral Communications*

The Omnibus Crime Control Act regulates the government's interception of »wire« and »oral communication.«[199] These terms have specific statutory definitions. A »wire communication« is any message conveyed wholly or partially through a wire, cable or like connection operated by a common carrier. An »oral communication« is any communication by a person who reasonably expects that his or her conversation is private and not subject to interception by third parties. An »interception« occurs when a communication is achieved through the use of mechanical, electrical or other devices.[200]

A party to a communication may intercept the communication without violating the Act, however, unless the purpose of the interception is to commit a crime or other injurious act. The theory behind this provision is that the conversation is no longer private, because at least one participant has consented to the interception. Unless an interception is exempt, a person may be fined up to $10,000 and imprisoned up to five years for wire tapping.[201] For example, agents of a common carrier may intercept wire communications in the course of their employment. FCC employees may intercept communications while performing official duties. Law enforcement personnel may intercept communications if they have the consent of one or more of the communicating parties or act with a court order.[202]

The use of intercepted communications as evidence in judicial, administrative or legislative proceedings is restricted.[203] Evidence is not admissible in federal, state or local proceedings if its gathering was not authorized by the Act. The Act provides for disclosure of intercepted information if it is derived from a court-authorized interception and if the parties opposed to disclosure have been notified of the impending disclosure and furnished with a copy of the court order authorizing the interception.[204] A person may move to suppress disclosure of wire or oral communications on the grounds that the authorization for the interception was insufficient or that

199 18 U.S.C. § 2510 (1982).
200 *Id.* § 2510(1), (2), (4).
201 *Id.* § 2511(1).
202 *Id.* § 2511(2).
203 *Id.* § 2515.
204 *Id.* § 2517.

the interception did not conform to the authorizing order.[205] A person whose communication is intercepted or disclosed in violation of the law can sue the perpetrators. Good-faith reliance on a court-ordered interception, however, is a complete defense to such a lawsuit.[206]

A court may order the interception of a communication if there is probable cause to believe that: (a) an individual is involved in one of several enumerated crimes (e.g., transmission of betting information, bribery, extortion); (b) information relating to that offense will be obtained through an interception; (c) normal investigative techniques have failed or appear unlikely to succeed; and (d) the communications at issue are commonly used by suspects in the case.[207] Another clause provides emergency grounds for interception without prior court approval for communications concerning activities that threaten national security or involve organized crime. In these cases, however, application for court approval must be made within forty-eight hours of the interception.[208]

In addition, under the Foreign Intelligence Surveillance Act, the president, through the attorney general, may authorize electronic surveillance to obtain foreign intelligence information without a court order.[209] The surveillance must be directed solely at intercepting communications between foreign powers or at acquiring technical intelligence information emanating from premises under a foreign country's exclusive control. There must be no substantial likelihood that the surveillance will intercept communications with a U.S. citizen.[210] Where communications of U.S. citizens are involved or are likely to be involved, surveillance cannot be undertaken without court approval.[211] The attorney general may direct a common carrier to furnish all information, facilities or technical assistance necessary to carry out surveillance and to keep records of the communications under strict security procedures.[212]

3. *Governmental Access to Financial Data*

The Right to Financial Privacy Act of 1978 generally denies government

205 *Id.* § 2518(a).
206 *Id.* § 2520.
207 *Id.* § 2518(3).
208 *Id.* § 2518(5).
209 50 U.S.C. § 1801 (1982).
210 *Id.* § 1802(a).
211 *Id.* § 1802(b).
212 *Id.* § 1802(4).

authorities access to customer financial information held by banking and other financial institutions.[213] But exceptions exist, such as authorization by the customer, compliance with an administrative subpoena, a valid search warrant or court order or a formal written request.[214] All of these activities must further a legitimate law enforcement inquiry in order to create an exemption.

A government agency must notify the subjects of an inquiry that their financial records are being sought and disclose the purpose of the request. A person subject to an inquiry may challenge the inquiry in federal court on the ground that the information sought is not relevant to a legitimate law enforcement inquiry.[215] The government may obtain a court order for direct access without notice, upon a showing that notice would allow the subject party to flee or to destroy evidence.[216] Upon receipt of financial records, one government agency may not disclose them to another agency without notifying the subject-party and without a certification from the receiving agency that the records are relevant to a legitimate law enforcement inquiry.[217]

4. *Electronic Funds Transfer Act*

The Electronic Funds Transfer Act (EFTA) requires financial institutions to inform their customers about their rights and obligations for EFT services.[218] It provides procedures for resolving inaccuracies in customer accounts and penalties for banks' errors in transmitting or documenting EFT transactions.

The EFTA defines an »electronic funds transfer« as any transfer of funds initiated through an electronic terminal, telephonic instrument, computer or magnetic medium (e.g., tape, disc, RAM) to authorize a financial institution to debit or credit an account. This includes point-of-sale transfers, automated teller machine transactions, direct deposits or withdrawals and transfers by telephone.[219] The Act covers state and national banks, state and federal savings and loan associations, mutual savings banks, state and fed-

213 12 U.S.C. § 3401 (1982).
214 *Id.* §§ 3405–3408.
215 *Id.* § 3408.
216 *Id.* § 3409.
217 *Id.* § 3412(a).
218 15 U.S.C. § 1693 (1982).
219 *Id.* § 1693a(6).

eral credit unions, and any other entity that directly or indirectly holds customer accounts.[220]

The Act requires a financial institution to disclose the terms and conditions of EFT accounts when a consumer orders EFT service, including information on issues such as: the consumer's liability for unauthorized transfers; the types of services offered; rates for all services; the institution's liability to the consumer; and the conditions under which EFT consumer information will be disclosed to third parties.[221] The consumer is liable for an unauthorized EFT transaction if it took place either with an access card or device issued by the institution for EFT transactions or through a code or other means of access issued by the institution. A consumer's liability for an unauthorized transaction, however, does not exceed fifty dollars.[222] A financial institution is liable for failing to make a transfer in the correct amount or time period if it had proper instructions from the consumer – subject to exceptions, of course, such as insufficient funds in the account or force majeure.[223]

A financial institution is liable to a consumer for failure to comply with the Act's provisions. But an unintentional violation – that is, a bona fide error that took place despite all reasonable precautions – does not create liability.[224] Compliance with EFTA's provisions is enforced by the Comptroller of the Currency, the Federal Reserve Board, the Federal Deposit Insurance Commission and other federal agencies.[225]

5. *Private Collection of Credit and Other Financial Information*

The Fair Credit Reporting Act (FCRA) regulates the information-gathering and -disclosure practices of »consumer reporting agencies« (CRAs) and the use of »consumer credit reports.«[226] A CRA is »any person which, for monetary fees, dues, or on a cooperative nonprofit basis, regularly engages in whole or in part in the practice of assembling or evaluating consumer credit information or other information on consumers for the purpose of furnishing consumer reports to third parties.«[227] If businesses gather but

220 *Id.* § 1693a(8).
221 *Id.* § 1693c.
222 *Id.* § 1693g.
223 *Id.* § 1693h.
224 *Id.* § 1693m(a), (c).
225 *Id.* § 1693.
226 *Id.* § 1681.
227 *Id.* § 1681a(f).

do not disclose information to third parties or disclose only information about their own dealings with a consumer, they are not deemed to be »reporting agencies.« A »consumer report« is »any written, oral, or other communication of any information by a consumer reporting agency bearing on a consumer's credit worthiness, credit standing, credit capacity, character, general reputation, personal characteristics, or mode of living which is used ... as a factor in establishing a consumer's eligibility for (1) credit or insurance, ... (2) employment purposes, or (3) other purposes« (i.e. government benefits, licenses or business transactions).[228]

A consumer reporting agency may furnish a financial report under the following circumstances:

1. in response to a valid court order;
2. with the consumer's permission;
3. to parties that intend to use the information for a consumer credit transaction (e.g., extension of credit, review or collection of an account) or for employment purposes;
4. for underwriting insurance for a consumer;
5. to parties using the information to determine a consumer's elegibility for a government license or benefit; or
6. to parties with a legitimate business need for the information in connection with a business transaction with the consumer.[229]

A CRA need not allow consumers to see their files but must disclose to them the »nature and substance« of all information (except medical information) in its files, the source of the information and any third-party access to the data within the last six months. The Act prohibits reporting of obsolete information – e.g., paid tax liens that antedate the report by seven years.[230]

Consumers may dispute the contents of their file.[231] Upon verification of discrepancies, the agency must delete inaccuracies and notify parties who had received the information.[232] If a third party denies credit, insurance or employment to a consumer on the basis of a CRA's report, the third party must identify the CRA to the consumer.[233]

Willful noncompliance with these provisions by CRAs or third parties creates liability for actual and punitive damages.[234] Negligent noncom-

228 *Id.* § 1681a(d) (1982).
229 *Id.* § 1681b.
230 *Id.* § 1681c.
231 *Id.* § 1681i.
232 *Id.* § 1681i(d).
233 *Id.* § 1681m(a).
234 *Id.* § 1681n.

pliance also gives rise to liability. The Act's requirements are enforced primarily by the Federal Trade Commission and secondarily by the Federal Deposit Insurance Corporation, the Comptroller of the Currency and others.[235]

6. *Collection of Information by Cable Television Systems*

a. *Federal law*

The Cable Communications Policy Act of 1984 (Cable Act) is a general codification of cable television law, including provisions on subscriber privacy.[236] The Act requires cable operators to give initial and thereafter annual written notice to cable subscribers informing them of: (1) the type of personally identifiable information to be collected on them and the nature of its use; (2) the nature, purpose and frequency of disclosure of such data, as well as the types of persons to whom disclosure will be made; (3) the time period during which data will be maintained by the operator; and (4) the times and places at which subscribers can examine this information.[237]

The Cable Act prohibits a cable operator from collecting personally identifiable information concerning any subscriber without the subscriber's prior written or electronic consent.[238] For example, on an interactive or two-way system, a computer might need to ask subscribers whether they consented to the release of information about their transaction before processing transaction requests. Without a subscriber's consent, a cable operator may only collect data necessary to render cable service or to detect unauthorized reception of cable communications.[239]

A cable operator may not disclose personally identifiable information about subscribers without their consent.[240] An exception to this prohibition exists if disclosure is necessary to conduct a legitimate cable television business activity or is pursuant to a court order, after the subscriber has received notice of the order.

Cable subscribers have access to all information about them maintained by

235 *Id.* § 1686s.
236 47 U.S.C. § 521 (Supp. 1986).
237 *Id.* § 551(a)(1).
238 *Id.* § 551(b)(1).
239 *Id.* § 551(b)(2)(A), (B).
240 *Id.* § 551(c)(1).

a cable operator.[241] A subscriber must have a reasonable opportunity to correct any error in such data. A cable operator must destroy personally identifiable information that is no longer necessary.[242] Any person aggrieved by a cable operator's violation may bring a civil action in a federal district court. The court may award punitive as well as actual damages and reasonable attorneys fees as well as litigation costs.[243]

As a corollary to a subscriber's access rights, a government agency may obtain information about a subscriber only if it shows a court through clear and convincing evidence that the subject of the request is reasonably suspected of engaging in criminal activity and that the information would be material evidence in the case. In any event, the subscriber has a right to contest the government's claim.[244]

The Act does not prevent state or local franchising authorities from enacting or enforcing laws consistent with the Act in order to protect subscriber privacy.[245] An number of states and cities in fact do so, as discussed below.

b. *State law: The Wisconsin, California and Illinois examples*

Under Wisconsin law, upon a subscriber's request, any terminal capable of transmitting a message from a subscriber's location to an operator's central processing facilities must provide the subscriber with equipment to prevent transmission of such messages – except for signals necessary to monitor security, fire and utility services.[246] A cable operator must notify each subscriber in writing of the availability of such devices and may not make any additional charge for them.[247]

Unless an operator obtains the written consent of a cable subscriber every two years, an operator may not: (1) monitor the subscriber's cable equipment or use, except for purposes of billing or of checking the system's technical performance; (2) disclose information on a subscriber's personal behavior, including individual viewing habits, finances or programming preferences; or (3) conduct research that requires subscriber response (except by mail or personal interview), unless the subscriber has been notified in writ-

241 *Id.* § 551(d).
242 *Id.* § 551(e).
243 *Id.* § 551(f).
244 *Id.* § 551(h).
245 *Id.* § 551(g).
246 WIS. STAT. ANN. § 134.43(1)(a) (1982).
247 *Id.* § 134.43(1)(c), (d).

ing before the research begins.[248] Violators are subject to a forfeiture of up to $50,000 for a first offense and $100,000 for subsequent offences.

The Illinois Communications Consumer Privacy Act makes it unlawful for a cable operator to: (1) observe activities in a subscriber's household without the subscriber's knowledge or permission; (2) provide lists of subscribers without prior notice to them; (3) disclose a subscriber's television viewing habits without his or her prior consent; or (4) install a home security device without the resident's express written consent.[249] Violations of the Act are punishable by fines of up to $10,000.

California prohibits cable operators from recording or monitoring conversations without the subscriber's express written consent. A cable operator also may not disclose any individually identifiable information – such as a subscriber's viewing habits, shopping choices, interests, opinions, banking data or any other personal or private information – without the subscriber's written consent.[250]

The California statute also prohibits a cable operator from giving individually identifiable subscriber data to government agencies in the absence of legal compulsion, such as a court order or subpoena. An operator must notify a subscriber of the nature and origin of any request prior to disclosing information, unless otherwise prohibited by law.[251] Individually identifiable subscriber information gathered by a cable operator must be made available for subscriber inspection. If a subscriber shows that the information is inaccurate, an operator must correct the data.[252] A cable operator must notify all subscribers of their privacy protections.[253]

7. *Unauthorized Interception of Programming*

The Communications Act includes a general prohibition on the unauthorized interception and commercial exploitation of signals not transmitted to the general public.[254] Divulging the contents of these signals to third parties without the sender's consent violates the Act. The prohibition does not apply, however, to radio communications relating to ships, aircraft,

248 *Id.* § 134.43(2)(a), (b), (c).
249 ILL. STAT. ANN., ch. 38, § 87–1 (1982).
250 CALIF. STAT. ANN. § 637.5(a)(1), (2) (1982).
251 *Id.* § 637.5(c).
252 *Id.* § 637.5(d).
253 *Id.* § 637.5(e).
254 47 U.S.C. § 705(a) (Supp. 1985).

vehicles or persons in distress, or transmitted by amateur or citizens band operators.

As amended by the Cable Act, section 705 also prohibits the interception of channels on a cable television system without the program supplier's specific authorization. In effect, it creates a federal »theft of service« statute to prevent viewers from receiving programming without paying for cable service. The severity of criminal penalties for violating this section depends on the nature of the intercepted signal. Willful violations for personal use may result in fines of up to $1,000 and imprisonment for up to six months. But if a person willfully intercepts signals for purposes of »commercial gain« (e.g., to attract customers to a restaurant), he or she is liable for fines of up to $50,000 and imprisonment for up to two years.

Along somewhat similar lines, another Cable Act amendment attempts to create a new »marketplace« system for cable and other programming transmitted by satellite.[255] Most cable channels – such as the pay channel Home Box Office (HBO) – are transmitted via satellite and intended for receipt only by cable television operators, who then resell them to their subscribers. Many viewers have bought inexpensive – $1,000 to $2,000 – satellite receivers, in order to pick up these signals for free. Section 705 now allows reception of programs if they are not encrypted and if a »marketing system« is not established by the national programming source, such as HBO.

If a marketing system has been established, a user may receive such programming upon paying the programmer for a license.[256] Unauthorized private viewing of these signals is punishable by a fine of up to $1,000 and imprisonment for up to six months. If people intercept these signals without authorization and for commercial gain, however, they may be fined up to $50,000 and imprisoned for up to two years.[257] Violators face civil liability for all revenues received by their interceptions. Programmers also may seek injunctions and damages.

In practice, the unauthorized reception of satellite transmissions has been growing by leaps and bounds, particularly in rural areas that are not served by cable television. Some observers believe that almost two million homes now have satellite receivers.[258] Satellite programmers recently adopted a uniform scambling protocol, however, and will begin encrypting their signals in 1986 – a move that naturally will force viewers to buy service from

255 *Id.* § 705(b).
256 *Id.* § 705(b)(1), (2).
257 *Id.* § 705(d)(1), (2).
258 Cablevision, Dec. 9, 1985, at 11.

the programmers.[259] The trend appears to be that local cable operators will sell programming for satellite reception within their operating areas, thus adding a new revenue flow to their operations.

C. *Anti-Espionage Laws and Classified Information Statutes*

U.S. law contains a large number of data-classification provisions relating to espionage.[260] An intensive discussion of these provisions is not feasible here. Nevertheless, a brief description of several major provisions may be in order, since all of them impact upon the availability of data for international transmission.

The Espionage Act imposes fines of up to $10,000 and imprisonment for up to ten years on persons convicted of engaging or conspiring to engage in three broad categories of proscribed activity.[261] The terms of the Act are quite comprehensive in scope. They include the following.

1. *Gathering, Transmitting or Losing Defense Information*

It is illegal to obtain information regarding national defense by entering military installations, government buildings or research laboratories, or by intercepting defense-related telephone, telegraph or radio transmission.[262] Unauthorized copying or other obtaining of documents, plans, photographs and items connected with the national defense also violates the Act.[263] If a person receives or attempts to receive illegally procured national defense materials, he or she is in violation of the Act.[264] If people

259 *Id.*

260 *See, e.g.*, 50 U.S.C. § 401 note, Ex. Ord. No. 12356, section 1.3(1) (1982) (classification of military plans); 50 U.S.C. § 401 note, Ex. Ord. No. 12356, section 1.3(2) (1982) (information regarding national security installations); 50 U.S.C. § 401 note, Ex. Ord. No. 12356, section 1.3(3) (1982) (information regarding foreign governments); 50 U.S.C. § 401, Ex. Ord. No. 132356, section 1.3(40) (1982) (information regarding intelligence activities); 50 U.S.C. § 401 note, Ex. Ord. No. 12356, section 1.3(5) (1982) (information regarding foreign relations); 50 U.S.C. § 401 note, Ex. Ord. No. 12356, section 1.3(7) (1982) (information regarding nuclear materials and facilities).

261 18 U.S.C. § 791 (1982).

262 *Id.* § 793(a).

263 *Id.* § 793(b).

264 *Id.* § 793(c).

with lawful access to defense-related materials communicate such information to unauthorized persons or fail to deliver such information to an authorized U.S. official, they also violate the Act.[265]

2. *Delivering Defense Information to Foreign Governments*

If people have reason to believe that information in their possession may be used to jeopardize national security, they may not communicate it to any foreign government or its agents.[266] Violation of this section is subject to punishment by execution or life imprisonment. Attempting to communicate defense and security-related information to an enemy in wartime also may be punished by execution or life imprisonment.[267]

3. *Disclosure of Classified Information*

The law prohibits any knowing communication to unauthorized persons of classified information concerning: (1) the nature, preparation or use of any U.S. or foreign code, cipher or cryptographic system; (2) the design, construction or use of U.S. or foreign cryptographic or intelligence-related devices; (3) the communications intelligence activities of the United States or any foreign government; or (4) confidential communications of foreign governments.[268]

265 *Id.* § 793(d).
266 *Id.* § 794(a).
267 *Id.* § 794(b).
268 *Id.* § 798(a)(1), (2), (3), and (4).

Conclusion

This survey of restrictions on data flows out of or into the United States shows that such restrictions are relatively limited and are diminishing outside the area of national security. Historically, the United States has exercised some control over international communications by regulation of the channels of communication rather than the content of the communications themselves. This regulation was premised initially on the scarcity of the electromagnetic spectrum and later of geosynchronous orbit positions. Coupled with the absence of a governmental monopoly, this scarcity necessitated an allocation among private firms. The regulation of communications channels, in turn, focused primarily on industry *structure* rather than on *behavior*, on the grounds that structure determines behavior and that structural regulation avoids free speech problems under the first amendment of the U.S. Constitution.

Historically, the U.S. policy in international telecommunications had been to carve up the market into distinct segments, each assigned to different types of carriers. Underlying the restrictive licensing scheme was the desire to regulate behavior and at least partly limit AT&T's power – by restricting it to the voice market, regulating its rates and insulating the international record carriers from competition. When satellite communications emerged as a potential disruption to this system, fear of AT&T's expanding powers led the U.S. government to create Comsat as a monopoly, initially serving as a carriers' carrier without any competition for users' business.[269]

This system of neat, compartmentalized service categories functioned as a cartel mechanism by dividing markets and separating competitors from each other. Partly because it was profitable, it proved unstable when its underlying conditions changed, namely, when: (a) voice and record service distinctions broke down as telephone carriers became major data carriers; (b) new entrants did not conform to traditional market divisions; (c) transmission capacity grew and costs fell rapidly due to high-capacity satellites as well as submarine cables; and (d) government policies opened competition in domestic telecommunications, dismembered AT&T and extended deregulation to the international sector.[270]

269 *See* discussion in text at note 155 *supra*.
270 *See* discussion in text at note 141 *supra*.

These factors combined to eliminate in rapid succession many of the structural rules that had characterized U.S. communications. The few remaining rules may also change, along with INTELSAT's position. The United States is in transition to an environment in which carriers – such as AT&T, MCI, Sprint, RCA, Western Union, Comsat, Tel-Optic and Orion – will compete to provide all types of domestic as well as international transmission services, with little governmental supervision except for initial frequency and orbital allocations.[271]

The limit on this scenario, of course, is the necessity of accommodation with overseas carriers and governments, which do not share the United States' competitive views for reasons of ideology, politics or economics. The United States faces in every international telecommunications body a front that includes most of its traditional allies and trading partners. At the same time, the competition among U.S. carriers allows those countries' telecommunications authorities to play off U.S. carriers against each other, thus transforming a previously bilateral monopoly situation into a unilateral one.

At the extreme, foreign carriers could enter the U.S. market by connecting with local BOC exchange companies; they thus could bypass U.S. long-distance and international carriers while discriminating against the latter's access in their home territories. In this situation, a variety of U.S. measures – such as the »anti-whipsawing« rules – may survive and even expand. While inconsistent with true deregulation, these rules would be a rational response to the realities of an international environment that prevents unilateral deregulation in a multilateral world.

With these caveats, most U.S. regulation of transmission channels and market segments is about to disappear. In terms of regulation of international communications flows, this leaves primarily those restrictions that also affect domestic communications. In other words, the international effect is merely an extension of domestic law, including special provisions as to national security. Among the former category – that is, general restrictions on information flows – are the following, which for purposes of brevity have not been discussed in this paper:

(a) privileged information (such as medical or accounting data);
(b) defamation;
(c) proprietary information, protected by copyright or contract;
(d) financial information, which the financial securities laws may require to conform to certain standards of completeness, timeliness and accuracy;

271 *See* discussion in text at note 147 *supra*.

(e) false advertising;
(f) obscenity and indecency;
(g) information that can be construed to be part of the unauthorized practice of a profession requiring a license;
(h) information violating people's privacy, appropriating their likeness or personality, holding them up to ridicule, causing mental and emotional distress or interfering with their civil rights;
(i) »fighting words« that are likely to provoke an immediate violent response;
(j) advocacy of violent behavior, where such behavior is imminent, intended and likely;
(k) advertising of controlled products and services, such as liquor, cigarettes and gambling;
(l) the manner of political speech, in instances where public campaign financing is accepted; and
(m) in general, regulation concerning the reasonableness of time, place and manner of information dissemination. For example, the provision of sexually oriented »adult« pornographic telephone tape messages outside of evening hours may be limited.

While these general categories of restrictions exist, they almost never prohibit information flows in advance. Only *after* such dissemination has taken place can an injured individual or the state seek damages or penalties.[272] Exceptions to this principle against »prior restraints« are obscenity, some national-security threats and imminent danger of violence. Most of the other restrictions listed above are interpreted very narrowly and are difficult to enforce because of the presumption in favor of free speech. The major exception is securities-trading regulations, which control dissemination and use of stock-market-related information. These restrictions recently have become subject to constitutional challenge under the free speech clause of the U.S. Constitution.[273]

All of these restrictions affect information flows into or out of the U.S. Their scope is in continuing flux because of vague statutes and regulations, which are subject to judicial, common-law, case-by-case review. While it is difficult to generalize, the past trend was to limit restrictions on information flows, and this has continued under the current Supreme Court.

The major restriction on international and U.S. domestic information flows lies in the area of national security. Unilateral and cooperative restrictions

272 *E.g.*, Near v. Minnesota, 283 U.S. 697 (1931).
273 *See* Penny Stock Newsletter, Nos. 801–19962, 801–15347 (S.E.C., Dec. 19, 1984).

on the transfer of technological and strategic information to non-allied countries exist in a variety of forms, and their enforcement has received priority in recent years. These regulations center on nuclear information, arms information and dual-use (civilian and military) information. Multinational coordination attempts to harmonize Western efforts.[274]

Concerning the protection of data privacy, there is a frequent but erroneous view that such protections are weak or non-existent in the United States. There is no comprehensive national statute, possibly because of a general U.S. reluctance for centralized legislation. The thrust of U.S. protection is to restrict, through piecemeal legislation, governmental intrusion into personal data by requiring search warrants, notification, opportunity to challenge searches, access by individuals to information about themselves and the right to correct such data. Restrictions on the private collection of data are more lax where the information is not distributed to third parties. Here the underlying assumption is that an individual seeking credit or employment relinquishes some privacy in order to reduce transactions costs. But consumers have access to credit files kept on them, and employers cannot divulge information freely.

Some characteristics of U.S. international communications regulation conflict both with each other and with other industrialized countries' policies. These characteristics are:

(a) withdrawal of the governmental role in establishing channels of communications and encouragement of competition;

(b) freedom of speech (tempered by common-law and regulatory safeguards of special policy concern)

(c) national security;

(d) acceptance of private data collection as an integral part of economic activity; and

(e) support of the commercial activities of U.S. firms internationally.

As befits this multiplicity of goals, there are not enough »degrees of freedom« to structure a consistent and stable policy, nor is every goal achieved in a pure form. Hence, foreign critics easily can point to inconsistencies as a sign of ideological hypocricy or commerical greed. As Ralph Waldo Emerson said, however, »A foolish consistency is the hobgoblin of little men.«[275] It is precisely in the nature of the common law and of a federal state that policies emerge piecemeal, without necessarily being coordinated in time and purpose.

274 *See* discussion in text at note 188 *et seq. supra*.

275 R.W. EMERSON, SELF-RELIANCE.

On the other hand, such a mechanism permits frequent adjustment. Indeed, U.S. policies on information and telecommunications have changed quite rapidly in the past fifteen years, with little major legislation. Overall, the tendency clearly has been towards withdrawal of the governmental role. In the international sphere, the concurrent stress on national security has been the major counter-trend.

This is not ideological inconsistency; even most advocates of a minimalist state seek a strong protective role for government in foreign affairs. But it creates practical problems, as well as the need to negotiate with foreign governments on international communications matters. It keeps the U.S. government active in communications regulation and creates a built-in friction with its allies, which is not likely to disappear in the near future.

PART II: REGULATION OF MASS MEDIA

by *Stephen R. Barnett*[*]

* The author is grateful to Tze Lee Tien, a law and doctoral student at the University of California, Berkeley, for his skilled research and editorial assistance on this project over an extended period. The author is also grateful to Berkeley law students Randy P. Baker, Glenn F. MacGilvra, Alfred M. Mamlet and Jeffrey E. Thomas for their valuable research and editorial assistance.

Introduction

Government regulation of the mass media has produced in the United States an extensive and intricate body of law. The fountainhead of this law is the First Amendment to the United States Constitution. That Amendment states, in apparently absolute and simple terms, that »Congress shall make no law ... abridging the freedom of speech, or of the press.«[1] Although United States law under the First Amendment is indeed highly protective of speech and press, as compared with the law of most other countries, it is neither as simple nor as minimal as the language of the Amendment might suggest.

Even with respect to the print media, First Amendment law draws distinctions between categories of speech. Some categories receive full constitutional protection, some receive no protection (e.g., »obscenity«), and some receive partial protection (e.g., defamation and commercial speech).[2] Further distinctions are drawn, and different First Amendment »tests« applied, depending on whether a particular regulation aims at the »communicative impact« of speech or only »incidentally« restricts speech while pursuing some other objective.[3] Meanwhile, a variety of special doctrines – such as »prior restraint,« the »public forum« and »content neutrality« – further complicate government regulation of speech.[4]

Different media add their own complications. Broadcasting has been accorded significantly less constitutional protection than the print media,[5] and the Supreme Court indeed has suggested that each new medium requires its own First Amendment analysis.[6] Although the traditional treatment of broadcasting, based on the notion of spectrum scarcity, is now

1 U.S. CONST. amend. I
2 *See infra* notes 35–40 and accompanying text.
3 *See infra* notes 58–66 and accompanying text.
4 *See infra* notes 41–55 and accompanying text.
5 *See infra* note 529 and accompanying text.
6 Red Lion Broadcasting Co. v. FCC, 395 U.S. 367, ___ (1969); *see infra* note 156 and accompanying text.

under question,[7] there is no reason to think that differences in the characteristics of new media will not continue to call forth differences in the First Amendment standards applied to them.

Given the elaborate development and high visibility of media law in the United States, one would expect that law to have devoted special attention to media flows that cross the borders of the United States. In today's world, the mass media are highly international in their operation and impact, preeminently so with respect to the United States. An article in a Lebanese magazine in November 1986 set off a political crisis in the United States.[8] Foreign journalists based in the United States number more than 1,400.[9] Foreign opponents of United States policies regularly take their cases to the American public. The distinction between domestic and international issues increasingly blurs. Many issues of national security, economics, health, the environment, culture and even politics that are debated within a country, especially a country as conspicuous as the United States, have international or worldwide dimensions.

Nevertheless, U.S. media law, as of the end of 1986, had devoted surprisingly little attention to the First Amendment questions raised by governmental regulation of transborder speech. The Supreme Court had touched on the subject both in an immigration law case involving the government's power to deny a visitor a visa on the basis of his ideological or political persuasions[10] and in cases involving the government's power to restrict the foreign travel of U.S. citizens.[11] But the Court only once had confronted a restriction on »pure speech« crossing the border. This was in *Lamont v. Postmaster General*,[12] decided in 1965, where the Court held invalid under the First Amendment a statute requiring that »communist political propaganda« mailed into the United States be detained at the Post Office until the addressee was notified and requested its delivery.

There now appears to be growing attention in the United States to legal

7 *See infra* notes 158–63 and accompanying text.

8 *See A Watchdog Asleep: The Press in the Iran Affair*, Int'l Herald Trib., Mar. 5, 1987, at 3, cols. 4–7 (N.Y. Times dispatch).

9 The Foreign Press Center, a division of the United States Information Agency, reports that its mailing list of foreign journalists based in the United States includes about 750 in New York City, 525 in Washington, D.C., and 150 in Los Angeles. Telephone interview with Nicholas King, director of the Foreign Press Center (New York) (Mar. 16, 1987); telephone interview with Don Jones, director of the Foreign Press Center's Los Angeles office (Mar. 16, 1987).

10 Kleindienst v. Mandel, 408 U.S. 753 (1952); *see infra* notes 346–58 and accompanying text.

11 *E.g.*, Regan v. Wald, 468 U.S. 222, 240–42 (1984); Haig v. Agee, 453 U.S. 280 (1981); Aptheker v. Secretary of State, 378 U.S. 500 (19864); *see infra* notes 373–91 and accompanying text.

12 381 U.S. 301 (1965); *see infra* notes 308–13 and accompanying text.

restrictions on transborder speech. The Supreme Court as of December 1986 was considering a case challenging under the First Amendment the provisions of the Foreign Agents Registration Act, which regulate as »political propaganda« speech disseminated in the United States by agents of foreign entities, that were applied to three documentary films from Canada concerning nuclear war and acid rain.[13] In October 1986, a federal district court held invalid under the First Amendment the regulations used by the United States Information Agency in deciding whether to certify films as »educational« for the purpose of duty-free import to other countries under an international agreement.[14] In addition, the Supreme Court in 1986 accepted for review a new case dealing with the denial of visitors' visas for reasons based on the ideological or political leanings of the would-be visitors.[15]

Meanwhile, the technology of communications, particularly of communications satellites, increasingly can reach across national frontiers. As a result, the existing U.S. restrictions on transborder speech are growing in their impact and, at the same time, are coming under increased scrutiny in the United States.

From another perspective, U.S. regulation of transborder speech invites a comparison with the position the United States has taken in the international debate on transborder speech. In that debate, the United States has stood staunchly for a »free flow« of information across national frontiers. It has championed article 19 of the Universal Declaration of Human Rights, which declares a right to »seek, receive and impart information and ideas through any media and regardless of frontiers.«[16]

The »free flow« position of the United States has been particularly evident in debates at the United Nations over control of direct-broadcast satellites (DBS).[17] The United States has opposed almost any restriction on transborder DBS, especially any requirement of »prior consent« by the country

13 Meese v. Keene, 107 S. Ct. 1862 (1987). The case was decided April 28, 1987; *see infra* note 470. *See also infra* notes 419–69 and accompanying text.

14 Bullfrog Films, Inc. v. Wick, 646 F. Supp. 492 (C.D. Cal. 1986), *appeal docketed*, No. 86–6630 (9th Cir.); *see infra* notes 919–35 and accompanying text.

15 Abourezk v. Reagan, 785 F.2d 1043 (D.C. Cir. 1986), *cert. granted,* 107 S. Ct. 666 (1986) [*aff'd*, 56 U.S.L.W. 4001 (Oct. 19, 1987)]; *see infra* notes 362-67 and accompanying text.

16 G.A. Res. 217, U.N. Doc. A/810 (1948); *see infra* notes 7–19, 319–24 and accompanying text.

17 *See, e.g.*, K. QUEENEY, DIRECT BROADCAST SATELLITES AND THE UNITED NATIONS 79 (1978).

whose residents would receive the broadcasts.[18] In 1982, for example, in opposing a General Assembly Resolution supporting the principle of prior consent, the United States delegate declared that:

> [A]ny principle requiring that [a] broadcaster must obtain the consent of a foreign Government would violate United States obligations towards both the broadcasters and the intended audience; it would also violate article 19 of the Universal Declaration of Human Rights on the right to freedom of expression.[19]

This international posture of the United States makes it appropriate to consider to what extent the United States allows a »free flow« of information across its own borders. The »free flow« concept provides an external benchmark, while the First Amendment provides a domestic benchmark, for appraising U.S. laws regulating transborder media flows. Those laws thus can be compared both with the laws of other countries and with the principles espoused by the United States itself.

With those perspectives in mind, Part II presents a survey and commentary on the United States law regulating transborder media flows. By way of background, Chapter IV sets forth the domestic framework of media regulation under U.S. law. Chapter V deals with regulation of media flow into the United States, and Chapter VI with regulation of outgoing flow. Each chapter focuses first on laws regulating media flow in general and then on laws addressed specifically to the electronic media.

18 *See, e.g., id.*; Gorove, *International Direct Television Broadcasting by Satellites: »Prior Consent« Revisited*, 24 COLUM. J. TRANSNATL L. 1, 5 (1985); Price, *The First Amendment and Television Broadcasting by Satellite*, 23 UCLA L. REV 879, 879–80, 883–84 (1976); Hagelin, *Prior Consent or the Free Flow of Information Over International Satellite Radio and Television: A Comparison and Critique of U.S. Domestic and International Broadcast Policy*, 8 SYR. J. INT'L L. & COM. 265, 265 (1981); Magraw, *Telecommunications: Building a Consensus*, Harv. Int'l Rev., Nov. 1984, at 27, 28–30.

19 37 U.N. GAOR Special Political Comm. (34th mtg.) at 11, U.N. Doc. A/APC/37 34 (1982).

Chapter IV: Framework of National Law: Regulation of Domestic Media

A. *Constitutional Framework: The First Amendment*

1. *Scope and Purposes of First Amendment Freedoms of Speech and Press*

The First Amendment to the United States Constitution, which states that »Congress shall make no law ... abridging the freedom of speech, or of the press,«[20] limits the scope and character of all government action that regulates or restricts expression. It applies, by virtue of the Fourteenth Amendment to the Constitution, to the states (and cities) as well as the federal government,[21] and it limits the action of all branches of government: legislative, executive, administrative, judicial. Primary responsibility for interpreting and enforcing the First Amendment guarantees lies with the judicial branch, since the power of judicial review enables the courts to invalidate government action inconsistent with the Constitution.[22]

While no theory, or collection of theories, fully or indisputedly captures the purposes of the freedoms of speech and press guaranteed by the First Amendment, four rationales have achieved broad acceptance. Advanced in seminal opinions by United States Supreme Court Justices Oliver Wendell Holmes, Jr. and Louis D. Brandeis following the First World War,[23] these rationales have provided the classic premises on which First Amendment doctrine has developed.

Three of the rationales justify freedom of expression by its social purposes, the benefits it provides for society in general and democracy in par-

20 U.S. CONST. amend. I (1791).

21 The Fourteenth Amendment, adopted in 1868, provides that no state shall »deprive any person of life, liberty, or property, without due process of law.« The freedoms of speech and press that were established against congressional action by the First Amendment are considered part of the »liberty« that the due process clause of the Fourteenth Amendment forbids the states from violating as well. Gitlow v. New York, 268 U.S. 652 (1925).

22 Marbury v. Madison, 5 U.S. 137 (1803).

23 Abrams v. United States, 250 U.S. 616, 624 (1919) (Holmes, J., dissenting); Whitney v. California, 274 U.S. 357, 372 (1927) (Brandeis, J., concurring).

ticular. First, in a concept derived from John Milton[24] and John Mill,[25] free expression is considered essential to the advancement of knowledge and the discovery of truth. As Justice Holmes put it, »The ultimate good desired is better reached by free trade in ideas ... the best test of truth is the power of the thought to get itself accepted in the competition of the market.«[26] Second, free expression is especially necessary in the context of American democracy, because it enables citizens to enlighten themselves and hence govern themselves.[27] As Professor Alexander Meiklejohn influentially argued, »the necessities of self-government by universal suffrage« explain the First Amendment.[28] Third, free expression gives society a »safety valve,« a way for disgruntled citizens to express their grievances peacefully. In the words of Justice Brandeis, »The path of safety lies in the opportunity to discuss freely supposed grievances and proposed remedies.«[29]

The fourth of the classic theories, increasingly prominent in recent years, emphasizes not the social ends of freedom of expression but its role in promoting self-fulfillment of the individual. As Professor C. Edwin Baker has put it, »Speech is protected not as a means to a collective good but because of the value of speech conduct to the individual.«[30]

Other writers have supplemented and elaborated the basic theories. Professor Vincent Blasi has distinguished a »checking« function that free expression performs in a democracy:[31] Apart from promoting self-government, the public knowledge and public debate made possible by

24 *See* JOHN MILTON, AREOPAGITICA 409 (Encycl. Britannica ed. 1948).

25 JOHN MILL, ON LIBERTY 76 (Penguin ed. 1982).

26 Abrams v. United States, 250 U.S. 616, 630 (1919) (Holmes, J., dissenting); *see also* United States v. Associated Press, 52 F. Supp. 362 (S.D.N.Y. 1943), *aff'd*, 326 U.S. 1 (1944) (Learned Hand, J.) (» ... right conclusions are more likely to be gathered out of a multitude of tongues, than through any kind of authoritative selection«); T. EMERSON, THE SYSTEM OF FREEDOM OF EXPRESSION 6 (1970).

27 *See* Whitney v. California, 274 U.S. 357, 375–77 (1927) (Brandeis, J., concurring) (»freedom to think as you will and speak as you think are means indispensable to the discovery and spread of political truth; ... public discussion is a political duty ...«); T. EMERSON, *supra* note 26, at 7.

28 A. MEIKLEJOHN, FREE SPEECH AND ITS RELATION TO SELF-GOVERNMENT 37–39 (1948); *see also* T. EMERSON, *supra* note 26, at 7.

29 Whitney v. California, 274 U.S. 357, 375 (1927) (Brandeis, J., concurring).

30 Baker, *Scope of the First Amendment Freedom of Speech*, 25 UCLA L. REV. 964, 966 (1978); *see also* Whitney v. California 274 U.S. 357, 375 (1927) (Brandeis, J., concurring); T. EMERSON, *supra* note 26, at 6.

31 Blasi, *The Checking Value in First Amendment Theory*, 1977 AM. B. FOUND. RESEARCH J. 521.

the First Amendment enable the public to check governmental abuses of power.[32] In a parallel vein, Supreme Court Justice Potter Stewart suggested that one way the framers of the First Amendment sought to check governmental power was by recognizing freedom of the press separately from freedom of speech.[33] In Justice Stewart's view, the »press clause« of the First Amendment provides protection for the press as an institution, additional to the protection the »speech clause« provides for speakers generally, so the press can act as »a fourth institution outside the Government as an additional check on the three official branches.«[34]

2. *General Categories of Constitutionally Protected Speech*

It is possible to identify three general categories of constitutionally protected speech. (More specific categories, such as defamation, are considered below.) Political speech, particularly speech concerning issues or persons of civic importance, is the central object of First Amendment protection. »Whatever differences may exist about interpretation of the First Amendment, there is practically universal agreement that a major purpose of that amendment was to protect the free discussion of governmental affairs.«[35] Art, literature, and entertainment are also fully protected,[36] although a few writers would give them less protection than political speech.[37]

The third category is commercial speech, defined as expression »related solely to the economic interests of the speaker and its audience«[38] – in particular, commercial advertising. First Amendment protection for commercial speech is based on »the informational function of advertising«[39] rather than on more fundamental First Amendment values,

32 *Id.*
33 Stewart, *»Or of the Press,«* 26 HASTINGS L.J. 631 (1975).
34 *Id.* at 634; *see also* Anderson, *The Origins of the Press Clause,* 30 UCLA L. REV. 455, 533–37 (1983).
35 Mills v. Alabama, 384 U.S. 214, 218 (1966).
36 *See, e.g.*, Joseph Burstyn, Inc. v. Wilson, 343 U.S. 495, 502 (1952); *see also* Miller v. California, 413 U.S. 15, 34 (1973).
37 *E.g.*, Bork, *Neutral Principles and Some First Amendment Problems*, 47 IND. L.J. 1, 20 (1971).
38 Cent. Hudson Gas & Elec. Co. v. Pub. Serv. Comm'n, 447 U.S. 557, 561 (1980).
39 *Id.* at 563.

such as democracy or personal autonomy, and is therefore weaker than for the other categories. To justify a purposeful restriction on commercial speech, the government does not need to show a »compelling« interest; it needs only to show an interest that is substantial – that is, directly promoted by the restriction – and that could not be as effectively promoted by an alternative means less restrictive of speech.[40]

3. *Special Aspects of Constitutional Protection: Prior Restraint, Content Neutrality, and the Public Forum*

a. *Prior restraint*

One of the fundamental principles of First Amendment law is that regulation taking the form of a »prior restraint« of expression, as distinguished from penalties or other sanctions that take effect after material has been published, faces a very strong presumption of unconstitutionality. This principle derives from the main historical purpose of the First Amendment, which was to repudiate the schemes for licensing the press that had been employed in seventeenth-century England and also in the American colonies.[41] The principle has been extended, however, to »prior restraints« that have little in common with any licensing scheme.[42] The Supreme Court has used it, for example, to strike down a court order prohibiting journalists from publishing information about a criminal defendant's alleged confession until after a jury for his trial had been chosen.[43]

In the *Pentagon Papers* case,[44] the strong presumption against prior restraint prevailed against government claims that publication would damage national security. The Supreme Court rejected the federal government's attempt to enjoin the *New York Times* and the *Washington Post* from publishing the »Pentagon Papers,« even though these documents contained classified information and had been

40 *Id.* at 564; *accord*, Posadas de Puerto Rico Associates v. Tourism Co. of Puerto Rico, 106 S.Ct. 2968, 2976–80 (1986).

41 *See* Near v. Minnesota, 283 U.S. 697, 713–714 (1931).

42 *See* Barnett, *The Puzzle of Prior Restraint*, 29 STAN. L. REV. 539 (1977). *But see* Blasi, *Toward A Theory of Prior Restraint: The Central Linkage*, 66 MINN. L. REV. 11 (1981).

43 Nebraska Press Ass'n v. Stuart, 427 U.S. 539, 559 (1976).

44 New York Times Co. v. United States, 403 U.S. 713 (1971).

obtained from the government surreptitiously. The Court ruled that, at least in the absence of authorizing legislation from Congress, prior restraints on publication are not permissible even to protect national security unless, in the words of the concurring opinion of Justice Stewart, the failure to issue the injunction would »surely result in direct, immediate and irreparable damage« to the country.[45]

On the other hand, the licensing type of prior restraint sometimes is allowed, but only for certain media – principally films, where the content is fixed and time is not crucial – and under strict procedural safeguards. Where such safeguards were lacking, the Supreme Court overturned a system requiring movie exhibitors to obtain a license from a state censorship board, certifying that the film was not obscene, before showing the film to the public.[46] The Court held that such a system would be constitutional only if the censor were obligated to prove in a judicial proceeding that the film was obscene, and further that there must be a prompt final decision and that any interim restraint must be »for the shortest fixed period compatible with sound judicial resolution« of the obscenity question.[47]

While such procedural safeguards can make licensing procedures acceptable for the purpose of preventing obscenity in media like films and plays,[48] it by no means follows that they would be acceptable in the print media or broadcasting. In those media not only is time more crucial, but the content is more spontaneous and hence more vulnerable to both external and internal censorship.

b. *Content neutrality*

Even when a government regulation of expression would otherwise be permissible, it will be ruled unconstitutional if it is not »content neutral« – if it favors or disfavors particular ideas, points of view or speakers. The leading case for this important proposition is *Police Department of Chicago v. Mosley*.[49] The Supreme Court there overturned a local ordinance that prohibited picketing, except labor picketing, on the grounds of a public school. The Court said the city could have

45 *Id.* at 730 (Stewart, J., concurring).
46 Freedman v. Maryland, 380 U.S. 51 (1965).
47 *Id.* at 59.
48 *See* Southeastern Promotions, Ltd. v. Conrad, 420 U.S. 546 (1975).
49 408 U.S. 92 (1972).

banned picketing entirely in order to prevent noise or other disruption from affecting the classrooms but that the city could not discriminate on the basis of the content of the picketers' speech.[50]

c. *The public forum*

In addition to the other restrictions it imposes on government regulation of speech, the First Amendment requires the government to allow public access for speech and assembly in certain public places that traditionally have been held open for expressive activity, such as the streets and parks.[51] Expression in these »public forums« is subject to regulation of the »time, place, and manner« in which it occurs – as by requiring a parade permit, for instance, in order to minimize the disruption of traffic and assure adequate police protection.[52] But such regulation must be content-neutral, and speech in public forums may not be cut off or unduly restricted. Thus an ordinance that prohibited the distribution of leaflets in the streets, for the purpose of preventing litter, was held invalid because litter-free streets are not a sufficiently important governmental interest to warrant banning an entire medium of expression from a public forum, especially a medium that may be the only one available to people of small economic means.[53]

Obviously, not all public property – not the Oval Office in the White House, for example – is a public forum. If public property has not traditionally been open to the public for expressive activities and has not been »designated« for that purpose by the government, speech there may be restricted in ways consistent with the property's basic purpose.[54] Thus the Supreme Court has held that an Army base that was otherwise open to the public did not constitute a public forum, in part on the ground (questionable, it would seem) that speech on the base by members of the public would be incompatible with its military function.[55]

50 *Id.* at 101, 102. *See generally* Karst, *Equality As a Central Principle in the First Amendment*, 43 U. CHI. L. REV. 20 (1975); Stone, *Content Regulation and the First Amendment*, 25 WM. & MARY L. REV. 189 (1983).

51 *See* Hague v. CIO, 307 U.S. 496, 515 (1939) (Roberts, J.); Kalven, *The Concept of the Public Forum: Cox v. Lousiana*, 1965 SUP. CT. REV. 1 (1965).

52 Cox v. New Hampshire, 312 U.S. 569 (1941).

53 Schneider v. State, 308 U.S. 147 (1939).

54 *See, e.g.*, Perry Educ. Ass'n v. Perry Local Educators Ass'n, 460 U.S. 37 (1983).

55 Greer v. Spock, 424 U.S. 828 (1976).

4. *Limitations on the Constitutional Protection of Speech*

a. *Unprotected speech*

A few categories of speech are simply unprotected by the First Amendment. One is *deceptive commercial speech*. The Supreme Court has explained that since the limited purpose of constitutional protection for commercial speech is to inform the public, deceptive commercial speech, »communication more likely to deceive the public than to inform it,« is inconsistent with this objective.[56]

Also beyond the pale of First Amendment protection is *obscenity*. The Supreme Court has had great difficulty defining obscenity. Its current definition holds that a work of expression is obscene if »a) the average person, applying contemporary community standards, would find that the work, taken as a whole, appeals to the prurient interest, b) the work depicts or describes, in a patently offensive way, sexual conduct specifically defined by the applicable state law, and c) the work, taken as a whole, lacks serious literary, artistic, political, or scientific value.«[57]

b. *»Clear and present danger« of public harm*

Speech that is constitutionally protected may nonetheless be regulated. In general there are two ways in which government may abridge speech and two corresponding modes of First Amendment analysis. One way – which Professor Laurence Tribe calls »track one« – is government action that aims purposefully at ideas or information, seeking to regulate the »communicative impact« of speech.[58] The other way, »track two,« involves government action that is content-neutral and seeks non-speech-related goals – clean streets, for example – but that »incidentally« limits the opportunities for speech.[59]

The current test for government regulation on »track one« holds that one may advocate with constitutional protection even the most hateful or offensive program (the right of American Nazis to speak and parade has been

56 Cent. Hudson Gas & Elec. Co. v. Pub. Serv. Comm'n, 447 U.S. 557, 563 (1980). *See generally* Baker, *Commercial Speech: A Problem in the Theory of Freedom*, 62 IOWA L. REV. 1 (1976).

57 Miller v. California, 413 U.S. 15, 24 (1973). *See generally* Lockhart, *Escape from the Chill of Uncertainty: Explicit Sex and the First Amendment*, 9 GA. L. REV. 533 (1975).

58 L. TRIBE, AMERICAN CONSTITUTIONAL LAW 580–84 (1978).

59 *Id.*

upheld) and that speech may be suppressed for its content only if it is »directed to inciting or producing imminent lawless action and is likely to incite or produce such action.«[60] The Supreme Court laid down this tightened version of the older »clear and present danger« test in 1969 in *Brandenburg v. Ohio*,[61] in the course of striking down a law that generally prohibited advocacy of unlawful violence.[62]

The *Brandenburg* principle may be tested in connection with a law passed by the U.S. Congress. This statute makes it a crime to publish the names of U.S. intelligence agents, where the publisher has reason to believe that the publication might bring harm to the agents.[63] The statute does not require that the publication of the agents' names be likely to produce »imminent« lawless action and apparently applies even if the names already have been published elsewhere. The statute could well have the effect of deterring press accounts about the activities of U.S. intelligence agencies – accounts that may not be credible if they cannot use names – and thus may impair the First Amendment objective of keeping the public fully informed about the activities of their government. This law that directly punishes speech about government could well be held to violate the First Amendment.

c. *Regulations that »incidentally« restrict speech*

Content-neutral regulations having an »incidental« impact of restricting speech are judged on »track two« by a less severe constitutional test, derived from the case of *United States v. O'Brien*.[64] Under this test the regulation will be upheld if it furthers »an important or substantial governmental interest« and »if the incidental restriction on alleged First Amendment freedoms is no greater than is essential to the furtherance of that interest.«[65] In essence, the governmental interest is »balanced« against the restriction on speech, with the court deciding which value weighs more heavily in the particular case. In one recent application of this test, the Supreme Court considered a Los Angeles city ordinance that prohibited the posting of all signs – including political campaign signs – on public pro-

60 Brandenburg v. Ohio, 395 U.S. 444, 447 (1969).

61 *Id. See generally* Linde, *»Clear and Present Danger« Reexamined: Dissonance in the Brandenburg Concerto*, 22 STAN. L. REV. 1163 (1970).

62 395 U.S. at 447.

63 50 U.S.C. § 421 (1982).

64 391 U.S. 367 (1968).

65 *Id.* at 377. *See also* United States v. Albertini, 105 S. Ct. 2897, 2907 (1985) (regulation permissible under *O'Brien* if the substantial government interest »would be achieved less effectively absent the regulation«).

perty, including utility poles and other fixtures on streets and sidewalks.[66] The Court, by the vote of 6 to 3, upheld the ordinance. It reasoned that the city had a »sufficiently substantial« esthetic interest in eliminating the »visual clutter« of signs, that the ordinance went no further than was necessary to promote that interest, and that there remained adequate modes of communication by which political candidates could get their messages to the public.

Thus »track two,« at least as applied by the majority of the present Supreme Court, fairly easily allows government regulation that can broadly limit opportunities for speech, even the political speech that lies at the heart of First Amendment protection.

d. *Defamation*

Defamation is a category of speech that has partial constitutional protection. U.S. civil law has always included the right to sue and collect damages for libel or slander. In the 1964 case of *New York Times Co. v. Sullivan*,[67] however, the Supreme Court held that the First Amendment limits this right. In a defamation suit brought by a public official for statements relating to his official conduct, the Court said, the First Amendment prohibits an award of damages (or any other remedy) unless the official can show that the statements were made with knowledge that they were false or with disregard of whether they were false or not. To impose liability for statements about the official conduct of a public official that did not meet this test would compromise the »profound national commitment to the principle that debate on public issues should be uninhibited, robust, and wide-open.«[68]

The protection of the *New York Times* rule has since been extended beyond public officials to »public figures.«[69] In addition the Court has announced that defamation consisting of statements of opinion, rather than statements of fact, may not be sued on at all, by anyone. This is because »[u]nder the First Amendment there is no such thing as a false idea. However pernicious an opinion may seem, we depend for its correction not on the conscience of judges and juries but on the competition of other ideas.«[70]

66 Members of City Council v. Taxpayers for Vincent, 466 U.S. 789 (1984).
67 376 U.S. 254 (1964)
68 *Id.* at 270.
69 Curtis Publishing Co. v. Butts, 388 U.S. 130 (1967).
70 Gertz v. Robert Welch, Inc., 418 U.S. 323, 339 (1974).

Persons who are not public officials or public figures may still recover for libel or slander without showing knowing or reckless falsity; they need only show that the defendant was negligent in publishing the material.[71] (Much turns therefore on whether a particular plaintiff is a »public figure« or not, a point on which the law is chaotically unclear.) But even a »private« plaintiff may not recover punitive or general damages – only »actual damages« – unless he or she does show that the statement was knowingly or recklessly false.[72]

The reason the First Amendment is held to impose lesser restrictions on defamation suits by private persons than on suits by public officials or public figures is, in part, that speech about private persons is less important to democratic government. But persons considered »private« under present law may in fact be involved in matters of significant public interest, and the speech for which they are suing may be about those matters; so this reason for the public figure-private person distinction often seems questionable. The Supreme Court seems to put more weight, in fact, on the notion that public officials and public figures »assume the risk« of negative attention and comment that may injure their reputation, while private persons do not.[73]

e. *Invasion of privacy*

Also partially protected by the First Amendment, though to a less certain extent, is speech that »invades the privacy« of a person via the publication of private facts about him or her. The Supreme Court has held that a suit for invasion of privacy is blocked by the First Amendment when the facts that were disclosed consist of true information obtained from public records (in that case, the name of a crime victim that the defendant broadcaster had

71 *Id.* at 347 f. But »private« plaintiffs, like »public« plaintiffs, must bear the constitutional burden of proving that the statement was false, in contrast to the common-law rule requiring the defendant to prove truth. Philadelphia Newspapers, Inc. v. Hepps, 106 S. Ct. 1558, 1563 (1986).

72 Gertz v. Robert Welch, Inc., 418 U.S. 323, 349 (1974). However, the Supreme Court in 1985 threw constitutional defamation law into turmoil by holding that this requirement does not apply when the defamatory statements »do not involve matters of public concern.« Dun & Bradstreet, Inc. v. Greenmoss Builders, Inc., 105 S. Ct. 2939, 2948 (1985) (opinion of Powell, J.). The decision leaves open whether any or all of the other constitutional limits on defamation law likewise do not apply to such speech. It also leaves open what is meant by speech that is not of »public concern.« (*Dun & Bradstreet* itself involved a credit agency's report to its subscribers that the plaintiff company had filed for bankruptcy). *See also* Philadelphia Newspapers, Inc. v. Hepps, 106 S. Ct. 1558, 1559 (1986).

73 Gertz v. Robert Welch, Inc. 418 U.S. 323, 344 f. (1974).

obtained from court records).[74] The Supreme Court has not decided whether suits for invasion of privacy may be constitutionally maintained when the facts disclosed were true but were not taken from a public record. Lower courts have allowed such suits if the facts were »private« ones and were »not of legitimate concern to the public.«[75]

f. *Copyright infringement*

Another category of expression that may be limited without violating the First Amendment is copyright infringement. Such infringement not only produces an action for damages, but, if the action is brought before publication of the infringing material, that publication normally will be enjoined, despite the First Amendment's repugnance for prior restraint.[76] Yet the First Amendment does have an impact on copyright law. Since copyright protects only an author's »expression« and not the ideas or the facts presented, those ideas or facts can be made available to the public in different words without infringing the copyright. Moreover, even appropriation of the author's »expression« is protected to some extent by the copyright doctrine of »fair use.« This doctrine employs an ad hoc balancing test to determine whether the use of an author's work »for purposes such as criticism, comment, news reporting, teaching ... scholarship, or research«[77] was justified in the particular case.

In a recent application of these principles, the Supreme Court held that the magazine *The Nation* infringed the copyright on the memoirs of former President Gerald Ford when it published an article about them prior to their first authorized publication.[78] The Court said that the First Amendment does not create a separate defense to copyright infringement, even for works by high public officials that have substantial news value. Rather, First Amendment values are adequately embodied in the fair-use defense and in the distinction between »idea« and »expression.« The Court's decision was accordingly based not on the magazine's having reported »the news« of Ford's memoirs before he could publish them but on its having used too many quotations from the memoirs and thus taken too much of his copyrighted »expression.«

74 Cox Broadcasting Co. v. Cohn, 420 U.S. 469 (1975).
75 *E.g.*, Virgil v. Time, Inc., 527 F.2d 1122 (9th Cir. 1975), *cert. denied*, 425 U.S. 998 (1976).
76 *See* 17 U.S.C. §§ 501–04 (1982).
77 17 U.S.C. § 107 (1982).
78 Harper & Row Publishers Inc. v. Nation Enters. Inc., 105 S. Ct. 2218 (1985).

g. *Censorship of government employes by contract*

A newly important government device for limiting constitutionally protected speech, and specifically speech about the activities of government, was upheld by the Supreme Court in the 1980 case of *Snepp v. United States*.[79] Snepp was a former employe of the Central Intelligence Agency who published a book about events that took place while he worked for the agency. The government did not claim that the book contained classified information, but it claimed he had violated a provision of his employment contract, which required that he submit to the agency, for pre-publication review, anything he might ever publish that contained information gained during his service with the agency. The Court upheld the government's position and its use of such contracts, saying the requirement of pre-publication review was constitutional in this context because it was a »reasonable means« for »protecting both the secrecy of information important to our national security and the appearance of confidentiality so essential to the effective operation of our foreign intelligence.«[80] Snepp accordingly was compelled to turn over to the government all the profits he made from his book.

Without condoning Snepp's personal conduct in breaking his agreement with the government, the Supreme Court's decision has been widely criticized for its likely impact on protected speech.[81] The prior-review procedure seems very likely to curtail the flow of information to the public about the activities of government from writers who are in a uniquely competent position to know what they are talking about.[82] Moreover, the Court approved this rather drastic approach without demanding from the government any evidence to confirm its claim that a less restrictive approach would have been incompatible with the national security.[83]

President Reagan has since acted to expand the scope of the censorship system approved by the Court in *Snepp*. National Security Directive No. 84, issued by the president in 1983,[84] required all federal employes with

79 444 U.S. 507 (1980).

80 *Id.* at 509 n.3.

81 *E.g.*, Medow, *The First Amendment and the Secrecy State: Snepp v. United States*, 130 U. PA. L. REV. 775 (1982).

82 *See* Cheh, *Judicial Supervision of Executive Secrecy: Rethinking Freedom of Expression for Government Employees and the Public Right of Access to Government Information*, 69 CORNELL L. Q. 690 (1984)

83 *See* Snepp v. United States, 444 U.S. at 522 f. (Stevens, J. dissenting).

84 The directive, issued March 11, 1983, is reprinted in *National Security Decision Directive 84, Hearings Before the Senate Comm. on Governmental Affairs*, 98th Cong., 1st Sess. 85–86 (1984).

high-level security clearances – employes numbering in the hundreds of thousands – to sign contracts that would require them to submit to the government for pre-publication review – during their lifetimes – any speeches, books, articles or other writings based on their government work, even if the writings contained no classified information and even if they were based entirely on matter already public.[85]

Directive 84, even more than the *Snepp* decision, was criticized as likely to discourage a wide range of writings that inform the U.S. public about the conduct of its government.[86] Faced with strong opposition in Congress, the administration in 1984 suspended the pre-publication review requirements of Directive 84. However, it was reported in 1986 by a congressional agency that the suspension of Directive 84 »has had little effect on prepublication review requirements,« because the government was still requiring employes to sign another document, »Form 4193,« whereby they agree to submit to such review.[87]

In 1983 a committee of the House of Representatives approved a bill to prohibit pre-publication review agreements for federal employes outside the Central Intelligence Agency and other national security agencies.[88] Until such legislation is enacted, or until the courts overturn the administration's program, federal employes who have signed these agreements (or forms) presumably are obligated to submit to the pre-publication review. The administration's pursuit of this program designed to restrict the flow of information about the U.S. government to the U.S. public may seem difficult to square with the U.S. government's insistence on the »free flow« of information across international borders.

85 *See* HOUSE COMM. ON GOVERNMENT OPERATIONS, THE ADMINISTRATION'S INITIATIVES TO EXPAND POLYGRAPH USE AND IMPOSE LIFELONG CENSORSHIP ON THOUSANDS OF GOVERNMENT EMPLOYEES, H.R. REP. No. 98–578, 98th Cong., 1st Sess. 15 (1983).

86 *E.g.*, Abrams, *The New Effort to Control Information*, New York Times Magazine, Sept. 25, 1983.

87 *Security Rule Died but Lived On*, N.Y. Times, Oct. 23, 1986, at 12, cols. 4–6 (national ed.). The article describes a report of the General Accounting Office as stating that »more than 290,000 present and former Federal employees have now promised to submit material to prepublication review,« including some 224,000 connected with the Department of Defense but not including employees of the CIA or the National Security Agency, which have their own requirements. The number of writings submitted for review was said to be some 13,000 in 1984 and 14,000 in 1985. *Id.*

88 *See* Burnham, *Censorship*, N.Y. Times, Aug. 16, 1984, sec. 2, at 14.

B. *Regulatory Framework for the Print Media*

1. *Special Applications of Constitutional Protection*

The constitutional freedoms of speech and press, as described above, apply most fully to newspapers, books, magazines and other print media. Any licensing of newspapers or other print media is generally prohibited; their publication may be subjected to prior restraint only under the most extraordinary circumstances; and the other aspects of First Amendment protection noted above are at their strongest.

The press is also exempt from any special taxes. Thus in the 1983 case of *Minneapolis Star and Tribune Co. v. Minnesota Commissioner of Revenue*,[89] the Supreme Court struck down a state »use tax« on the ink and paper used in producing newspapers. The State of Minnesota had argued that under this tax newspapers actually were treated more favorably than other businesses, because this tax was accompanied by an exemption from the generally applicable sales tax. The Supreme Court conceded that this might be so and also that the general sales tax could be applied to newspapers, but it nonetheless held the special use tax invalid:

> When the State imposes a generally applicable tax, there is little cause for concern. We need not fear that a government will destroy a selected group of taxpayers by burdensome taxation if it must impose the same burden on the rest of its constituency ... When the State singles out the press, though, the political constraints that prevent a legislature from passing crippling taxes of general applicability are weakened, and the threat of burdensome taxes becomes acute. That threat can operate as effectively as a censor to check critical comment by the press, undercutting the basic assumption of our political system that the press will often serve as an important restraint on government.[90]

Also distinctive of the printed press – at least quite different from the rule applied to broadcasters, as will be seen – is constitutional exemption from right-of-reply statutes. Thus in *Miami Herald Publishing Co. v. Tornillo*,[91] the Supreme Court struck down a Florida statute requiring a newspaper that attacked a candidate for public office to give the candidate an opportunity for reply in the newspaper. While acknowledging the legitimacy of the state's goal of assuring that the public hear both sides of the

89 460 U.S. 575 (1983).
90 *Id.* at 585.
91 418 U.S. 241 (1974).

controversy, the Court presented two reasons why the statute was inconsistent with the First Amendment. First, under the statute »editors might well conclude that the safe course is to avoid controversy« and thus avoid triggering the right of reply, with the result that coverage and criticism of election campaigns »would be blunted or reduced.« Second, even if that did not happen, the law would still be invalid because of »its intrusion into the function of editors.« Government regulation of »the choice of material to go into a newspaper,« the Court declared, is simply inconsistent »with First Amendment guarantees of a free press as they have evolved to this time.«[92]

2. *Applicability of General Laws*

The print media are not exempt from valid laws of general applicability, whether their focus is on speech or on other activities. Thus laws prohibiting obscenity are applicable to the print media,[93] as are legal sanctions against false advertising, copyright infringement, defamation, invasion of privacy and the like. Similarly, speech related to criminal conduct is punishable when it is printed. The Supreme Court made this clear when it held, by the vote of 5 to 4, that a newspaper could be prohibited from publishing job advertisements listed in terms of sex if it were illegal for employers to consider sex in their employment decisions.[94]

The print media are also subject to generally applicable non-speech laws, such as general taxes, labor laws, anti-discrimination laws and antitrust laws.[95] In the Newspaper Preservation Act,[96] however, Congress has given newspapers a special exemption from the antitrust laws. The Act enables competing newspapers in the same city to merge their business operations while maintaining separate editorial staffs and policies, where in the absence of the exemption it was likely that one of the newspapers would have failed. Passed in 1970, the Act not only applies to some twenty-two of these »joint-operating agreements« that already existed at that time but also authorizes the attorney general of the United States to confer the antitrust

92 *Id.* at 257 f. *See also* Baker, *Government Power to Structure the Press*, 34 U. MIAMI L. REV. 819 (1980).

93 Kaplan v. California, 413 U.S. 115 (1973).

94 Pittsburgh Press Co. v. Human Relations Comm'n, 413 U.S. 376 (1973).

95 *E.g.*, Minneapolis Star & Tribune Co. v. Minnesota Comm'r of Revenue, 460 U.S. 575, 586 n. 9 (1983) (tax); Associated Press v. NLRB, 301 U.S. 103, 132–33 (1937) (labor); Pittsburgh Press Co. v. Human Relations Comm'n, 413 U.S. 376, 376 (anti-discrimination); Citizen Publishing Co. v. United States, 394 U.S. 131, 139 (1969) (antitrust).

96 15 U.S.C. §§ 1801–04 (1982).

exemption on newly created agreements if he determines that one of the newspapers involved is failing. Through 1985, attorneys general had ruled on four applications for new agreements and in all cases granted the exemption.[97] These proceedings are strangely reminiscent of newspaper licensing. Since the attorney general's decision carries immense financial value for the publishers seeking the exemption, it presents an open field for political favoritism or retaliation.[98] The exemption granted to the two daily newspapers in Seattle, Washington was challenged in a federal court of appeals, which upheld it. The court rejected claims that the Act is unconstitutional because it gives the attorney general undue discretionary power over the press and because it enables the exempted newspapers to do economic injury to competing newspapers and other media.[99] The court conceded the possible harm to competing papers but held that this did not render the Act invalid, since such harm was only an incidental effect of the Act's legitimate attempt to prevent newspaper failures.[100]

C. *Regulatory Framework for Movies, Plays and Other Nonelectronic Audiovisuals*

Movies, plays and other nonelectronic audiovisuals are subject to slightly greater levels of government regulation than the print media. For example, films, as noted earlier, are subject to prior review for obscenity. Such review is unconstitutional if it commits the censorship decision to an administrative official rather than a court, if it is not conducted in an expedited proceeding, or if the would-be censor does not carry the burden of proving that the film contains unprotected (obscene) material.[101] Plays are entitled to at least as much protection. The Supreme Court has overturned a municipal-

97 The cities involved were Anchorage, Alaska; Cincinnati, Ohio; Chattanooga, Tennessee; and Seattle, Washington. *See, e.g.*, Barnett, *Monopoly Games*, COLUM. JOURNALISM REV. May/June 1980, at 40. In 1986 an application was filed from Detroit, Michigan, the largest city yet involved. *See* Wall St. J., July 25, 1986, at 8, cols. 2–3.

98 *See, e.g.*, Barnett, *Fast Shuffle in Chattanooga*, COLUM. JOURNALISM REV, November/December 1980, at 65. Enactment of the Newspaper Preservation Act was brought about, in part, by political pressure exerted on President Nixon and his administration by newspaper publishers. *See* B. BAGDIKIAN, THE MEDIA MONOPOLY 92–103 (1983).

99 Committee for an Independent P-I v. Hearst Corp., 704 F.2d 467 (9th Cir. 1983), *cert. denied*, 464 U.S. 892 (1983).

100 *Id.* at 482.

101 Freedman v. Maryland, 380 U.S. 51, 51 (1965).

permit system authorizing local officials to limit access to a municipal theater to plays that comported with their standards of propriety.[102]
But government regulation of films with sexual content does not have to be entirely content-neutral. The Supreme Court has upheld zoning regulations that restrict the locations of theaters showing films whose content is sexual but not obscene.[103] This decision suggests the emergence, at least in the context of film, of a new, intermediate category of constitutionally protected speech. Such a »variable« approach, championed by Justice John Paul Stevens of the Supreme Court, has shown indications of spreading to other media and other forms of »less protected« content as well.[104]

D. *Regulatory Framework for Radio and Television Broadcasting*

1. *The Federal Communications Commission and the Radio Spectrum*

Radio and television broadcasting is regulated by the Federal Communications Commission (FCC) under the Federal Communications Act of 1934.[105] The FCC is composed of five commissioners appointed by the president with the advice and consent of the Senate; no more than three may belong to the same political party.[106] Under the 1934 Act, the FCC is given broad power to formulate and administer rules governing broadcasting. This includes the power to assign frequencies, power levels, areas and times of operation to broadcast stations; to classify stations; and to prescribe the type of service to be rendered by each class of stations. The FCC may make rules as needed to carry out either the provisions of the Communications Act or those of any international treaty or convention concerning broadcasting to which the United States becomes a party. If a broadcaster violates any of the laws or rules administered by the FCC, the Commission has authority to suspend the broadcaster's license or impose other sanctions.[107]

102 Southeastern Promotions, Ltd. v. Conrad, 420 U.S. 546, 546 (1982).
103 Young v. American Mini-Theaters, Inc., 427 U.S. 40 (1976); City of Renton v. Playtime Theatres, Inc., 106 S. Ct. 925 (1986).
104 *See, e.g.*, FCC v. Pacifica Found., 438 U.S. 726 (1978); Cent. Hudson Gas & Elec. Co. v. Pub. Serv. Comm'n, 447 U.S. 557, 557 (1980).
105 47 U.S.C. §§ 151 *et seq* (1982).
106 47 U.S.C. § 154(a), (b)(5) (1982 & Supp. II 1984).
107 47 U.S.C. § 303 (1982).

The FCC has allocated to various uses the portions of the electromagnetic spectrum that are under its authority. Some portions have been designated for nonbroadcast uses, such as aviation, civil emergency communications and common carriers. The public broadcast portion of the spectrum comprises four categories: AM radio, FM radio, VHF television and UHF television. The following chart shows the number of each type of broadcast station, subdivided between commercial and noncommercial, on the air in the United States as of June 30, 1986:[108]

	VHF Television	UHF Television
Commercial	542	422
Noncommercial	113	187
Totals	655	609

	AM Radio	FM Radio
Commercial	4839	3923
Noncommercial	0	1247
Totals	4839	5170

In making its original station allocations, the FCC gave heavy weight to the »local service« objective of the Communications Act – the establishment of stations in as many localities as possible.[109] Thus in its crucial 1952 Table of Assignments for television, the FCC placed the objective of providing »each community with at least one television broadcast station« ahead of providing »a choice of at least two television services to all parts of the United States.«[110] Instead of establishing powerful regional or even national stations that could have provided the entire country with six or more VHF television program services, the decision was made to diffuse less powerful stations widely so they could provide local service in their communities. The result was, since most cities had no more than three stations, that only three national networks developed (and the local stations became network affiliates and provided very little local programming). The local-service principle has remained a keystone of broadcast regulation. One of the FCC's chief justifications for restricting the development of cable television in the 1960s, for example, was that by bringing in distant

108 Broadcasting, Dec. 1, 1986, at 122.

109 The textual basis is section 307(b) of the Act, which does no more than call on the FCC to »make such distribution of licenses, frequencies, hours of operation, and of power among the several States and communities as to provide a fair, efficient, and equitable distribution of radio service to each of the same.« 47 U.S.C. § 307(b).

110 Television Allocations, 41 F.C.C. 148, 167 (1952).

programs to compete with local stations, cable would impair the ability of those stations to provide the local service for which they were established.[111]

As the chart above indicates, the great majority of radio and television stations are commercial – that is, privately owned and operated for profit. They earn revenue by selling broadcast time to advertisers. The scheme of the Communications Act does not include the regulation of advertising rates, and hence broadcasters are free to set their own prices. They are also legally free to broadcast as much advertising as they like and to place their »commercials« not only at the beginning and end of programs but interspersed throughout. They use this freedom with a vengeance.

On the other hand, with the unimportant exception of STV (subscription television), all over-the-air broadcasting in the United States is »free,« in the sense that members of the public do not pay any direct charge for the right to receive it. (Of course, they may pay indirectly by way of higher prices for advertised products.) There are no license fees on radio or television receiving sets, for example.

As the chart indicates, the FCC has reserved a portion of the television and FM radio bands for noncommercial – also called educational or public – broadcasters. Most of these stations are licensed to governmental entities, such as school boards, local governments or universities, but many – including the most prominent public television stations – are licensed to private nonprofit organizations. Some nonprofit licensees are religious organizations.

Noncommercial broadcasters are financed by a variety of sources, including the federal government (mainly through the Corporation for Public Broadcasting), state and local governments, their own listeners and viewers (public broadcast stations are notorious for the amount of air time they devote to raising money), universities, businesses, foundations and private donors.[112]

Increasingly, noncommercial stations are also financed by advertising. While originally they were barred from selling broadcast time, recently this restriction has been relaxed, in large part as a result of decreasing federal support for public broadcasting.[113] Thus public broadcast stations are receiving growing revenues from corporations in return for displaying on the air their names, insignia and slogans, though the airing of actual »com-

111 *See* United States v. Southwestern Cable Co., 392 U.S. 157, 175 (1968).

112 *See generally* THE CARNEGIE COMMISSION ON THE FUTURE OF PUBLIC BROADCASTING, A PUBLIC TRUST (1979).

113 *See* 90 F.C.C.2d 895 (1982).

mercials« by public stations remains prohibited.[114] Despite the increasing advertising revenues, the financial condition of public broadcasting remains precarious. Attention has therefore focused on a variety of novel fund-raising possibilities. Among these was a proposal, subsequently shelved by the FCC because of broad opposition, that public TV stations holding valuable VHF frequencies enter into trades with commercial broadcasters holding much less desirable UHF frequencies and receive in return for their VHF slots enough money to create permanent programming endowments.[115]

2. *The Licensing of Broadcasters*

The Federal Communications Act directs the FCC to grant a station license to an applicant if the »public convenience, interest, or necessity« will thus be served.[116] The license term is now five years for a radio station and seven years for a television station, with renewals readily allowed.[117] In the seminal case of *National Broadcasting Co. v. United States*,[118] the Supreme Court concluded that the Act's vague charge to the FCC entailed more than the mere technical management of the airwaves:

> [T]he radio spectrum simply is not large enough to accommodate everybody. There is a fixed natural limitation upon the number of stations that can operate without interfering with one another. Regulation of radio was therefore as vital to its development as traffic control was to the development of the automobile ... But the Act does not restrict the Commission to supervision of traffic. It puts upon the Commission the burden of determining the composition of that traffic.[119]

The notion was that a broadcast licensee would hold and operate a frequency as a »trustee« for the public, and the FCC's licensing process was designed to choose the licensee that would best serve the public interest.

114 *See* N.Y. Times, Apr. 1, 1985 (national ed.), at 17, col. 3.

115 The FCC in 1985 received public comments on the proposal that public broadcasters be allowed to enter into such trades. Broadcasting, Feb. 18, 1985, at 45. The comments were mainly negative, with opposition coming particularly from commercial broadcasters who already had VHF frequencies and did not want the competition. *See* Broadcasting, June 24, 1985, at 38–43. The FCC therefore decided to leave the proposal in suspension for the foreseeable future. *See* Broadcasting, Mar. 17, 1986, at 7.

116 47 U.S.C. § 307(a) (1982).

117 47 U.S.C. § 307(c) (1982).

118 319 U.S. 190 (1943).

119 *Id.* at 213, 215 f.

To achieve this end, the licensing process is divided into two phases. First, an applicant must demonstrate that it is qualified to hold a broadcasting license. The qualifications include U.S. citizenship (to be discussed below), adequate financial resources, appropriate broadcasting equipment and an »affirmative action« program to insure adequate recruitment, training and promotion of disadvantaged minority groups and women.[120] In addition, the applicant's other media holdings must not exceed the legal limits (see below), and the applicant must have adequate »character« qualifications.[121] When the same license is sought by more than one qualified applicant, the process enters a second, »comparative« phase, in which the FCC seeks to decide which applicant is »best.« In choosing between applicants, the FCC seeks to promote a variety of goals that have included diversification of media control, promotion of ownership by women and members of minority groups, »integration« of ownership and management, local ownership and broadcasting experience.[122]

This comparative process has attracted over the years devastating criticism that is now virtually unanimous. Comparative contests for the extremely valuable VHF television licenses in large cities have been known to go on for as long as twenty years, bouncing between the FCC and the courts, and no serious person sees any reason to think that the eventual winners serve the public interest better than the eventual losers would have.[123] The various criteria by which the FCC judges the applicants are so manipulable, and so often inconsistent with each other, that the Commission can easily justify any decision it may want to make. It has been suggested that some of the decisions made during the 1950s, the heyday of the granting of the most valuable television licenses, correlated most closely not with any of the legal criteria but with the political allegiance of the applicants.[124]

The comparative licensing process is especially absurd because once an applicant has won the contest and received a license from the FCC – for which the applicant pays only a nominal fee (though its lawyers' fees may be substantial) – the applicant is then entitled to sell that license on the open market for whatever price it will bring (it can even be sold to the

120 47 U.S.C. §§ 310(b), 308(b) (1982); 47 C.F.R. § 73.125 (1985).

121 47 U.S.C. § 308(b) (1982).

122 *See* Policy Statement on Comparative Broadcast Hearing, 1 F.C.C.2d 393 (1965); W. Michigan Broadcasting Co. v. FCC, 735 F.2d 601 (D.C. Cir. 1984). In September 1986, however, the FCC – reversing a position it had taken for more than ten years – told the federal court of appeals that it now thought the preferences it had been giving to women and members of minority groups exceeded its statutory and constitutional authority. *See* Broadcasting, Sept. 22, 1986, at 42.

123 *See* Kinsley, *Gifts of the Nation*, The New Republic, Oct. 14, 1981, at 21.

124 *See* Schwartz, *Comparative Television and the Chancellor's Foot*, 47 GEO. L.J. 655 (1959).

applicant who lost before the FCC). Although the Communications Act states expressly, several times, that a license granted under the Act creates no right beyond the term of the license,[125] practice under the Act has accorded to the licensee a property right in the license. Not only is license renewal almost automatic, but the Act was amended to provide that when a licensee seeks the FCC's approval to transfer its license, the FCC may not compare the proposed transferee with other applicants for the license to see who would best serve the public interest; it may only consider whether the proposed transferee is qualified to hold a license.[126] The remarkable result is that broadcast licenses, awarded free by the government after an elaborate attempt to determine which applicant will best serve the public interest, can then be sold on the market to whomever will pay the highest price. Recent years have seen a dramatic surge in purchases, and purchase prices, of broadcast licenses. As of 1986, the record for sale of a single station belonged to a television station in Los Angeles that was sold in May 1985 to the Tribune Company of Chicago for $510 million.[127]

Many people propose, not surprisingly, that the government should sell the licenses itself and thus at least obtain their value for the public.[128] But such a solution, however attractive it might have been originally, is out of the question now. Not only does the political power of the broadcast industry stand in the way, but in addition it would not be fair, given the reliance interests built up under the present system, for the government now to take away and sell for its own gain licenses that have in fact been purchased on the open market. The most that might be achieved toward compensating the public for the value of the radio spectrum would be annual license fees for broadcasters. But broadcasters wield their formidable political power to resist even this, and even when it is proposed as a trade-off for deregulation of broadcasting.

Consistently with the de facto recognition of property rights in broadcast licenses, the FCC's renewal of a license is almost automatic. Although the Communications Act allows competing applications at renewal time and thus another comparative process,[129] the FCC has consistently sought a way to give the incumbent licensee a strong preference over any renewal challengers. The FCC's present doctrine, approved by the federal court of appeals, largely achieves this goal by according the incumbent a preference for

125 47 U.S.C. §§ 301, 304, 307(d), 309(h) (1982 & Supp. II 1984).
126 47 U.S.C. § 310(d) (1982).
127 Broadcasting, May 20, 1985, at 39.
128 *E.g.*, N.Y. Times, Dec. 3, 1984, at 22 (editorial).
129 47 U.S.C. § 309(e) (1982)

the quality of its past performance that is strong enough to override a challenger's superior merit on such criteria as diversification of ownership or minority ownership.[130] Nonetheless renewal is not guaranteed, especially if the incumbent has gotten into trouble with the FCC or otherwise has black marks on its record.

The FCC has authority to deny renewal, even in the absence of a competing application, if it finds that the licensee's performance has not served the public interest.[131] Thus in one case, the court of appeals reversed the FCC's renewal of a license where there was substantial evidence that the station has discriminated against black people in its programming.[132] Some fifty years ago, the FCC itself denied renewal, and was upheld by the court, where the station's broadcasts had »offend[ed] the religious susceptibilities of thousands, [or] inspire[d] political distrust and civic discord.«[133] That kind of decision today might well collide with modern First Amendment doctrine. Indeed the FCC in 1985, apparently overruling its earlier case, refused to deny renewal to a radio station that had aired many hours of programs containing »crude, derogatory and defamatory« remarks about blacks and Jews, as well as attacks on the government, lawyers, judges and bureaucrats that were found to encourage disregard of the law. Citing cases such as *Brandenburg v. Ohio*, the FCC ruled that such broadcasts fell within the First Amendment's protection of freedom of speech and therefore could not be a basis for denying license renewal.[134]

3. *Ownership Restrictions*

To promote diversity of ownership in the mass media, the FCC has adopted a variety of rules limiting the number and location of media outlets that may be under common control. On the national level, the FCC's »multiple ownership« rule now provides that no person or company may own (or have a significant interest in) more than twelve AM stations, twelve FM stations and twelve television stations anywhere in the country, with the further condition that the television stations may not reach more than twenty-five percent of the national viewing audience.[135] (Until 1984 the limits

130 *See* Cent. Florida Enters. Inc. v. FCC, 683 F.2d 503 (D.C. Cir. 1982).
131 47 U.S.C. § 309(d), (e) (1982 & Supp. 1982).
132 United Church of Christ v. FCC, 425 F.2d 543 (D.C. Cir. 1969).
133 Trinity Methodist Church v. FCC, 62 F.2d 850, 853 (1932), *cert. denied*, 288 U.S. 599 (1933).
134 *F.C.C. Bars Penalty on Racism on Air*, N.Y. Times, Apr. 29, 1985, at 16.
135 Broadcasting, Dec. 31, 1984, at 35.

were more strict – only seven stations of each kind. The relaxation of the rule spurred a wave of media mergers. The 1985 acquisition of the ABC company by Capital Cities Communications, for example, produced a company owning eight television stations and reaching 24.38 percent of the national audience, just under the new limit.)[136]

The FCC also has rules limiting ownership interests within the same city. Almost from the start, the Commission prohibited common ownership of more than one AM station, one FM station and one TV station serving the same city.[137] Since 1975 it has prohibited the acquisition or transfer – but not the continuing ownership – of both a radio station and a VHF television station in the same city.[138] Since 1975 it has also prohibited the acquisition or transfer – but, again, not the continuing ownership – of a broadcast station and a daily newspaper serving the same city.[139] (Hence Rupert Murdoch, who in 1985 agreed to buy television stations in Chicago and New York, was required to sell his newspapers in Chicago and New York.) The FCC's rule on newspaper-broadcast combinations has been upheld by the Supreme Court.[140] The Court said it was reasonable for the FCC to conclude that the public interest was best served when broadcast stations and newspapers represented fully independent sources of information. The rule did not violate the First Amendment rights of newspaper owners, the Court continued, since they remained free to own broadcast stations in other cities and since the First Amendment does not guarantee a right to broadcast as it does a right to speak or print.

4. *Obligations to Promote the Electoral System*

Although broadcasters receive at virtually no cost licenses to use public resources worth many millions of dollars, they are not required by law to make any of their broadcast time available without charge to anyone, including candidates for public office. The Communications Act does impose on them, however, two obligations designed to promote the nation's electoral system (in addition to the more general »fairness doctrine« obligation, to be discussed next). The first is the »equal time« or »equal opportunities«

136 Broadcasting, May 20, 1985, at 40.

137 Genesee Radio Corp., 5 F.C.C. 183, 186 (1938); 47 C.F.R. §§ 73.35 (AM), 73.240 (FM), 73.636 (TV) (1983).

138 47 C.F.R. § 76.401 (1981).

139 Multiple Ownership, 53 F.C.C.2d 589 (1975); 47 C.F.R. §§ 73.35(c), 73.240(c), 73.636(c) (1983).

140 FCC v. Nat'l Citizens Comm. for Broadcasting, 436 U.S. 773 (1978).

law.[141] It provides that if a station gives or sells air time to a candidate for public office, it must afford an »equal opportunity« – that is, the same amount and kind of time at the same price – to all other qualified candidates for the same office. (Since even a »nonpolitical« appearance by a candidate will trigger the equal-time law, old movies featuring Ronald Reagan, for example, were not shown on television during his electoral campaigns; the FCC never had to decide the interesting question of what would constitute an »equal opportunity« for an opposing candidate.) The equal-time law has four exceptions: appearances by candidates during newscasts, news interviews, news documentaries and on-the-spot coverage of bona fide news events.[142] The FCC has ruled that debates between candidates are »bona fide news events.« This ruling has made possible televised debates between the major-party candidates – President Reagan and Walter Mondale, for example – because it relieves the networks of having to give equal, free time to all the minor-party candidates as well.[143]
While the equal-time law comes into play only after a broadcaster has voluntarily decided to put a candidate on the air, the second electoral-system obligation does require broadcasters to provide some time whether they like it or not. Section 312(a)(7) of the Communications Act requires them to provide »reasonable amounts of time« – which need not be free – to legally qualified candidates for federal elective office. In the 1981 case of *CBS v. FCC*,[144] the Supreme Court upheld the constitutionality of this requirement. The Court noted that it created only a »limited« right of access to the broadcast medium and said it made »a significant contribution to freedom of expression by enhancing the ability of candidates to present, and the public to receive, information necessary for the effective operation of the democratic process.«[145]

5. *The Fairness Doctrine*

The fairness doctrine, originally promulgated by the FCC but now arguably ratified by Congress, imposes on broadcasters two general obligations: (1) to »devote a reasonable percentage of time to the coverage of public issues«

141 47 U.S.C. § 315 (1982).
142 47 U.S.C. § 315(a) (1982).
143 Aspen Institute on Communications, 55 F.C.C.2d 697 (1975), *aff'd sub nom.* Chisholm v. FCC, 538 F.2d 349 (D.C. Cir. 1976), *cert. denied*, 429 U.S. 89 (1976).
144 453 U.S. 367 (1981).
145 *Id.* at 396–97.

and (2) to make that coverage »fair,« in the sense of providing »an opportunity for the presentation of contrasting points of view.«[146] The FCC accords broadcasters wide latitude in deciding which issues to cover, so the first obligation is rarely invoked.[147] It is the obligation to present contrasting viewpoints once an issue has been covered that has generated most of the litigation and controversy under the fairness doctrine. Here again broadcasters are given considerable latitude. They need not give equal time to each side of an issue; they need not present each side in the same format (speeches by the president advocating one point of view can be »balanced,« for example, by newscasts and news-interview programs reflecting opposing viewpoints); and they can exercise their own news judgment in determining who shall be the spokesperson for a particular point of view.[148]

On the other hand, the fairness doctrine applies to all programming, regardless of the context in which a point of view on a controversial issue is presented. Even if the point of view is presented in advertising, the broadcaster is required to present the opposing points of view on the broadcaster's own time, if necessary.[149] While the FCC now holds that product commercials do not address a controversial issue of public importance if they simply urge the audience to buy the product,[150] commercials that otherwise address a public issue can still trigger the fairness doctrine if the station has not adequately covered the other side of the issue.[151] Thus, while the Reagan administration FCC has been extremely reluctant to find violations of the fairness doctrine, it did find one where a station had run a series of editorial advertisements for a public-utility trade association advocating continued construction of a nuclear generating plant. The plant's construction was shown to be a controversial issue in the locality, and the advertisements had consumed 182 minutes of coverage while the station had provided only 22 minutes to contrasting views.[152]

In addition to its general obligations, the fairness doctrine has two more specific corollaries – the personal-attack and political-editorializing rules.

146 Fairness Report, 48 F.C.C.2d 1 (1974) [On Aug. 4, 1987, the FCC repealed the fairness doctrine. Syracuse Peace Council, 63 Radio Reg.2d 541].

147 The FCC did invoke it once, where a radio station in a coal-mining area declined to cover the issue of strip mining. Rep. Patsy Mink, 49 F.C.C.2d 987 (1976).

148 *See* 48 F.C.C.2d 1 (1974); Democratic Nat'l Comm. v. FCC, 481 F.2d 453 (D.C. Cir. 1973); *cf.* Comm. for the Fair Broadcasting of Controversial Issues, 25 F.C.C.2d 283 (1970), *rev'd on other grounds sub nom.* CBS v. FCC, 454 F.2d 1018 (D.C. Cir. 1971).

149 Cullman Broadcasting Co., 40 F.C.C. 576 (1963).

150 The Handling of Public Issues Under the Fairness Doctrine and the Public Interest Standard, 58 F.C.C.2d 691, *rev'd in part*, Nat'l Citizens Comm. for Broadcasting v. FCC, 567 F.2d 1095 (D.C. Cir. 1977), *cert. denied*, 436 U.S. 926 (1978).

151 Energy Action Comm., Inc., 64 F.C.C.2d 787 (1977).

152 Syracuse Peace Council, 99 F.C.C.2d 1389 (1984).

Both require the giving of air time to a specific person (or group) to reply to what the station has said. When a station in discussing a controversial issue (subject to the same four exceptions as the equal-time law) airs a »personal attack« on the »honesty, character or like personal qualities« of an identified person or group, the station is required promptly to provide the person or group with a notice of the attack and a reasonable opportunity to reply over the air. As one would expect, the line separating a »personal attack« from mere criticism is hazy; a court has ruled that calling a congressman a »coward« for example, could appropriately be found to constitute a personal attack.[153]

The political-editorializing rule, which is both easier to implement and more useful, provides that when a station airs an editorial – that is, the station's own opinion – endorsing or opposing a candidate for public office, it must promptly notify the candidate whom it has opposed, or has not endorsed, and give that candidate an opportunity to reply over the air.[154]

The Supreme Court upheld the personal-attack and political-editorializing rules, and the fairness doctrine in general, in the 1969 case of *Red Lion Broadcasting Co. v. FCC.*[155] Responding to the broadcasters' claims that the reply and access obligations imposed by the fairness doctrine violated their First Amendment rights, the Court justified this regulation of speech on two grounds, namely, the scarcity of space in the radio spectrum and the First Amendment right of the public to receive a diversity of information and opinion:

> Because of the scarcity of radio frequencies, the Government is permitted to put restraints on licensees in favor of others whose views should be expressed on this unique medium. But the people as a whole retain their interest in free speech by radio and their collective right to have the medium function consistently with the ends and purposes of the First Amendment ... It is the right of the public to receive suitable access to social, political, esthetic, moral and other ideas and experiences which is crucial here. ...[156]

The Court's opinion in *Red Lion* sharply illuminates the difference in the First Amendment protections afforded to the broadcast and the print media. The case of *Miami Herald v. Tornillo*,[157] involving a right-of-reply

153 Strauss Communications Inc. v. FCC, 530 F.2d 1001 (2d Cir. 1976).
154 47 C.F.R. § 73.193(a) (1985).
155 395 U.S. 367 (1969).
156 *Id.* at 390.
157 418 U.S. 241 (1974).

statute for newspapers, presented almost the identical question yet drew from the Court a diametrically different opinion. Both of the arguments accepted by the Court in *Tornillo* – that the statute would deter the coverage of controversial issues and that it constituted impermissible government interference with editorial discretion – were made in *Red Lion* as well. So great was the gulf between the constitutional treatments of the two media that the Court's opinion in *Tornillo*, issued five years after *Red Lion*, did not even cite that decision, let alone explain why it was so different.

Today there is growing attack on the »second class« constitutional treatment accorded the broadcast medium by *Red Lion*. The basic theory that the scarcity of the radio spectrum distinguishes broadcasting from other media is much criticized. Critics argue that much of the scarcity is government-created (there is room for many more stations than the government has licensed); that the scarcity of the airwaves is no different from the scarcity of other resources, such as the paper and ink that go into newspapers; that in fact newspapers – at least daily newspapers – are more scarce in almost all U.S. cities than are radio or even television stations; and that the development of cable and other new technologies is removing scarcity from the broadcast context.[158] The present FCC shares these views and would like to repeal the fairness doctrine,[159] though it probably cannot do so without the approval of Congress.[160] The Supreme Court itself, recognizing that »[t]he prevailing rationale for broadcast regulation based on spectrum scarcity has come under increasing criticism in recent years,« has indicated that it would be prepared to »reconsider our longstanding approach« if it had »some signal from Congress or the FCC that technological developments have advanced so far that some revision of the system of broadcast regulation may be required.«[161] At the same time, the Court indicated it might reconsider *Red Lion* more specifically if it were shown that the fairness doctrine, by deterring broadcasters from addressing controversial issues,

158 *E.g.*, Fowler & Brenner, *A Marketplace Approach to Broadcast Regulation*, 60 TEX. L. REV. 207 (1982); *see also* Coase, *The Federal Communications Commission*, 2 J. LAW & ECON. 1 (1959).

159 *See* General Fairness Doctrine Obligations of Broadcast Licensees, 102 F.C.C.2d 145 (1985).

160 Congress probably codified the doctrine in its 1959 amendment to section 315 of the Communications Act. 47 U.S.C. § 315(a). *See* Broadcasting, Apr. 1, 1985, at 121 (FCC commissioner so concluding). A decision of the federal court of appeals in 1986, however, expressed the view that Congress had not ratified the doctrine. Telecommunications Research and Action Center v. FCC, 801 F.2d 501 (D.C. Cir. 1986). *See* Broadcasting, Sept. 29, 1986, at 72. [*But see supra* note 146].

161 FCC v. League of Women Voters, 468 U.S. 364, 376–77 n. 11 (1984).

did more to reduce than to enhance speech.[162] On the other hand, the Court's 1981 decision in *CBS v. FCC*,[163] upholding the statutory requirement of reasonable access for federal political candidates, suggests that the *Red Lion* approach to broadcast regulation has not lost all its force.

6. *Aspects of Broadcasters' Independence*

Within the extensive regulatory framework that governs broadcasting, broadcasters retain substantial spheres of editorial discretion protected by the First Amendment. Thus in the 1983 case of *CBS v. Democratic National Committee*,[164] the Supreme Court held that neither the First Amendment nor the Communications Act requires broadcasters, while they accept commercial advertising, also to accept »editorial advertising« on public issues. The Court declared:

> In the delicate balancing historically followed in the regulation of broadcasting, Congress and the Commission could appropriately conclude that the allocation of journalistic priorities should be concentrated in the licensee rather than diffused among many. This policy gives the public some assurance that the broadcaster will be answerable if he fails to meet its legitimate needs ...[165]

Somewhat ironically, in view of today's attacks on the fairness doctrine, the Court in *CBS v. Democratic National Committee* relied in part on the obligation broadcasters have under that doctrine – their »affirmative and independent statutory obligation to provide full and fair coverage of public issues.«[166] Thus the opinion fell distinctly short of recognizing full journalistic discretion for broadcasters under the First Amendment.

The Court endorsed another aspect of broadcasters' journalistic autonomy in the 1984 case of *FCC v. League of Women Voters*.[167] That decision held unconstitutional under the First Amendment a provision in the Public Broadcasting Act that barred noncommercial broadcasters from editorializing. None of the justifications offered for the statute – such as a desire to prevent stations partly financed by the government from becoming vehicles for government propagandizing – was found by the Court to be sufficiently

162 *Id.* at 378–79 n. 12.
163 CBS v. FCC, 453 U.S. 367, 367 ff.
164 412 U.S. 94 (1973).
165 *Id.* at 125.
166 *Id.* at 129.
167 468 U.S. 364 (1984).

important and sufficiently related to the statute to justify such a flat ban on highly protected political speech.

In addition, charges of falsity or distortion in broadcasters' news or documentaries – aside from charges of fairness doctrine violations – are regularly rejected by the FCC. While the Commission condemns »slanting« or »staging« of the news as a violation of the broadcaster's public-interest responsibility, it also refuses to become »the national arbiter of truth.«[168] It therefore will not investigate charges of news distortion unless presented with »extrinsic evidence of deliberate distortion,« evidence apart from both the program itself and the alleged »true facts.«[169] Since such evidence for obvious reasons is rarely presented, broadcasters' news judgments are normally free – defamation lawsuits aside – from official inquiry into their accuracy.

7. *Regulation of Programming Content*

As a result of recent deregulation by the FCC, broadcasters are now subject to very little formal regulation of their programming content. The FCC no longer concerns itself – except in comparative renewal contests and other special situations – with the amount of time a broadcaster devotes to public affairs, to locally originated programming, to agricultural or religious programming, and so forth. Industry-supported guidelines limiting the amount of time devoted to commercials also have been dropped (in the face of antitrust attack by the government). Indirect regulatory approaches to program content, such as the FCC's former requirement that broadcasters interview numerous local leaders to »ascertain« the issues of importance to their communities, have been largely lifted as well. All that remains in this connection is a broadcaster's obligation to keep a public list of five to ten local issues and how the broadcaster's programming has treated them in the past three months, plus a general obligation – enforceable in extreme cases at renewal time – to provide programming that covers issues of public concern and that generally serves the public interest.[170]

168 Hunger in America, 20 F.C.C.2d 143 (1969); Chet Huntley, 14 F.C.C.2d 713 (1968). *Compare also*, Broadcasting, Mar. 11, 1985, at 79.
169 *Id.; see* Chronicle Broadcasting Co., 27 Radio Reg.2d 743 (1973); 30 F.C.C.2d 150 (1971).
170 *See* Broadcasting, July 2, 1984, at 31.

8. *Informal Regulation of Programming*

Apart from what the law provides, there is informal regulation of broadcasting, sometimes by »raised eyebrow« and sometimes by rougher gestures. These methods vary widely in nature and efficacy. In 1979 the FCC issued a »nonbinding« policy statement encouraging broadcasters to do more programming for children.[171] Broadcasters largely ignored the request. But when the FCC, after receiving complaints about the broadcasting of »drug-oriented« song lyrics, notified licensees that as part of their public-interest duties they were responsible for knowing what they broadcast, the Commission's action – upheld by the court of appeals[172] – apparently had its intended effect of reducing the play of the targeted songs.

A less formal kind of regulation occurred in 1974 when the chairman of the FCC, responding to pressure from Congress to curb the amount of »sex« and »violence« on television, lobbied and cajoled the three networks and the broadcasters' trade association to establish a »family viewing hour« early each evening that would be free of such programming. The broadcasters initially gave in to this pressure,[173] but then a suit was brought challenging the chairman's actions as violating the First Amendment.[174] The suit dragged on for ten years and was eventually settled,[175] and in the meantime broadcasters drifted back to their old ways, and the »family hour« languished.[176] It was only because of the lawsuit that the scope and nature of the interventions by the FCC chairman became known to the public.

Another effort came to public light only because of the extensive Watergate investigation into the administration of President Richard Nixon. A memorandum from presidential assistant Charles W. Colson to presidential assistant H.R. Haldeman, dated September 25, 1970, reported that Colson had met with the chief executives of the three television networks to discourage them from airing replies to televised speeches by the president and to let them know, among other things, »that we are not going to let them get away with anything that interferes with the President's ability to communicate.« Colson told Haldeman he would pursue with the then-

171 Children's Television Programming and Advertising Practices, 75 F.C.C.2d 138 (1979).

172 Yale Broadcasting Co. v. FCC, 478 F.2d 594 (D.C. Cir. 1973), *cert. denied*, 414 U.S. 914 (1973).

173 *See* Writers Guild of America v. FCC, 423 F. Supp. 1064, 1092-1128 (C.D. Cal. 1976), *rev'd*, 609 F.2d 355 (9th Cir. 1979).

174 *See* 609 F.2d at 355 ff.

175 Broadcasting, Jan. 7, 1985, at 204.

176 *See* M. FRANKLIN, MASS MEDIA LAW 843 (3d ed. 1987).

chairman of the FCC »the possibility of an interpretive ruling by the FCC on the role of the President when he uses TV, as soon as we have a majority.«

Since the president appoints the members of the FCC and since the FCC holds great power over broadcasters, any president can exert weighty influence over broadcasters through his FCC appointments. The government's capacity for informal regulation of broadcasters must be taken into account along with the independence they are formally accorded by the law.

9. *Regulation of »Offensive« Programming*

One clear difference between the broadcast and print media under current law is that »offensive« speech may be restricted more readily in broadcasting. In *FCC v. Pacifica Foundation,*[177] the Supreme Court upheld the FCC's power to regulate broadcast speech that is »indecent« but not »obscene.« By the vote of 5 to 4, the Court said the Commission had acted permissibly in imposing sanctions on a radio station for presenting a satirical monologue entitled, and consisting of, »Filthy Words.« Although the material was not obscene under the constitutional standard, it »did not conform to accepted standards of morality« – at least not in the afternoon, when children would be in the audience – and therefore could be found »indecent« under a federal statute banning the use of »any obscene, indecent, or profane language by means of radio communications.«[178] The Court upheld the statute's constitutionality as thus interpreted, notwithstanding that in other media »indecent« speech has constitutional protection. The Court rested the lower standard of constitutional protection for broadcast speech on two considerations: the »uniquely pervasive« presence of the broadcast media »in the lives of all Americans,« and the fact that broadcasting »is uniquely accessible to children.«[179]

177 438 U.S. 726 (1978).

178 18 U.S.C. § 1464 (1982); *see* 438 U.S. at 735.

179 438 U.S. at 748 f. A federal appeals court has struck down under the First Amendment a state law attempting to apply the »indecency« standard of *Pacifica* to cable television. Jones v. Wilkinson, ____ F.2d ____ (10th Cir., Sept. 8, 1986) [*aff'd mem.*, 107 S. Ct. 1559 (1987)].

10. *Regulation for Reasons of Public Health*

In 1967 the FCC rather surprisingly ruled, in response to a citizen's complaint, that broadcast cigarette advertisements presented one point of view on a controversial issue of public importance – the desirability of smoking – and therefore required, under the fairness doctrine, that broadcasters air (without charge) anti-smoking announcements from public-health organizations.[180] The court of appeals upheld the Commission's ruling, relying not so much on the fairness doctrine as on the public-health component of the public interest that the FCC is charged to promote.[181] Congress responded with a law prohibiting all cigarette advertising on radio and television.[182] Under constitutional challenge by broadcasters, the law was upheld by a federal district court.[183] The court stressed the legitimacy of the government's objective, the lower level of First Amendment protection accorded to the broadcast media and the marginal amount of First Amendment protection that was accorded (at that time) to commercial speech. The Supreme Court affirmed the decision without issuing an opinion.[184] Since then, while adhering to a differential standard for broadcasting in cases like *Pacifica*, the Court has substantially strengthened the constitutional protection accorded to commercial speech.[185] It therefore has been thought questionable whether the cigarette-advertising law, flatly banning a form of expression because of the message it conveys, would survive constitutional review under today's standards. A 1986 decision of the Supreme Court, however, indicates that laws banning tobacco advertising would be upheld, and not only in the broadcast media.[186]

180 Television Station WCBS-TV, 9 F.C.C.2d 921 (1967).

181 Banzhaf v. FCC, 405 F.2d 1082 (D.C. Cir. 1968), *cert. denied*, 396 U.S. 842 (1969).

182 15 U.S.C. § 1335 (1982).

183 Capital Broadcasting Co. v. Mitchell, 333 F. Supp. 582 (D.D.C. 1971).

184 405 U.S. 1000 (1972) *(per curiam)*.

185 *See, e.g.*, Cent. Hudson Gas & Elec. Corp. v. Public Serv. Comm'n, 447 U.S. 557 (1980); Carey v. Population Servs. Int'l, 431 U.S. 678 (1977); Bigelow v. Virginia, 421 U.S. 809 (1975).

186 Posadas de Puerto Rico Associates v. Tourism Co. of Puerto Rico, 106 S. Ct. 2968 (1986). The Court held that Puerto Rico's power to completely ban casino gambling »necessarily includes the lesser power to ban advertising of casino gambling.« *Id.* at 2979. The decision, though surprising and questionable, presumably means – if the Court adheres to it – that all cigarette advertising could be prohibited, since cigarettes themselves could be prohibited.

11. *General Laws Regulating Broadcasters*

Like the print media, the broadcast media are subject to general laws that affect speech – those concerning defamation, invasion of privacy, copyright infringement and the like. The broadcasting of a movie, television program, or other copyrighted work is a »performance« of the work that, if unauthorized, constitutes copyright infringement.[187] Broadcasters are also subject to generally applicable taxes, labor laws and other economic regulation. In addition to actions taken by the FCC to limit concentrations of control in broadcasting, broadcasters in theory are fully subject to the antitrust laws,[188] though in practice it appears that only extreme cases will bring forth government antitrust action against either broadcasters or newspaper publishers. Broadcasters are also subject to the general anti-discrimination laws and, in addition, to extensive »affirmative action« requirements imposed by the FCC.[189]

False advertising on the broadcast media is subject to sanction by both the FCC and the Federal Trade Commission (FTC).[190] The FCC has stated that licensees are required to »take all reasonable measures to eliminate any false, misleading or deceptive matter« from the advertising they carry.[191] Both the FCC and the FTC have attempted to protect children from television advertising that is considered unfair to them. The FTC under the Carter Administration took major steps in this direction but was blocked in Congress.[192] The FCC has taken more limited steps, such as ordering a clear separation during children's programming between the programming material and the advertising.[193]

12. *Deregulation of Broadcasting*

In recent years, consistent with the trend in other areas of government regulation, a movement has developed to reduce or abolish government regulation of the broadcast media. The primary arguments have been (1) that the rationale of spectrum scarcity, which has provided the basic justifi-

187 17 U.S.C. § 101 (1982); *see, e.g.,* Roy Export Co. v. CBS, 672 F.2d 1095 (2d Cir. 1982).
188 United States v. RCA, 358 U.S. 334 (1959).
189 47 C.F.R. § 73.2080 (1985).
190 *See* FTC v. Colgate Palmolive Co., 380 U.S. 374 (1965).
191 False, Misleading or Deceptive Advertising, 40 F.C.C. 125 (1961).
192 *See* M. FRANKLIN, MASS MEDIA LAW 892 (2d ed. 1982).
193 *See* Action for Children's Television v. FCC, 564 F.2d 458 (D.C. Cir. 1977).

cation for broadcast regulation, is no longer plausible (if it ever was) because of the proliferation of new media such as cable, and (2) that »regulation« by the free market would more effectively respond to public desires and promote the public interest than regulation by a government agency like the FCC.[194] In 1984 the FCC chairman, Mark Fowler, cited the greater efficacy of market regulation in explaining the FCC's elimination of most of its general regulation (the political obligations aside) of radio and television programming content.[195] Congress has joined in the move toward deregulation. In 1982 it amended the Communications Act to empower the FCC to allocate new broadcast licenses by a lottery – but still not a money-making auction – instead of the traditional comparative hearings.[196]

In the 1981 case of *FCC v. WNCN Listeners Guild*,[197] the Supreme Court approved the FCC's decision to eschew regulation of radio station »formats.« The court of appeals had held that when a proposed sale of a radio station involved a change in its program format so that, for example, the city's only classical-music format would be eliminated, the FCC, before approving the license transfer, was obligated to consider whether the proposed format change would be in the public interest. The FCC said it preferred to leave format decisions to broadcasters, who in seeking to maximize their audiences and incomes in the marketplace would respond to public desires more quickly and effectively than the FCC could. The Supreme Court upheld the FCC's position.

The FCC has also expressed a strong interest, as noted above, in abolishing the fairness doctrine.[198] The Supreme Court, in the *League of Women Voters* case, has indicated that it might be sympathetic.[199]

Meanwhile in Congress every year there are bills to deregulate the broadcast media and give them full First Amendment protection.[200] These measures founder, typically, on the refusal of broadcasters to pay anything for their use of the spectrum, such as annual license fees (not to mention something approaching the true value of their licenses). To at least some extent, then, U.S. broadcasters have themselves to blame for their continued failure to achieve full First Amendment rights; they simply place a higher value on money.

194 *See, e.g.*, Fowler & Brenner, *supra* note 158.
195 *See* Broadcasting, July 2, 1984, at 31.
196 47 U.S.C. § 309(i)(1) (1982).
197 450 U.S. 582 (1981).
198 *See supra* note 159 and accompanying text [*but see supra* note 146].
199 *See supra* text accompanying notes 161–62.
200 *See, e.g.,* Broadcasting, Jan. 14, 1985, at 216.

The constitutional question is reemerging in the Supreme Court, however. Both there and in Congress, the essential nature of broadcast regulation in the U.S. legal scheme remains unsettled.

E. *Regulation of Other Electronic Media Delivery Systems (Excluding Cable and DBS)*

1. *Subscription Television (STV)*

Over-the-air pay television, or subscription television (STV), uses a conventional, full-powered television broadcast station to broadcast commercial-free programming, in scrambled form, which subscribers decode and view for a fee. STV operators obtain revenue from the subscription fees and also from leasing or selling decoders. At the end of 1984, there were fewer than twenty STV operations, serving 560,000 homes, a sharp drop from about 1.4 million homes in 1982. STV appears to be, if not dying, at best short-lived. With its single station and its high operating costs, it apparently cannot compete with cable, and it survives mainly in cities where cable has been slow to develop.[201]
At one time the FCC regulated STV quite aggressively, imposing limits on the kinds of movies, sports events and other programming that STV could carry, in an effort to prevent the »siphoning« of such programs away from conventional »free« television.[202] In recent years regulation of STV has been reduced almost to the vanishing point. Under present regulations, any television licensee may become an STV operator simply on ten days' notice given to the FCC.[203] STV operators are relieved of some of the rules still applicable to regular broadcasters, such as the ban on owning more than one station in the same city.[204]

2. *Low Power Television (LPTV)*

Low power television (LPTV) evolved from »translator« television stations. A translator uses conventional broadcast technology at a low power

201 *See* Broadcasting, Dec. 10, 1984, at 44.
202 *See* Home Box Office, Inc. v. FCC, 567 F.2d 9, 19, 59–60 (D.C. Cir. 1977).
203 *See* 47 C.F.R. § 73.642-.644 (1984).
204 *See* Subscription Television Service Amendment, 48 Fed. Reg. 56,386 (1983).

level to strengthen and rebroadcast a weak signal from an affiliated station, typically to bring that station's signal to a remote area. LPTV was born when the FCC allowed translator stations to begin broadcasting their own programming. The primary difference between conventional television and LPTV is that an LPTV station has a much more limited range, and a great many LPTV stations can therefore be licensed without interfering with one another.[205]

When the FCC in 1980 first proposed to license LPTV, it set off a gold rush that at one time brought forth more than 30,000 applications.[206] The Commission was overwhelmed, and even though it subsequently adopted a lottery system to award the licenses between mutually exclusive applicants, the awards have been slow and the medium remains stunted. But the number of licensed stations is now rising rapidly. As of June 30, 1986, there were 408 LPTV stations on the air (248 VHF, 160 UHF), and construction permits had been granted for another 210 stations.[207]

The FCC decided to minimize regulation of LPTV. In addition to adopting the lottery procedure, it declined to impose ownership restrictions, minimum hours of broadcasting or requirements to ascertain community needs. On the other hand, restrictions on network-affiliation agreements do apply, as do the equal-time and reasonable-access laws for political candidates and the fairness doctrine.[208]

3. *Multipoint Distribution Services (MDS)*

In 1974 the FCC authorized two channels in each city to be used for multipoint distribution services (MDS). An MDS system transmits an omnidirectional microwave signal that can be received by subscribers with special antennas.[209] The MDS signal can carry large amounts of information, including television programming; MDS may be thought of as a »wireless cable system.« In 1983 the FCC reallocated some of the electromagnetic

205 An Inquiry into the Future Role of Low Power Television Broadcasting and Television Translators in the National Telecommunication System, 47 Fed. Reg. 21,468 (1982).

206 Broadcasting, Dec. 10, 1984, at 58.

207 Broadcasting, Dec. 1, 1986, at 122. (These are in addition to the conventional television stations listed in the chart in the text at note 108 *supra*.)

208 *See* The Future Role of Low Power Television Broadcasting and Television Translators in the National Telecommunication System, 48 Fed. Reg. 21,478 (1983); 47 C.F.R. §§ 74.780, 74.784 (1985); 47 Fed. Reg. at 468.

209 Amendment of Parts 1, 2, 21, and 43, 45 F.C.C.2d 616 (1974).

spectrum from the Instructional Television Fixed Service to MDS in order to allow for eight more MDS channels in each city. These new channels are allocated in two groups of four, creating Multichannel MDS (MMDS).[210] MMDS operators thus are able to offer four or five channels, still a good deal less than cable but perhaps at lower capital costs.[211]
For reasons that are less than clear, both MDS and MMDS have been classified by the FCC under the Communications Act as »common carriers« rather than »broadcasters.«[212] This means that they lease their channels rather than do their own programming. Single-channel MDS operators have typically leased their entire capacity to a single programmer, such as a pay-movie entrepreneur who provides programming to hotels, apartment houses and homes. Under the common-carrier rules, MDS operators are prohibited from substantial involvement in the programming they transmit, and they can devote no more than half of their broadcast time to programming supplied by an entity with which they are affiliated.[213] Broadcasting regulations, such as equal time, reasonable access and the fairness doctrine, probably apply to the customers who lease the MDS channels – not because the FCC has said so but because the court of appeals did in a parallel case involving DBS.[214]
As with other new technologies, there has been a tremendous interest in obtaining MMDS licenses. Overwhelmed by more than 16,500 applications, the FCC adopted a lottery procedure to choose between mutually exclusive ones, though it still held comparative hearings for the few remaining single-channel MDS licenses.[215] At the end of 1984, there were some 450,000 subscribers to MDS – down from 570,000 in 1982 – but the first MMDS licenses had yet to be awarded.[216] Enthusiasm about the prospects of MMDS declined in the years 1982–85, and it remains to be seen how

210 Amendment of the Commission's Rules with Regard to the Instructional Television Fixed Service, the Multipoint Distribution Service, and Private Operation Fixed Microwave Service, 48 Fed. Reg. 33,873 (1983).
211 *See* Broadcasting, Dec. 10, 1984, at 45 f.
212 47 C.F.R. §§ 21.900 *et seq.* (1985); *see also* Common Carrier, 45 F.C.C.2d 616 (1974); Homet, *Getting the Message: Statutory Approaches to Electronic Information Delivery and the Duty of Carriage*, 37 FED. COM. L.J. 217, 238–40 (1985).
213 47 C.F.R. § 21.903 (1985).
214 *See* Nat'l Ass'n of Broadcasters v. FCC, 740 F.2d 1190, 1199–1205 (D.C. Cir. 1984).
215 *See* 50 Fed. Reg. 5983 (1985).
216 Broadcasting, Dec. 10, 1984, at 46. The first awards were made in September 1985; lotteries and resulting awards continued through 1986. *See* Broadcasting, Oct. 6, 1986, at 73. Quincy Cable TV, Inc. v. FCC, 768 F.2d 1434 (D.C. Cir. 1985), *cert. denied*, 106 S. Ct. 2889 (1986).

effectively the medium can compete against the much greater channel capacity of cable.

F. *Regulatory Framework of Cable Television*

1. *Description and Background of Cable*

Cable television has existed in the United States since about 1950. The first cable systems – called at that time community antenna television (CATV) - were located in communities perhaps sixty miles away from the nearest television station, or surrounded by mountains, and therefore afflicted with poor television reception. The CATV operator erected an antenna on high ground near the town, picked the television signals off the air, and sent them by wire to the homes of local residents, who paid a monthly fee for the service. Cable's original purpose, thus, was to overcome natural obstacles to good television reception in communities that were more or less within the »natural« range of the stations being received.

The next step was to increase the program offerings available by using microwave relays to bring in the signals of »distant« stations. With this attraction cable could appeal to viewers even in large cities enjoying a full complement of off-the-air stations. It could, for example, bring the independent (i.e., not network-affiliated) stations in the very largest cities, such as Los Angeles or Chicago, into cities (say Denver) that had three network affiliates but no independent VHF station. What made cable's distant-signal appeal a commercial reality was the introduction in the mid-1970s of domestic satellites to replace terrestrial microwave relay stations as cross-country program carriers. The satellites have made possible the carriage of television »superstations« – three independent VHF stations in Chicago, New York and Atlanta – to thousands of cable systems throughout the country.

The satellites have also brought to cable systems something new and even more important than distant broadcast signals: a legion of new »cable networks« that provide original cable programming in a wide diversity of formats. There are cable networks showing full-time news (Cable News Network), full-time coverage of the proceedings of the U.S. Congress (C-Span), full-time music (MTV), full-time sports, full-time movies, full-time foreign-language programs and numerous other formats. The cable networks are provided for a fee to individual cable systems, and the systems provide them to their subscribers either as part of the »basic tier« of cable services that every subscriber receives in return for the monthly subscription fee or as part of an added tier for which the subscriber pays extra (»pay cable,« exemplified by entertainment networks such as Home Box Office or Showtime). In addition cable systems can, and often do, originate their own local programming. This has rarely been an important factor in attracting audiences, though it is commercially important insofar as it involves the origination of commercials. Advertising, however, still provides only a small part of cable revenues (less than five percent) as of 1985).[217] Although cable systems still carry the signals of local television stations, regardless of being required to do so by the FCC's »must carry« rule,[218] the variety of specialized programming provided by the cable networks is the principal thing that has made cable today a successful, fast-growing and increasingly important medium.

In mid-1985 there were in the U.S. some 6,600 operating cable systems serving about 37 million homes, or fourty-four percent of the nation's television households.[219] The cable industry's revenues in 1984 totaled about $3.6 billion, and the industry was starting to be profitable as well. Most cable systems have at least twelve channels. Those built after March 1972 must have at least twenty. It is now common for systems to have around fifty channels, and fifty-four is typical for systems built today. Many systems now being built in large cities have two cables and thus the ability to transmit more than one hundred channels. The average monthly subscription fee for basic cable service in late 1986 was $10.50 and rising rapidly.[220]

2. *Local Franchising Regulation of Cable*

Originally, and to a significant extent still, cable has been regulated largely at the local level through the »franchising« process. Because the cables must be laid over or under the city's streets, a cable operator cannot begin construction without a permit, or »franchise,« from the city. Contests among cable companies to obtain a city's franchise – assuming there will be only one franchise, a question discussed below – have often been fierce,

217 BROADCASTING YEARBOOK 1985, at D-3.
218 *See* text at notes 237–38 *infra*.
219 Broadcasting, May 13, 1985, at 11.
220 Wall St. J., Dec. 12, 1986, at 29, cols. 4–6.

and cities have developed elaborate auction procedures designed to obtain as much as possible for the city in the franchise terms. Thus a city might set franchise conditions specifying the minimum channel capacity of the cable system; the area it would serve; a timetable for wiring the entire area; the cable networks or other program services the system would provide; the subscription rates it would charge; the setting aside of one or more channels for use by the city government and the school system and for free public-access programming; construction of network and studio facilities in connection with the channels so set aside; the length of the franchise (typically fifteen years); procedures for deciding whether the franchise would be renewed; and a minimum franchise fee – typically a percentage of the system's revenues – to be paid to the city each year. All bidders for the franchise would be expected to meet these basic conditions, and the franchise would then be awarded to whichever company agreed to pay the highest franchise fee or otherwise made the most attractive bid (or, in many cases, had the most political influence with the city government; or, in some cases, paid the most effective bribes).[221]

3. *Cable and Copyright*

When cable began to develop in earnest in the 1960s, the question naturally arose whether a cable system, when it received broadcast signals (either off the air or by microwave relay) and retransmitted them by wire to its subscribers, was infringing the copyrights on the movies or other television programs being broadcast. If so, then the television networks and the motion picture companies, which owned most of the copyrights, might be able either to close down or to take over the emerging cable industry and end the competitive threat it represented. Under the copyright law, the question was whether a cable retransmission of a broadcast signal constituted a »performance« of the work being broadcast (or, if it did, whether there was an »implied license« to perform a work by aiding the reception of a signal broadcast to the public).

The Supreme Court decided the question twice. In 1968 it held in *Fortnightly Corp. v. United Artists Television, Inc.*,[222] dealing with a tradition-

221 *See* Cable Franchise Policy and Communications Act of 1984, H.R. REP. No. 934, 98th Cong., 2d Sess. 23 (1984) (hereinafter cited as »House Report«); Barnett, *State, Federal, and Local Regulation of Cable Television*, 47 NOTRE DAME LAW. 685 (1972).

222 392 U.S. 390 (1968). The author was among the counsel for the defendant cable operator in *Fortnightly*.

al cable system that took its signals off the air from a station some sixty miles away, that such retransmission did not constitute a performance of the broadcast work. In 1974, in *Teleprompter Corp. v. CBS*,[223] the Court dealt with a more advanced cable system that received signals by microwave relay from more than a thousand miles away, and it reached the same conclusion. In both cases the Court's reasoning – that cable did not »perform,« because it was more like a receiver than like a broadcaster – was unsatisfactory, but its result was sound. Not only were better legal reasons available, but the result, as a Supreme Court Justice has since observed, »had the arguably desirable effect of protecting an infant industry from a premature death.«[224]

In the Copyright Act of 1976, Congress reached a complicated compromise on the cable copyright question. The Act establishes that cable retransmission does constitute performance, but it relieves cable systems of copyright liability for carrying local signals and further gives them a compulsory license for the carriage of distant signals. The statutory royalty fees for distant-signal carriage are set, periodically adjusted and distributed among copyright owners by a new federal agency called the Copyright Royalty Tribunal.[225]

4. *Cable Regulation by the FCC*

Cable regulation by the FCC rose in the 1960s, crested in 1972 and has since subsided. Designed originally to protect television broadcasters against cable, it exists today largely to protect cable against local franchise regulation.

The FCC began in 1959 by deciding that its regulatory jurisdiction under the Communications Act gave it no authority to regulate cable, which was neither a broadcaster nor a common carrier.[226] But as cable grew in the 1960s and began to import distant signals that competed for the audience of local broadcasters, the FCC changed its mind. In 1966 it adopted rules designed to protect broadcasters against cable competition.[227] These rules (i) required cable systems to carry the signals of local stations (the »must

223 415 U.S. 394 (1974).

224 Twentieth Century Music Corp. v. Aiken, 422 U.S. 151, 166 (1975) (Blackmun, J., concurring).

225 17 U.S.C. § 111 (1982).

226 CATV and TV Repeater Services, 26 F.C.C. 403 (1959).

227 Community Antenna Television, Second Report and Order, 2 F.C.C. 725 (1966).

carry« rule); (ii) barred them from duplicating a locally broadcast program with an imported signal on the same day; and (iii) prohibited cable systems from importing distant signals into the 100 largest cities – and thus, effectively, from getting started in those cities – without a cumbersome hearing into the effect the cable operation would have on local broadcasting. The Supreme Court in 1968, in the *Southwestern Cable* case,[228] upheld these rules on the ground that they were reasonably considered necessary to protect local broadcasting and therefore were within the FCC's power to regulate things »ancillary to broadcasting.«

The FCC in 1972 moved further by adopting a comprehensive set of rules governing the aspects of cable that were subject to local franchise regulation.[229] These rules required franchising authorities to hold a public hearing before granting a franchise; required newly built systems to have at least twenty channels; required cable systems to provide channels for governmental, educational, public access and leased use; limited franchise terms to fifteen years; limited franchise fees to three percent (or, on a special showing, five percent) of the cable system's annual revenues; and so forth. In addition, the FCC already had barred ownership of cable systems by any of the television networks and by television stations and telephone companies in the same locality as the system.[230]

Not long after the 1972 rules were issued, the regulatory tide began to turn, as the advent of satellites brought cable new growth and political influence and as it was increasingly recognized that the FCC's regulation had functioned largely to protect broadcasters against a new competitive industry. Contributing to the trend was a 1979 Supreme Court decision holding that the access-channel requirements in the FCC's 1972 rules went beyond the Commission's existing jurisdiction over cable.[231] Contributing also was the 1976 Copyright Act, which removed the justification for the FCC's distant-signal restrictions on cable.[232] The 1970s thus saw a progressive dismantling of the regulatory structure the FCC had erected. The various rules governing the local aspects of cable were reduced to nonbinding recommendations, except that the ceiling on franchise fees remained in effect.[233] The FCC also »preempted,« or used its superior federal authority to prohibit, any local regulation of the rates charged by cable systems for pay-cable

228 United States v. Southwestern Cable Co., 392 U.S. 157 (1968).
229 Cable Television Report and Order, 36 F.C.C.2d 143 (1972).
230 47 C.F.R. §§ 63.54 (telephone), 76.501 (networks, broadcasters) (1985).
231 FCC v. Midwest Video Corp., 440 U.S. 689 (1979).
232 *See* text at note 225 *supra*.
233 47 C.F.R. § 76.31 (1985).

programming (but not of the basic rates for subscribing to cable).[234] FCC rules restricting distant-signal carriage by cable systems – adopted as a substitute for copyright liability – were lifted in 1980.[235] The rule banning network ownership of cable systems has been effectively lifted, though the bans on ownership by local television stations and local telephone companies remain.[236] Also remaining were the »must carry« rules, until they were struck down by a federal court of appeals in 1985 as violating the First Amendment rights of cable operators.[237] The FCC in late 1986 readopted the rules in more limited form, no longer requiring cable systems to carry *all* local broadcast stations regardless of the number of channels available on the system.[238] It remained unclear whether these new rules would withstand court attack.

That FCC regulation of cable serves largely now to protect cable from local (or state) regulation was illustrated by the 1984 Supreme Court decision in *Capital Cities Cable Inc. v. Crisp.*[239] The Court held that an Oklahoma statute prohibiting commercials for alcoholic beverages could not be applied to cable programming. Requiring cable systems to remove such commercials would impose a heavy burden and would conflict, the Court said, with FCC regulations permitting cable carriage of distant signals and also with the compulsory-license provisions of the 1976 Copyright Act.

5. *The Cable Communications Policy Act of 1984*

Despite the deregulation at the FCC, cable still chafed under the demands of cities in the local franchising process and, in particular, under their regulation of cable's subscription rates. At the same time, the power of cities to regulate cable through the franchising process – for example, to grant an exclusive franchise – was coming under increasing challenge in court. A 1982 Supreme Court decision struck dread into the hearts and pocketbooks of cities by holding that they could be subject to antitrust liability for

234 *See* Brookhaven Cable TV Inc. v. Kelly, 573 F.2d 765 (2d Cir. 1978), *cert. denied*, 441 U.S. 904 (1979).

235 Cable Television Syndicated Program Exclusivity Rules, 79 F.C.C.2d 663 (1980); *see* Malrite T.V. of New York, Inc. v. FCC, 652 F.2d 1140 (2d Cir. 1981), *cert. denied*, 454 U.S. 1143 (1982).

236 47 C.F.R. §§ 63.54, 76.501 (1984).

237 Quincy Cable TV, Inc. v. FCC, 768 F.2d 1434 (D.C. Cir. 1985), *cert. denied,* 106 S. Ct. 2889 (1986).

238 Broadcasting, Dec. 1, 1986, at 43.

239 104 S. Ct. 2694 (1984).

actions taken in cable franchising.[240] With the cable industry wanting less local regulation and the cities wanting legal protection for some local regulation, a bargain was struck that produced congressional passage of the Cable Communications Policy Act of 1984 (the »Cable Act«),[241] the most important amendment yet of the Communications Act of 1934. The essence of the bargain was that regulation of cable subscription rates was lifted, while the power of cities to grant franchises and impose other regulations on cable as part of the franchising process was confirmed.

The Cable Act states that every cable system must have a franchise and authorizes a city to award »1 or more franchises.«[242] The House Committee Report makes clear that this means the city may decide to grant only one franchise.[243] The Act limits franchise regulation in several ways: the city's franchise fee may not exceed five percent of the cable system's annual revenues;[244] the city (at least in new franchises) may not regulate the content of cable programming (except for programming that is obscene or »otherwise unprotected by the Constitution of the United States«);[245] and – the big prize for the cable industry – after January 1, 1987, the city may not regulate the cable system's subscription rates.[246] The Act also has provisions for modification of the franchise at the behest of the cable operator and a complex franchise-renewal section that seeks to balance the competing interests of the city and the franchise holder.[247]

The Act has important provisions regarding »mandatory access« to cable systems by parties other than the system owner. It allows cities as part of the franchising process to require that channels be set aside for use by the city, the schools and the public, with studios and other facilities provided by the cable operator.[248] More important, the Act requires all cable systems having thirty-six or more channels to set aside some of them – ten percent on systems with up to fifty-four channels, fifteen percent on systems with more than fifty-four – for commercial leased access by other programmers.[249] The likely effectiveness of this requirement is weakened, however, by provisions allowing the cable system owner to set the rates for channel leasing so as to

240 Community Communications Co. v. City of Boulder, 455 U.S. 40 (1982).
241 98 Stat. 2779 (1984), 47 U.S.C. §§ 521–59 (Supp. 1985)
242 47 U.S.C. § 541(a)(1), (b).
243 House Report, *supra* note 221, at 59.
244 47 U.S.C. § 542(b).
245 47 U.S.C. § 544(b), (d).
246 47 U.S.C. § 543; *see also* Note following 47 U.S.C. § 521.
247 47 U.S.C. §§ 545, 546.
248 47 U.S.C. § 531.
249 47 U.S.C. § 532.

protect his own programming against the competition provided by the leased offerings.[250] (Yet the antitrust laws, in turn, might undercut these provisions.)[251]

The Act confirms the preexisting restrictions on ownership of cable systems by television broadcasters or telephone companies in the same locality.[252] (Last-minute lobbying by newspaper publishers knocked out a similar ban on ownership by local newspapers.) It provides that cable systems, insofar as they carry television programming, are not subject to regulation as common carriers (apart from the access requirements imposed or approved by the Act).[253] Government entities are allowed to own cable systems, but if they do, they may not exercise editorial control except through a separate entity.[254]

The Act requires cable operators to protect the privacy of their subscribers. They may collect and use personally identifiable information only to the extent necessary to render service or to detect unauthorized reception. Subscribers are given the right to know what information has been collected about them, how it will be used and when it is available for inspection. They also have a right to recover damages in court for violation of the Act's privacy provisions.[255]

Various content regulations apply to cable programming under the Act and the preexisting law. Except with respect to programming on access channels, a cable operator remains liable – just as a broadcaster is – for defamation, invasion of privacy, false advertising or other generally applicable speech offenses.[256] The operator is also subject to criminal laws on obscenity; since sex-oriented material on cable has been a sharp political issue in some parts of the country, the Act adds its own criminal prohibition for transmitting over cable any matter that is obscene or »otherwise unprotected by the Constitution of the United States.«[257] (The quoted phrase reflects a hope that the special constitutional standard applied to broadcasting in the *Pacifica* case[258] will be applied to cable as well. This seems unlikely, particularly since the Act requires cable operators to sell or lease to

250 *See* 47 U.S.C. (c)(1), (2), (d), (f); House Report, *supra* note 221, at 50–54; Homet, *supra* note 212, at 268.
251 *See* House Report, *supra* note 221, at 50.
252 47 U.S.C. § 533.
253 47 U.S.C. § 541(c).
254 47 U.S.C. § 533(e).
255 47 U.S.C. § 551.
256 *See* 47 U.S.C. § 558.
257 47 U.S.C. § 559.
258 FCC v. Pacifica Foundation, 438 U.S. 726 (1978); *see supra* notes 177–79 and accompanying text

subscribers, on demand, a »lock box« to prevent viewing by children.[259])
Finally, the FCC had previously extended to cable-originated programming such broadcast-content regulations as the equal-time and reasonable-access requirements and the fairness doctrine,[260] and the Cable Act does nothing to change that.[261]

6. *Cable Regulation and the First Amendment*

The existing scheme of cable regulation, as confirmed and adjusted by the Cable Act, raises some serious First Amendment questions. There is room here only to outline the most important ones.

a. *The constitutionality of access requirements*

The provision of the Cable Act requiring cable systems with thirty-six or more channels to set aside channels for commercial leased access is under attack – as are franchise provisions requiring that channels be set aside for governmental, educational and public-access use – as an unconstitutional intrusion on the editorial discretion of the cable operator as a First Amendment speaker. That discretion is said to comprehend the programming or program selection for all channels on the system. A requirement that some channels be made available to other programmers is thus said to violate the constitutional principle of *Miami Herald Publishing Co. v. Tornillo,*[262] which held that newspapers could not be required to make reply space available. One federal appeals court has supported this argument,[263] two others have indicated some sympathy for it,[264] and the Supreme Court has observed that the argument is »not frivolous.«[265] But another appeals court has viewed cable access requirements as distinguishable from the right-of-reply statute in

259 47 U.S.C. § 544(d)(2).
260 47 C.F.R. § 76.205–.221 (1985).
261 *See* 47 U.S.C. § 544(f).
262 418 U.S. 241 (1974); *see supra* text at notes 91–92.
263 Midwest Video Corp. v. FCC, 571 F.2d 1025, 1055–56 (8th Cir. 1978), *aff'd on other grounds*, 440 U.S. 689 (1979).
264 Preferred Communications, Inc. v. City of Los Angeles, 754 F.2d 1396, 1401 n.4 (9th Cir. 1985), *aff'd as modified*, 106 S. Ct. 2034 (1986); Quincy Cable TV, Inc. v. FCC, 768 F.2d 1434, 1450 (D.C. Cir. 1985).
265 FCC v. Midwest Video Corp., 440 U.S. 689, 709 n. 19 (1979).

Tornillo,[266] while a federal district court has squarely upheld such requirements.[267]

The Supreme Court, one would think, will uphold them. *Tornillo* seems different not only because it involved newspapers, traditionally a specially protected medium under the First Amendment, but also because the Court there emphasized that the reply-space requirement could deter the newspaper from printing controversial campaign coverage in the first place. There is no such danger with respect to channel access requirements, since they are independent of the content of the cable system's own programming. A more pertinent precedent than *Tornillo* may be found in *Prune-Yard Shopping Center v. Robins*.[268] There the Supreme Court, distinguishing *Tornillo*, held that a state could require the owner of a private shopping center to allow First Amendment activities, such as picketing and leafleting, on his property – that imposing this right of speech by others did not violate the owner's First Amendment rights.

The argument that access requirements nonetheless intrude on the cable operator's editorial discretion in the same manner as telling a newspaper what to print begs the question whether the cable operator's editorial discretion extends, as a matter of constitutional right, to all the channels on the system. While the cable operator, to the extent that he programs or selects programming, is a First Amendment speaker, he is also something else: the owner of a cable grid. This grid is capable of carrying 50 or 100 channels of television programming (and other communications) running to homes throughout the city, and, given the natural-monopoly characteristics of cable, it is very likely to be and remain the only such grid available to homes in the area it serves. The government, it would seem, has power to regulate this grid as it regulates other public utilities, and such regulation can include requiring that some channels on the grid be made available to programmers other than the system owner. This requirement has only the most attenuated impact on speech by the cable owner, who remains entitled to program all the other channels (and to add more of them at will). Meanwhile the access requirement does much to promote the First Amendment interests of the public by assuring that the cable medium in the community will not be monopolized but reflect a diversity of sources of information and opinion, including ones that disagree or compete with those of the cable system owner. The Supreme Court has recognized the First

266 Home Box Office, Inc. v. FCC, 567 F.2d 9, 46 n. 82. (1977).

267 Berkshire Cablevision of Rhode Island v. Burke, 571 F. Supp. 976, 983-88 (D.R.I. 1983).

268 447 U.S. 74 (1980).

Amendment interests of the public in a number of cases,[269] and one would expect it to do so again by upholding the congressionally approved access requirements for cable.[270]

b. *The constitutionality of exclusive franchising*

A more difficult question is whether cities may grant – as they have traditionally done and are apparently authorized to do by the Cable Act – only one cable franchise, thereby excluding other cable companies from constructing and operating systems in the city. In March 1985, the federal court of appeals in California, in *Preferred Communications, Inc. v. City of Los Angeles*,[271] held that the traditional method of auctioning a single franchise to the highest bidder violated the First Amendment rights of a cable company denied a franchise, if there were room on the utility poles (as there was conceded to be) for a second company's cable.

Forceful arguments exist on both sides of the question. Cable television is clearly a medium protected by the First Amendment, and denial of a franchise prevents a would-be cable operator from »speaking« in that medium in that locality, at least through the means of constructing and operating his own system. But the cities – relying on the First Amendment »balancing« test of *United States v. O'Brien*[272] – assert a number of governmental interests to justify the single-franchise approach to cable. These interests include avoiding repeated disruption of the streets and obtaining for the city various benefits of a cable franchise: benefits such as the wiring of the entire city (including low-income areas); maximum channel capacity and other state-of-the-art technology; channels and facilities for governmental, educational and public-access use; a maximum franchise fee; and so forth. These benefits represent legitimate and important government objectives, given the growing significance of the cable medium, and the cities say a cable operator will not agree to such franchise terms unless the city can assure the operator exclusivity in return. The cities further contend

269 Red Lion Broadcasting Co. v. FCC, 395 U.S. 367 (1969); CBS v. FCC, 453 U.S. 367 (1981); Nat'l Citizens Comm. for Broadcasting v. FCC, 436 U.S. 775 (1978); Associated Press v. United States, 326 U.S. 1 (1945).

270 See Barnett, *Franchising of Cable TV Systems to Get Airing at Supreme Court*, National Law Journal, Apr. 21, 1986, at 42, 43. The Supreme Court in City of Los Angeles v. Preferred Communications, Inc., 106 S. Ct. 2034, 2038 (1986), while not addressing the constitutionality of access requirements, appeared to disavow a strict analogy between cable and newspapers and to suggest application of a First Amendment »balancing« test that seems likely to accommodate access requirements. *See infra* notes 276–80 and accompanying text.

271 754 F. 2d 1396 (9th Cir. 1985), *aff'd as modified*, 106 S. Ct. 2034 (1986).

272 391 U.S. 367 (1968); *see supra* text at notes 45–47.

that, since leased access will be available (as the Cable Act requires) on the franchised system, other cable operators are not in fact excluded from »speaking« by way of cable in the city – they simply have to do so by leasing channel space on the single franchised system.

While the court of appeals in *Preferred* relied too heavily on the analogy between cable and newspapers, it was probably right in holding that denial of a franchise works too much restraint on speech to pass muster under the First Amendment. The test of *United States v. O'Brien* requires that a regulation of speech leave adequate alternative modes of communication by which the speaker can reach the public.[273] A would-be cable operator denied the right to construct and operate a cable system does not appear to have adequate alternative means of speaking by way of cable in that community. True, access to the franchised system presumably would be available under the Cable Act (assuming the constitutionality of the access requirement). But the Act's leased-access requirement applies to only ten or fifteen percent of a system's channels, is subject to discriminatory pricing by the system owner and is full of doubts about how much demand there will be and how much channel time will in fact be available and on what terms.[274] Leased access therefore seems an inadequate substitute for the right to build one's own system. This is particularly so because the Constitution's Equal Protection clause limits unequal treatment in the exercise of First Amendment rights.[275] Under that standard, the contrast is dramatic between the speech rights of the franchised cable operator, who controls numerous channels and further controls the pricing for the access channels, and those of the would-be cable operator, who is reduced to standing in line for problematic access to a few channels subject to price control by his competitor.

Finally, while the benefits sought by the city through granting a single franchise are substantial, it is not clear enough that the single-franchise approach is truly necessary in order to obtain them. All of those benefits, with the exception of highest-bid features, such as a maximum franchise fee (which in any event is capped by the Cable Act at five percent of revenues), can be demanded in all the franchises that a city grants to all qualified operators who want them. While one cannot conclusively reject the city's fear

273 City Council of Los Angeles v. Taxpayers for Vincent, 466 U.S. 789 (1984); City of Renton v. Playtime Theatres, Inc., 106 S. Ct. 925, 928, 932 (1986).

274 *See* 47 U.S.C. § 532; House Report, *supra* note 221, at 50–54; Homet, *supra* note 212, at 268–69 f.

275 *See* Williams v. Rhodes, 393 U.S. 23 (1968); Police Department of Chicago v. Mosley, 408 U.S. 92 (1972); Karst, *supra* note 50.

that cable operators will not accept such terms unless they are guaranteed protection from competition, the natural-monopoly character of cable makes it likely that whichever operator builds first in a particular area will be the only operator who builds there, thus providing de facto exclusivity in any event.

In 1986 the Supreme Court decided the *Preferred* case.[276] In a terse opinion, the Court recognized that the activities of cable television »plainly implicate First Amendment interests,« since cable »partakes of some of the aspects of speech and the communication of ideas as do the traditional enterprises of newspaper and book publishers, public speakers and pamphleteers.«[277] But the Court also stated, citing *O'Brien*, that »where speech and conduct are joined in a single course of action, the First Amendment values must be balanced against competing social interests.«[278] On this basis, the Court sent *Preferred* back to the lower courts for the development of more facts, particularly with respect to the city's claims that the operation of more than one cable system in a given area would disrupt its public ways and cause »permanent visual blight.«[279]

The Supreme Court in *Preferred* thus took a narrower view of cable's First Amendment rights than had the court of appeals and apparently called for application of the *O'Brien* »balancing« text instead of a strict analogy between cable and newspapers. Nonetheless, when the constitutionality of single franchising is finally decided, the *O'Brien* test itself should lead to the conclusion, as indicated above, that this approach to cable is inconsistent with the First Amendment.[280]

c. *The constitutionality of cable franchise fees*

A third question involves the franchise fees that cable systems traditionally have paid to their franchising cities – and that the Cable Act expressly authorizes cities to collect, though with a ceiling of five percent of gross revenues annually.[281] These fees are laid only on cable systems and are in addition to general taxes, such as a sales tax, that are laid on cable systems together with other businesses. Since the Supreme Court in the *Minneapolis Star* case[282] struck down a tax laid only on newspapers, one may ask

276 City of Los Angeles v. Preferred Communications, Inc., 106 S. Ct. 2034 (1986).
277 *Id.* at 2037.
278 *Id.* at 2038.
279 *Id.* at 2037–38.
280 *See* Barnett, *supra* note 270, at 42.
281 47 U.S.C. § 542..
282 460 U.S. 575 (1983); *see supra* text at notes 89–90.

why cable franchise fees are not likewise invalid as a state-imposed financial burden that singles out one communications medium. True, the five percent statutory ceiling removes the potential, relied on by the Court in *Minneapolis Star*, for escalating the fee to confiscatory levels. Moreover, the fees are traditional for cable systems. Presumably they will be defended as a charge for the use of public property – the streets and easements through which the cable is laid. Yet newspapers also »occupy« public property – through their forests of newsracks on public sidewalks – and are not charged a revenue-raising fee for the privilege. While a revenue-raising fee for newsracks within a public bus terminal has been upheld by a federal appeals court, the court's reasoning suggested that to impose the fee for newsracks on the sidewalk – which might well be a necessary location if newspapers are to reach their public – would be invalid.[283] For cable, the use of the public ways to lay the wires is a necessary way to reach the public. If revenue-raising cable franchise fees are upheld, then, it will be because tradition and the congressional five percent ceiling indicate that they are not in fact a threat to cable's financial health and growth. The constitutional case against them is substantial.

7. *Regulation of the Reception of Cable Programming from Non-broadcast Satellites*

Section 705 of the Federal Communications Act of 1934 (formerly section 605) prohibits any person not authorized by the sender to »intercept any radio communication« and any person »not being entitled thereto« to »receive or assist in receiving any interstate or foreign communication by radio.«[284] The 1984 Cable Act amended this provision insofar as it applies to the growing practice of using a satellite receiving dish to receive from a domestic satellite television programs that the satellite is transmitting to cable systems for retransmission to their subscribers. (By mid-1986, there were an estimated 1.5 million »backyard dishes« in the United States.[285]) The amended section 705 provides that the interception or receipt »of any satellite cable programming for private viewing« is not illegal if (1) the programming involved is not encrypted (scrambled) and (2) the owner of the programming has

283 Gannett Satellite Information Network v. Metropolitan Transportation Authority, 745 F.2d 767 (2d Cir. 1984).

284 47 U.S.C. § 705 (1985).

285 Broadcasting, Oct. 6, 1986, at 74.

not established a marketing system under which individuals can pay for the right to receive the programming for private viewing.[286] Thus, if pay-cable operators and other cable networks wish to control the practice of receiving their programming directly from satellites, they have the choice of scrambling their »satellite feeds« or selling the right to receive them. (Since enforcement of a marketing system would be difficult, cable programmers generally have decided to scramble their feeds, and by early 1987, most major programmers were expected to have done so.[287]) More broadly, the new amendment signifies that when program-bearing signals for cable television are being distributed in the United States in nonscrambled form, even by satellites engaged in point-to-point transmission, members of the public have a legal right to receive those signals for private viewing, either free or by paying for them.[288]

G. *Regulatory Framework for Direct-Broadcast Satellites*

The FCC has defined direct-broadcast satellites (DBS) as »a radiocommunication service in which signals transmitted or retransmitted by space stations are intended for direct reception by the general public.«[289] DBS is a medium of awesome potential power. The service area of a single DBS transmitter could encompass an entire U.S. time zone; using two or three satellites, a DBS operator could broadcast to virtually every home in the nation, bypassing »such earthbound media as broadcasting and cable.«[290] Moreover, DBS can broadcast multiple channels, and its powerful signal enables reception by dishes two to three feet in diameter instead of the ten to fifteen feet needed for conventional satellites. In 1982 the FCC authorized DBS service in the United States and granted construction permits to eight

286 47 U.S.C. § 705(b) (1985).
287 *See* Broadcasting, Oct. 6, 1986, at 74.
288 However, this is true only of signals being distributed for *cable* programming and not for broadcast programming. Broadcast television networks and program owners take the position, which seems correct, that their unscrambled »network feeds« may not be picked up by satellite dish antennas. *See* N.Y. Times, Dec. 11, 1986, at 16, cols. 1–2 (national ed.) (*War Over Satellites Pits N.F.L. Against Bars*). *See infra* notes 701–22 and accompanying text.
289 47 C.F.R. § 100.3 (1985).
290 Broadcasting, Dec. 10, 1984, at 46.

applicants (subjcct to the United States's receiving enough orbital slots at the 1983 Regional Administrative Radio Conference,[291] which was accomplished).[292]

In determining whether it would serve the »public interest« under the Communications Act to authorize DBS, the FCC weighed the potential benefits of the new service against the potential costs. It noted five major potential benefits: (1) DBS can bring service to isolated rural areas that presently have little or no television service; (2) DBS can provide additional channels of programming for rural or noncabled viewers; (3) since DBS can reach many people with many channels and is contemplated as a pay service, it offers the prospect of »narrowcast« programming for smaller audiences with more specialized tastes, a service potentially more responsive to consumer demand than advertiser-supported programming; (4) DBS can provide innovative services, such as high-definition television, stereo television, teletext and dual-language sound tracks, more easily than conventional broadcasting can; and (5) DBS can be used for non-video services, such as data transmission.[293] Against these potential benefits, the FCC weighed the economic harm that DBS might cause to the existing broadcast system and to the »local service« it provides. But the FCC found no »strong evidence that a significant net reduction of service to the public would result,«[294] concluding that the evidence of economic harm to existing broadcasters was at best speculative. The FCC also considered harm to existing users of the 12-GHz band, where DBS would be assigned, but concluded that they could be satisfactorily relocated. The Commission thus concluded that the public interest would be served by authorizing domestic DBS service.

The regulatory scheme the FCC erected for this service was designed to minimize regulation and to rely as heavily as possible on the competitive forces of the marketplace. DBS licensees were not made subject to any of the ownership limits that apply to conventional broadcasters, and thus no limit was imposed on the number of channels a single DBS operator could control. Nor was any access requirement imposed, as has been done for cable systems under the Cable Act (unless the DBS operator chooses to operate as a common carrier). The DBS rules do include, however, the

291 Direct Broadcast Satellites, 90 F.C.C.2d 676 (1982); STC Decision, 91 F.C.C.2d 953 (1982); In re Application of CBS, 92 F.C.C.2d 64 (1982).

292 *See DBS Under FCC and International Regulation*, 37 VAND. L. REV. 67, 82 f. (1984).

293 90 F.C.C.2d at 680–82.

294 *Id.* at 689.

same ban on alien ownership (discussed below) that is laid down for broadcast licensees by the Communications Act.[295]

While the Communications Act establishes separate regulatory schemes for »broadcasters« (in title III of the Act) and »common carriers« (in title II), the FCC, saying that technological changes had drained meaning from these classifications, declined to force DBS into either category. Instead, it proposed to make an individual determination that would depend on the nature of the service offered by a particular DBS operator or by the same operator on different channels. Thus, an operator who proposed direct-to-home service and retained control over program content presumably would be treated as a broadcaster and hence made subject to the equal-time, reasonable-access and fairness requirements; on the other hand, an operator who leased channels to others presumably would be treated as a common carrier and hence required to offer services to the public without discrimination.[296] The suggestion of common-carrier designation for DBS operations then raised the question of what regulation, if any, would be applied to the »customer-programmers« of a DBS common carrier. The FCC said these programmers would be subject only to the common-carrier regulation applied to the DBS operator and would not be regulated themselves as broadcasters.[297]

The DBS regulatory scheme took its final form in a 1984 decision of the U.S. Court of Appeals for the District of Columbia Circuit on appeal from the FCC's ruling. In this case, *National Association of Broadcasters v. FCC (NAB)*,[298] the court upheld the FCC's determination that authorizing DBS service was in the public interest. It had difficulty with the FCC's refusal to apply to DBS operators the ownership limitations that apply to terrestrial broadcasters, finding an inadequate empirical basis for the Commission's claim that competition in the market for video services made such a rule no longer necessary.[299] The court accepted, however, the Commission's alternative argument that, in view of the high costs and riskiness of the DBS business, there was a substantial economic need, at least initially, for DBS enterpreneurs to be able to offer more than one channel of service.[300]

What the court reversed was the FCC's refusal to impose the obligations of broadcasters on DBS in the case where the DBS operator leases channels

295 47 C.F.R. § 100.11 (1985), *see* 47 U.S.C. § 310 (1982); text at notes 579–82 *infra*.
296 90 F.C.C.2d at 709; *see* Homet, *supra* note 212, at 242.
297 90 F.C.C.2d at 709–11.
298 740 F.2d 1190 (D.C. Cir. 1984).
299 *Id.* at 1208.
300 *Id.* at 1207

as a common carrier. When the DBS customer programs a DBS channel and that programming is transmitted to the homes of the public, *somebody* is acting as a broadcaster within the meaning of the Communications Act, the court said. The FCC therefore had no authority to refuse to apply broadcast regulatory requirements. The court noted that under the FCC's scheme, a federal candidate for national office would have no right to obtain »equal time« or »reasonable access« on a DBS channel to reply to the opposing candidate and declared that the sheer power of DBS made application of the political-broadcasting rules even more critical than for conventional broadcasting.[301] While the court thus vacated the FCC's ruling on this point, it let the ruling stand otherwise, and it left to the FCC the remedy for this defect – whether by treating the customer-programmers as broadcasters or by making the DBS operator responsible for their compliance with the statutory obligations.[302]

While a regulatory framework for DBS is thus established, DBS itself is far from being established. The medium has enormous entry costs – an estimated $700 million to launch one satellite and provide just one year of service to homes on the East Coast.[303] As a result, as of 1986, none of the ten applicants granted permits by the FCC since 1982 had raised the necessary money and gone into operation. The first and most enthusiastic applicant, Satellite Television Corp., a division of Comsat, pulled out of DBS in 1984 after spending some $140 million. In 1986 at least two companies were still trying to raise capital to begin DBS service, but their prospects were not considered bright. This was especially so because the potential DBS market was shrinking as more and more homes acquired home earth stations (dishes) capable of receiving cable-network programming from conventional satellites.[304]

301 *Id.* at 1201–04.

302 *Id.* at 1205; *see also* United States Satellite Broadcasting Co. v. FCC, 740 F.2d 1177, 1187 (D.C. Cir. 1984).

303 Broadcasting, Dec. 10, 1984, at 50.

304 *Id.*; Broadcasting, Oct. 6, 1986, at 72. While high-power DBS thus foundered, low-power satellite broadcasting, an unexpected new medium, was showing distinct if limited promise. This medium consists of the transmission of scrambled satellite feeds, for a price, to the home earth stations that previously were receiving unscrambled satellite feeds for free. The medium was born in early 1986, when cable programmers began scrambling their feeds and selling subscriptions to them to dish owners and was expected to spread to almost all cable programmers. *See id.* at 72, 74. Of course, this type of satellite broadcasting, unlike DBS, is simply an alternative way of delivering programming that is already available on cable systems. It is not a new or additional programming medium.

Chapter V: Regulation of Media Flow Into the United States

A. *Regulation of Incoming Information Flow in General*

The legal response of the United States to the entry of information from abroad reflects a clash of opposing principles. On one side stands the concept, grounded in the First Amendment, that government should not interfere with the communication of information, at least when one party to the communication (in this case the listener) is a citizen or resident of the United States.[305] Opposing this concept is a battery of U.S. laws that restrict the incoming flow of information in the interests of national security, foreign policy, the nation's control over its borders, trade protectionism or other concerns.[306] Since there is also a tradition of judicial deference to the legislative and executive branches in matters foreign or international,[307] these laws rarely have been overturned by the courts. The result is something of a standard: U.S. citizens have a right to receive information from abroad, but this right frequently is limited by determinations of the legislative and executive branches.

1. *Principles and Practices Protecting Incoming Information Flow*

The First Amendment and related principles of United States law surely are not limited to communications that both originate and are received within the United States. Legal protections for freedom of speech must have some application to the import and export of information. For this self-evident proposition one finds, however, curiously little judicial support. As of the end of 1986, there were only two major Supreme Court cases. The Court's only squarely relevant holding came in *Lamont v. Postmaster General.*[308] There the Court struck down under the First Amend-

305 *See* Lamont v. Postmaster General, 381 U.S. 301 (1965).
306 *See infra* notes 337–520, 541–82, 603–785, 810–55 and accompanying text.
307 *See, e.g.,* Regan v. Wald, 468 U.S. 222, 242 (1984).
308 381 U.S. 301 (1965).

ment a federal postal statute prohibiting the delivery, except on specific written request by the addressee, of material mailed from abroad that the secretary of the Treasury had determined to be »communist political propaganda.«[309] The Court observed that the statute »sets administrative officials astride the flow of mail to inspect it, appraise it, write the addressee about it, and await a response before dispatching the mail.«[310] The Court held that by imposing on the addressee the »affirmative obligation« to request delivery, an obligation »almost certain to have a deterrent effect,« the statute violated the addressee's First Amendment rights.[311]

Three concurring Justices in *Lamont* saw the decision as reflecting a First Amendment right to receive information. »The dissemination of ideas can accomplish nothing if otherwise willing addressees are not free to receive and consider them. It would be a barren marketplace of ideas that had only sellers and no buyers.«[312] In subsequent cases, involving domestic rather than transborder communications, the Court provided further support for a First Amendment right to receive information from a willing speaker.[313]

The second major case on transborder speech was *Kleindienst v. Mandel.*[134] The case involved denial of a visitor's visa to a foreign academic invited to speak in the United States.[315] The Court indicated that U.S. citizens have a First Amendment right to receive information from a foreign speaker.[316] But it found that right outweighed, at least on the facts presented, by the government's power to exclude aliens.[317] *Mandel*, which represents a microcosm of both of the opposing approaches to transborder speech, will be discussed in more detail shortly.[318]

Apart from the First Amendment, endorsement of the principle of a free flow of incoming information is reflected in United States support for the Universal Declaration of Human Rights.[319] Article 19 of the Declaration provides: »Everyone has the right to freedom of opinion and expression; this

309 *Id.* at 302–07

310 *Id.* at 306.

311 *Id.* at 307.

312 *Id.* at 308 (Brennan, J., concurring).

313 *E.g.*, Virginia State Board of Pharmacy v. Virginia Citizens Consumer Council, 425 U.S. 748, 756 (1976); Red Lion Broadcasting Co. v. FCC, 395 U.S. 367, ___ (1969).

314 408 U.S. 753 (1972); *see infra* notes 346–58 and accompanying text.

315 *See* 408 U.S. at 757.

316 *Id.* at 763–64.

317 *Id.* at 769–70.

318 *See infra* notes 346–58 and accompanying text.

319 G.A. Res. 217A(III), U.N. Doc. A/810, at 71 (1948)

right includes the freedom to hold opinions without interference and to seek, receive and impart information and ideas through any media and regardless of frontiers.« The Universal Declaration was adopted unanimously by the United Nations General Assembly in 1948.[320] While it is not a treaty and thus not directly controlling law in the United States,[321] it has been cited by several courts[322] and arguably has legal effect, either as part of the customary law of nations or as an authoritative interpretation of the United Nations Charter.[323] Perhaps more important than the Declaration's legal status in the United States is the U.S. government's support for article 19 in international fora.[324] This support should make it politically and morally difficult for the United States to refuse to accept a free flow of information and ideas across its own frontiers, i.e., to fail to practice what it preaches.

In practice, the United States does have a basic openness to information from abroad. Foreign newspapers and periodicals, for example, circulate freely. Any government attempt to restrict their circulation surely would violate, if not the First Amendment rights of the publishers or distributors,[325] the First Amendment rights of Americans wishing to receive the information that the publications contain.[326]

Another way the United States observes a »free flow« commitment is by opening U.S. media, except broadcasting,[327] to alien or foreign ownership. Newspapers, magazines, news services, film and television producers, cable television networks, cable television systems and all other nonbroadcast media in the United States may be owned and controlled by foreign

320 *Id.* The Soviet Union and other East European nations abstained. *Id.*

321 *See* Burke, *et al., Application of International Human Rights Law in State and Federal Courts*, 18 TEXAS INT'L L.J. 291, 305 (1983).

322 *E.g.*, Filartiga v. Pena-Irala, 630 F.2d 876, 881–83 (2d Cir. 1980); Zemel v. Rusk, 381 U.S. 1, 14 n. 13 (1964)

323 *See* Burke, *et al., supra* note 321, at 305–08; Powell, *Toward a Negotiable Definition of Propaganda for International Agreements Related to Direct Broadcast Satellites*, 45 LAW & CONTEMP. PROBS., 3, 9 n. 29 (1982); Paust, *Transnational Freedom of Speech: Legal Aspects of the Helsinki Final Act*, 45 LAW & CONTEMP. PROBS. 53, n. 3 (1982)

324 *See, e.g.*, Hagelin *supra* note 18, at 294; *supra* notes 16–19 and accompanying text.

325 Publishers or distributors of foreign print media, at least if resident in the United States, probably would have First Amendment protection against restrictions on the distribution of those media. *See* Bridges v. Wixon, 326 U.S. 135, 148 (1945) (»Freedom of speech and of press is accorded aliens residing in this country«); Yick Wo v. Hopkins, 118 U.S. 356, 369 (1886). *See also, e.g.*, Bantam Books, Inc. v. Sullivan, 272 U.S. 58 (1963); Minneapolis Star and Tribune Co. v. Minnesota Commissioner of Revenue, 460 U.S. 575 (1983).

326 *See* Lamont v. Postmaster General, 381 U.S. 301; *supra* notes 308–18 and accompanying text.

327 *See infra* note 550 and accompanying text.

nationals, regardless of whether they are resident in the United States.[328] In other contexts, such as the production of television programming, the United States endorsement of the »free flow« principle may ring hollow, since in practice the »flow« consists overwhelmingly of American exports.[329] Foreign ownership of U.S. media, however, is a conspicuous reality, especially in newspapers and other publishing enterprises.[330] It is also notable in the cable television industry.[331]

In summary, while the case law remains sparse, the Supreme Court's decision in *Lamont*,[332] together with its opinion in *Mandel*[333] and its rulings in other right-to-receive cases,[334] goes far toward establishing a First Amendment right to receive information from abroad. These cases, combined with U.S. endorsement of the Universal Declaration of Human Rights[335] and with such practices as tolerance of foreign ownership of U.S. nonbroadcast media,[336] provide strong evidence of a national commitment to the concept of a free flow of information into the United States.

328 Restrictions on ownership by resident aliens, at least with regard to print media, might well be unconstitutional. *See* Bridges v. Wixon, 326 U.S. 135, 148 (1945); Yick Wo v. Hopkins, 118 U.S. 356, 369 (1886). *Cf.* Ambach v. Norwick, 441 U.S. 68, 83 (1979) (Blackmun, J., dissenting).

329 *See infra* notes 541-47 and accompanying text.

330 For example, the International Thomson Organization, a Canadian corporation headquartered in London, owns many newspapers in the United States. *See* 1986 EDITOR & PUBLISHER INTERNATIONAL YEARBOOK, at I-379; National Law Journal, May 26, 1980, at 2, col. 3. The Australian Rupert Murdoch owned major daily newspapers in New York, Chicago and Boston, plus other media properties in the U.S., before he acquired U.S. citizenship in 1985 in order to purchase major broadcast properties in the U.S. *See* 1984 EDITOR & PUBLISHER INTERNATIONAL YEARBOOK, at I-439. European publishers have increasingly entered the magazine, trade-journal and book-publishing industries in the United States. *See* Wall Street Journal, June 13, 1985, at 35, cols. 2–4; *see also* National Law Journal, May 26, 1980, at 2, col. 3 (Thomson organization buying a third U.S. speciality publishing company).

331 *See infra* text accompanying notes 591–602. The openness of United States media to foreign ownership apparently goes beyond what is required by the protections for alien investment embodied in the United States's bilateral trade and investment treaties with its major trade partners. These treaties typically exclude »communications,« along with banking, transport and other activities, from their protection of reciprocal investment. *See* Note, *The Rising Tide of Reverse Flow: Could a Legislative Breakwater Violate U.S. Trade Commitments?* 72 MICH. L. REV. 551, 568–71 (1974). The treaty with West Germany specifies that communications »includes radio and television, among other means of communication.« Treaty of Friendship, Commerce, and Navigation, Oct. 29, 1954, United States-Federal Republic of Germany, Protocol, para. 11, 2 U.S.T. 183a, T.I.A.S. No. 3593. The treaties do not otherwise define »communications,« but at least some of the U.S. media that are open to foreign ownership – cable television systems, for example – would appear to fall within that term.

332 *See supra* note 308 and accompanying text.

333 *See supra* note 314 and accompanying test.

334 *See supra* note 313 and accompanying text.

335 *See supra* note 324 and accompanying text.

336 *See supra* note 327 and accompanying text.

At the same time, however, the United States has a variety of laws, discussed in the next section, that restrict incoming information flow; despite the First Amendment, these laws, except for the one struck down in *Lamont*, to date have been upheld by the courts.

2. *Restrictions on Incoming Information Flow*

a. *Restrictions on visitors' visas under the McCarran-Walter Act*

The McCarran-Walter Immigration Act[337] contains two provisions that may bar the entry of aliens into the United States, even as short-term visitors, if they hold views offensive to the U.S. government. Subsection 28 of section 1182(a)[338] bars the entry of aliens who are, or at any time have been, »anarchists,« members or affiliates of the Communist Party »or any other totalitarian party,« or persons who »advocate the economic, international, and governmental doctrines of world communism.«[339] Subsection 27[340] bars the entry of aliens who the U.S. government has reason to believe seek to enter the United States »to engage in activities which would be prejudicial to the public interest, or endanger the welfare, safety, or security of the United States.«[341]

Under these provisions – which date from the Joseph McCarthy era of the 1950s – the U.S. government maintains a list, or »Lookout Book,« of aliens to be denied entry.[342] The list was reported in 1984 to include eight thousand persons from Canada alone.[343] In 1986 an official of the U.S. State Department told a congressional committee that in the previous year 47,500 persons had been formally excluded from the country under subsection 28. While the vast majority of these were granted automatic waivers, some 800 had been denied waivers.[344] In addition, 33 aliens had been excluded under subsection 27.[345]

337 8 U.S.C. §§ 1101–1503 (1985).
338 8 U.S.C. § 1182(a)(28) (1982 & Supp. II 1984).
339 *Id.*
340 *Id.* § 1182(a)(27).
341 *Id.* In addition, § 33, added in 1978, bars the entry of any alien who participated in Nazi war crimes or other activities amounting to persecution during the Second World War.
342 *See, e.g.,* Itzcouitz v. Selective Service Local Bd. No. 6, 447 F.2d 888 (2d Cir. 1971).
343 N.Y. Times, Feb. 19, 1984, at 21, col. 1
344 N.Y. Times, Aug. 12, 1986, at 6, cols. 1–2
345 *Id.*

In 1972, in *Kleindienst v. Mandel*,[346] the Supreme Court upheld the application of subsection 28 to deny a visitor's visa to a Marxist scholar from Belgium who was invited to speak at academic conferences in the United States. The attorney general had refused to grant a waiver to permit Mandel's entry, and the Court, by a 6–3 vote, upheld the attorney general's action.[347]

The Court indicated that while Mandel had no constitutional right to enter the country, American academics had a First Amendment right to receive information from him at the academic gatherings he would attend.[348] Such a right could not be denied simply because »the mode of regulation bears directly on physical movement,« rather than on speech, any more than the First Amendment right to receive in *Lamont* could have been denied because the regulation on its face »dealt only with the Government's undisputed power to control physical entry of mail into the country.«[349] Moreover, U.S. citizens' right to hear Mandel was not satisfied by the availability of alternative means for receiving his ideas, such as his books and published speeches, or tapes and telephone hookups. In view of »what may be particular qualities inherent in sustained, face-to-face debate, discussion and questioning,« the Court was »loath to hold on this record that existence of other alternatives extinguishes altogether any constitutional interest« in having direct, personal access to Mandel's ideas.[350]

Nonetheless, the Court held that this constitutional interest could not prevail against the »plenary congressional power to make policies and rules for exclusion of aliens.«[351] The Court previously had held that the power to exclude aliens was »›to be exercised exclusively by the political branches of government,‹«[352] and it was »not inclined in the present context to reconsider this line of cases.«[353]

The Court did stop short of recognizing power in the executive branch to deny a waiver, and hence a visa, to a particular alien because of his ideas. While the government had argued that it need not give any reason for its decision to exclude Mandel,[354] the Court went to some length to avoid

346 408 U.S. 753 (1972).
347 *Id.* at 753, 769.
348 *Id.* at 764.
349 *Id.* at 764–65.
350 *Id.* at 765.
351 *Id.* at 769.
352 *Id.* at 765 (quoting government brief).
353 *Id.* at 767.
354 *See id.* at 769.

confronting this position. Noting that earlier in the litigation the attorney general *had* given a reason for excluding Mandel – Mandel's unknowing and minor violations of the conditions of entry on a prior visit – the Court found that to be sufficient. Where a decision to exclude an alien was based on »facially legitimate and bona fide reasons,« it would not be scrutinized by the Court or weighed against the First Amendment interests in the case.[355]

Mandel thus left the opposing interests in precarious balance. The case confirms that, in accord with *Lamont*, U.S. citizens have a First Amendment right to receive information from foreign speakers, and probably to receive it face to face. At the same time, *Mandel* upholds the »plenary power« of Congress to exclude aliens and indicates that this power comprehends the exclusion of classes of aliens – such as the classes listed in subsection 28 – because of their ideas.[356] The power thus stands in contrast to the »content neutrality« usually required of government action affecting First Amendment rights.[357] Further, while shying away from holding that the government could deny a waiver to a particular alien because of his ideas, the Court said it would not scrutinize any colorable reason that the government put forward for such a denial.[358]

After *Mandel*, Congress moved in 1979 to shift the balance by adding to the McCarran-Walter Act the McGovern Amendment.[359] This provision was adopted »[f]or purposes of achieving greater United States compliance [and] ... encouraging other signatory countries to comply« with the Helsinki Accords of 1975.[360] The amendment provides that when an application for a visitor's visa is made by an alien excludable under subsection 28 »by reason of membership in or affiliation with a proscribed organization,« a waiver allowing the visa should be issued, unless the secretary of state

355 *Id.* at 770.
356 *See id.* at 770.
357 *See, e.g.,* Police Department of Chicago v. Mosley, 408 U.S. 92 (1972); Stone, *supra* note 50.
358 408 U.S. at 770.
359 22 U.S.C. § 2691(a) (1982).
360 *Id. See* Conference on Security and Cooperation in Europe: Final Act, Aug. 1, 1975, *reprinted in* 73 Dep't State Bull. 323 (1975); Paust, *supra* note 323, at 63; Carliner, *United States Compliance with the Helsinki Final Act: The Treatment of Aliens*, 13 VAND. J. TRANSNAT'L L. 397, 400, 407–08 (1980).

certifies to Congress that admission of the alien »would be contrary to the security interests of the United States.«[361]

The executive branch apparently has reacted to the McGovern Amendment by finding some aliens who otherwise would be covered by the amendment to be excludable under subsection 27 instead of subsection 28. In *Abourezk v. Reagan*,[362] the government denied visas under subsection 27 to four persons who might have fallen under subsection 28 and the McGovern Amendment.[363] The decision of the court of appeals somewhat restricted the government's power to act under subsection 27. The court held that when an alien is a member of a proscribed organization so that subsection 28 would apply, the government may not bypass the McGovern Amendment and proceed under subsection 27 unless the reason for the perceived threat to national interests under subsection 27 is independent of the fact of membership in the organization.[364]

In dissent, Judge Robert H. Bork thought subsection 27 properly could come into play if the alien's membership in the proscribed organization »raises additional concerns, as it does when it involves a connection to a government that implicates American foreign policy.«[365] Judge Bork warned that the majority's decision »begins, albeit cautiously, a process of judicial incursion into the United States' conduct of its foreign affairs.«[366] The government has successfully petitioned for Supreme Court review in *Abourezk.*[367]

Under either subsection 27 or subsection 28, a number of foreign intellectuals who hold views offensive to the U.S. government have been denied visitors' visas and thus prevented from expressing their views in the

361 22 U.S.C. § 2691(a).

362 785 F.2d 1043 (D.C. Cir. 1986), *cert. granted*, Dec. 15, 1986, No. 86–656.

363 The four were Tomas Borge, the Interior Minister of Nicaragua; Nino Pasti, former member of the Italien Senate, former general in the Italian armed forces and participant in the World Peace Council, an organization believed by the U.S. State Department to be controlled by the Soviet Communist Party; and Olga Finley and Leonor Rodriguez Lezcano, two Cuban women with expertise in family law who were said by the U.S. State Department to be members of an organization affiliated with the Communist Party of Cuba. 785 F.2d at 1048–49.

364 *Id.* at 1058.

365 *Id.* at 1071 (Bork, J., dissenting).

366 *Id.* at 1076 (Bork, J., dissenting).

367 107 S.Ct. 666 (No. 86–656, *cert. granted*, Dec. 15, 1986) [*aff'd* 56 U.S.L.W. 4001 (Oct. 19, 1987)].

United States.[368] In 1986 a U.S. Senate committee held hearings on a bill designed to prevent such exclusions.[369] Sponsored by Senator Mathias, the bill would have prevented the exclusion of any alien »because of any past or expected speech, activity, belief, affiliation, or membership which, if held or conducted within the United States by a United States citizen, would be protected by the First Amendment to the Constitution.«[370] The Reagan administration opposed the bill, though offering to support »reasonable changes« in subsection 28 to »ameliorate concerns about possible infringements on the First Amendment rights of Americans.«[371]

For a nation committed to the principles of the First Amendment, changes in the McCarran-Walter Act certainly are in order. Subsection 28, which

368 In 1985, Farley Mowat, a prominent Canadian writer on wildlife and conservation, was denied entry. Officials of the U.S. Immigration and Naturalization Service explained that he had been listed for many years in the Service's »Lookout Book,« because he was affiliated with »leftist organizations« and for other reasons that were »confidential.« N.Y. Times, Apr. 24, 1985, at B 10, col. 8. Others whose visa requests have been denied in recent years include Hortensia de Allende, widow of the president of Chile; Gerry Adams, leader of the political wing of the Irish Republican Army; Roberto d'Aubuisson, president of El Salvador's Constituent Assembly; Ruben Zamora, spokesman for the El Salvadoran Revolutionary Democratic Front; Dario Fo and Franca Rame, Italian political satirists; and Patricia Lara, a Colombian journalist. N.Y. Times, Nov. 12, 1986, at 10, cols. 3–7. Nobel laureates Gabriel Garcia Marquez and Carlos Fuentes are among other prominent writers and thinkers who have been barred or have declined to visit the United States because of these laws. N.Y. Times, Apr. 14, 1984, at 24.

The case of Patricia Lara, the Colombian journalist, was especially noteworthy. Ms. Lara came to New York in October 1986 at the invitation of Columbia University to attend ceremonies there honoring Latin American journalists. On arrival she was taken into custody by the Immigration and Naturalization Service, held for five days and then deported to Bogota. INS officials explained that her name had appeared in their Lookout Book and that she was excludable under subsection 27 and other sections of the law. They conducted no hearing and refused to be more specific, saying their information was »of a confidential nature that we can't disclose.« The president of Columbia University said the case was »anathema to a free society.« N.Y. Times, Oct. 15, 1986 at 17, cols. 1–4; N.Y. Times, Oct. 17, 1986, at 6, cols. 5–6. A U.S. assistant secretary of state subsequently said on television that Ms. Lara had been expelled because there was evidence that she was a member of a Colombian terrorist group – a charge the U.S. government had neither made public nor given Ms. Lara a chance to refute before expelling her. *See* Time, Dec. 29, 1986, at 68. Ms. Lara denied the charge. *Id.*

369 S. 2263, 99th Cong. 2d Sess. (1986).

370 *Id.; see* N.Y. Times, Aug. 12, 1986, at 6, cols. 1–2. Senator Mathias, sponsor of the bill, stated (*id.*):

> We are not talking about the rights of aliens. We are talking about the rights of Americans to hear the views of others. Why shouldn't Americans be able to hear unpopular views, even if they diverge from the views of a majority or disagree with official policy?

371 *Id.* The Reagan administration spokesman said: »It is not the policy of this Administration to deny visas to aliens merely because of their abstract political ideology.« He maintained, however, that the government must keep, for foreign-policy reasons, the subsection 27 power to exclude aliens who seek to engage in activities deemed »prejudicial to the public interest.« *Id.*

prima facie empowers the U.S. government to bar short-term visitors because of their ideas or political allegiances, is particularly offensive. To be sure, subsections 27 and 28 are immigration laws, designed to control the flow of people into the United States. As the Supreme Court emphasized in *Mandel*, »plenary congressional power to make policies and rules for exclusion of aliens has long been firmly established.«[372] But such policies and rules can operate to restrict the flow of ideas and information into the United States. At least where brief visits are concerned, a country that values free speech and champions a free flow of information across national borders cannot consistently bar visitors from entering its own borders because of their speech or ideas.

b. *Restrictions on foreign travel of U.S. citizens*

The United States restricts the incoming flow of information when it prevents U.S. citizens from traveling to other countries. Such travel provides the traveler, his associates and his domestic audiences with information about those countries – information that may relate to the policies or actions of the United States government as well. Travel restrictions can be divided into two kinds: a ban on travel anywhere by a particular person, and a ban on travel by all persons to a particular country.

The Supreme Court has held that freedom to travel abroad is »a constitutional liberty closely related to rights of free speech and association.«[373] Thus a U.S. citizen may not be denied a passport absent evidence that his proposed travel poses a serious threat to U.S. interests.[374] In *Aptheker v. Secretary of State*, [375] the Court invalidated a provision of the Subversive Activities Control Act of 1950 that denied passports to knowing members of communist organizations, saying the statute swept too broadly and hence abridged the freedom of travel.[376] By comparison, in *Haig v. Agee,*[377] the Court allowed the lifting of the passport of an ex-CIA agent, where it was stipulated that his activities abroad were a danger to the U.S. national security.[378]

While lifting an individual's passport for reasons particular to that individual may infringe his constitutional rights, such action is unlikely to have

372 408 U.S. at 769–70.
373 Aptheker v. Secretary of State, 378 U.S. 500, 517 (1964).
374 *See id.* at 514; *see also, e.g.*, Zemel v. Rusk, 381 U.S. 1, 14 (1965).
375 378 U.S. 500 (1964).
376 *Id.* at 514.
377 453 U.S. 280 (1981).
378 *Id.* at 287.

much impact on the incoming flow of information about foreign countries. Other U.S. travelers, including journalists, remain free to go to those countries and report on them. The same cannot be said of restrictions on all travel by U.S. citizens to particular countries. Such restrictions may substantially limit knowledge by the U.S. public of what is happening in those countries.[379] Nevertheless, the Supreme Court has upheld restrictions of this kind. In *Zemel v. Rusk*,[380] the Court upheld a law allowing the secretary of state to invalidate passports to Cuba, finding the right to travel to be outweighed by the national interest in restricting travel to a country belligerent to the United States.[381] The Court dismissed the direct freedom-of-speech claim by denying the existence of a »right to gather information.«[382]

In *Regan v. Wald*,[383] the Court reaffirmed *Zemel* in upholding an executive regulation prohibiting general business or tourist travel to Cuba.[384] The claim based on the constitutional right to travel was rejected as not overcoming »weighty concerns of foreign policy« – in this case, the desire of the U.S. government to deny to the Cuban government access to hard U.S. currency.[385] With respect to the freedom-of-speech claim, the Court said simply that no First Amendment right of the kind present in *Aptheker* was offended by an across-the-board travel restriction.[386] The Court did not consider possible First Amendment rights to receive or gather information, which had made substantial progress in the years since *Zemel*.[387] However, given the high premium that the Court in *Regan v. Wald* placed on deferring to the executive and legislative branches in matters of foreign affairs,[388] it is doubtful that recognition of any such First Amendment rights would have changed the outcome.[389]

The prohibitions on travel by U.S. citizens upheld in *Zemel v. Rusk* and *Regan v. Wald* probably have a significant impact in curtailing the flow into the United States of information about Cuba. Still, the information-

379 Of course, non-U.S. citizens can still go to those countries and report in the United States.

380 381 U.S. 1 (1965).

381 *Id.* at 15–16.

382 *Id.* at 17.

383 468 U.S. 222 (1984).

384 31 CFR § 515.201(b) (1985).

385 468 U.S. at 229.

386 *Id.* at 241–42.

387 *See, e.g.*, Lamont v. Postmaster General, 381 U.S. 301 (decided in 1965 after *Zemel v. Rusk*); Virginia State Board of Pharmacy v. Virginia Citizens Consumer Council, 425 U.S. 748; Kleindienst v. Mandel, 408 U.S. at 762–65.

388 *See* 468 U.S. at 242.

389 *Cf.* Kleindienst v. Mandel, 408 U.S. at 762–65; *supra* text accompanying notes 373–82.

blocking effects of these travel bans are incidental. Few would claim that the bans had the *purpose* of excluding information about Cuba, as the McCarran-Walter Act apparently has the purpose of excluding unwelcome ideas from the United States.[390] Further, restrictions on the movement of people do not necessarily establish precedents for restrictions on the flow of pure information. Where restrictions on pure information are concerned, the Supreme Court's only case in point remains *Lamont*, which struck down the law burdening the flow of mail into the United States.[391]

c. *Customs restrictions on communicative materials*

Along with broad power over the entry of persons into the United States, the legislative and executive branches have significant control over the entry of objects. With respect to communicative materials, the U.S. customs law prohibits the importation of any »obscene« matter, or »any matter advocating or urging treason or insurrection against the United States, or forcible resistance to any law of the United States.«[392]

The substantive restrictions thus imposed are not onerous. The Supreme Court has held that the applicable standard of »obscenity« is the same one used to judge domestic material.[393] Following this lead, the ban on materials advocating insurrection or illegality has been construed as reaching no farther than domestic law can.[394] Thus, insofar as their substance is concerned, communicative materials from abroad are as free as domestic materials to enter and circulate within the United States.

That freedom, however, may be deceptive, since Customs officials have broader enforcement powers than domestic officials. Searches and seizures within the United States usually require a warrant or probable cause, as provided in the Fourth Amendment to the federal Constitution.[395] The Supreme Court, however, has allowed a search without warrant or probable cause of an incoming letter suspected of carrying heroin.[396] The

390 *See supra* text accompanying notes 337–72.

391 *See supra* notes 308–13 accompanying text. *But see* the recent decision in *Meese v. Keene*, *infra* note 470.

392 19 U.S.C. § 1305(a) (1982). These provisions apply to the importation of »any book, pamphlet, paper, writing, advertisement, circular, print, picture, or drawing.« *Id.*

393 United States v. 12 200-Ft. Reels, 413 U.S. 123 (1973).

394 Church of Scientology v. Simon, 460 F. Supp. 56 (C.D. Cal. 1978), *aff'd mem.*, 441 U.S. 938 (1979). Thus, under Brandenburg v. Ohio, 395 U.S. 444, 447 (1969), materials cannot be excluded on these grounds unless they are »directed to inciting or producing imminent lawless action and ... likely to incite or produce such action.«

395 U.S. CONST., amend. IV; *see, e.g.,* Wong Sun v. United States, 371 U.S. 471 (1963).

396 United States v. Ramsey, 431 U.S. 606 (1977).

Court stated that Customs agents may search any luggage or effects crossing the border and that no one could reasonably expect privacy against a border search.[397]

Detention of incoming material for inspection at the border, moreover, delays its distribution in the United States. This delay is not subject to the stringent safeguards that would apply to any such »prior restraint« on the distribution of domestic materials.[398] Responding to a claim of unconstitutional restraint at Customs, a federal district court, in a decision affirmed by the Supreme Court, declared the problem *de minimis*:

> In this case, the Church of Scientology's papers ... were detained for a very short period by the Customs Service before the Service determined the papers to be importable. Under the Customs Service's broad power to restrict imports and conduct a search of material entering the country from abroad, the temporary delay and retention of documents do not constitute a constitutional deprivation.[399]

As this language suggests, a prolonged detention of communicative materials by Customs might amount to a constitutional deprivation.

One use of Customs searches has been recognized as improper. When Edward Haase, an American writer critical of U.S. policy toward Nicaragua, returned to the United States from a trip to Nicaragua in 1985, Customs agents at the Miami airport, together with an FBI agent, searched his luggage and seized and copied some of his papers.[400] In Haase's suit against the FBI and the Customs Service alleging violations of his constitutional rights, the government effectively confessed error, offering to undo everything that had been done to Haase.[401]

The court of appeals nonetheless held that Haase's suit for declaratory relief should not have been dismissed.[402] Haase alleged that other travelers had been similarly subjected to intrusive border searches on returning from Nicaragua, as part of an apparent government policy, and the court ruled

397 *Id.* at 618–19.

398 *See* Freedman v. Maryland, 380 U.S. 51 (1965).

399 Church of Scientology v. Simon, 460 F. Supp at 58, *aff'd mem.*, 441 U.S. 938 (1979).

400 *See* Haase v. Webster, 807 F.2d 208, 210 (D.C. Cir., Dec. 9, 1986).

401 The government offered to return all the copies of Haase's papers and certified that they had not been further copied or disseminated. *Id.* at 211.

402 *Id.* at 217. The court of appeals upheld the district court's dismissal of the claim for injunctive relief. *Id.*

that the government must respond to that allegation.[403] Meanwhile, the Customs Service in August 1986 issued internal directives designed to provide guidance to field agents in such situations.[404]

It thus appears that, at least in Haase's case and perhaps more broadly, the U.S. government improperly searched and seized the papers of travelers returning to the U.S. from Nicaragua. It also appears that this practice or policy was stopped, but only as a result of litigation. In this case, it seems, the legal protections of the U.S. Constitution have freed the incoming flow of information from a government attempt to monitor or restrict that flow.

d. *Customs exemptions for communicative materials under the Beirut Agreement*

The Beirut Agreement is a multination treaty designed to encourage the international circulation of audio-visual materials of an educational character by exempting them from import duties, license requirements, taxes and other restrictions of importing countries.[405] Under the Agreement, a person seeking duty-free treatment for audio-visual materials must apply for a certificate of educational character from the appropriate agency of the exporting country.[406] The certificate is then submitted to the importing country, which makes its own determination whether the material qualifies for exemption, but giving »due consideration« to the exporting country's determination.[407]

The president of the United States, as authorized by legislation implementing the treaty,[408] has designated the United States Information Agency

403 *Id.* at 216

404 The directives covered such subjects as personal searches, photocopying and the legal definitions of sedition and treason. Telephone conversation with Ellen McClain, attorney, U.S. Customs Service, Washington, D.C., Mar. 30, 1987).

405 Agreement for Facilitating the International Circulation of Visual and Auditory Materials of an Educational, Scientific, and Cultural Character, July 15, 1949, 17 U.S.T. 1579, T.I.A.S. No. 6116, 197 U.N.T.S. 3 (entered into force for the United States on Jan. 12, 1967). *See* Note, *USIA Censorship of Educational Films for Distribution Abroad*, 3 CARDOZO ARTS & ENT. L. REV. 403 (1984).

406 Agreement, *supra* note 405, at art. IV, 17 U.S.T. at 1582–84.

407 *Id.*

408 Pub. L. No. 89–634, 80 Stat. 879 (1966).

(USIA) to administer the Beirut Agreement for the U.S.[409] The functions thus conferred on the USIA include both the »certification« of materials for export from the United States and the »authentication« of materials certified by another country for duty-free import into the United States.[410] The regulations used by the USIA in issuing certificates for export were held to violate the First Amendment in *Bullfrog Films, Inc. v. Wick*,[411] a case discussed later in connection with outgoing media flows.[412]

The USIA's conduct in authenticating materials for import into the United States under the Beirut Agreement appears, to date, not to have attracted criticism. This is somewhat surprising. The regulations applied by the USIA in determining whether materials are »educational« for the purpose of U.S. import are identical to those struck down in *Bullfrog Films* with regard to U.S. export.[413]

Moreover, article V of the Beirut Agreement reserves the right of receiving states »to censor material in accordance with their own laws or to adopt measures to prohibit or limit the importation of material for reasons of public security or order.«[414] When the U.S. Congress was considering ratification of the Agreement in 1966, concern was expressed about the entry of foreign political materials. One congressman pointed to article V as assurance that the Agreement »does not require us to bring in a single film from Yugoslavia that is communistic in nature.«[415] To deny duty-free entry to a film because it was »communistic in nature,« regardless of whether such denial was authorized by the Beirut Agreement, would constitute discrimination based on political content that might well violate the First Amendment.[416]

The apparent absence of challenge to the USIA's implementation of the Beirut Agreement with respect to materials imported into the United States may indicate that the Agency has routinely accepted the certifications of exporting countries. Or perhaps would-be importers, located outside the United States, have had legal or practical difficulties in challenging

409 *See* 22 C.F.R. §§ 502.1–502.8 (1986); Bullfrog Films, Inc. v. Wick, 646 F. Supp. 492, 495 (C.D. Cal. 1986) [*appeal docketed*, No. 86–6630 (9th Cir.)].

410 *See* 22 C.F.R. §§ 502.2–502.6 (1986).

411 646 F. Supp. 492 (C.D. Cal. 1986).

412 *See infra* text accompanying notes 859–76.

413 *See* 22 C.F.R. § 502.6 (1986).

414 Agreement, *supra* note 405, at art. V, 17 U.S.T. at 1584.

415 *See* Note, *supra* note 405 at 408.

416 *See, e.g.*, Police Department of Chicago v. Mosley, 408 U.S. 92 (1972); Bullfrog Films, Inc. v. Wick, 646 F Supp. 492, 506 (C.D. Cal. 1986); *see also* Kinsella v. United States, 361 U.S. 234 (1960) (U.S. Constitution prevails over inconsistent treaty).

USIA rulings.[417] In any event, the decision on appeal in *Bullfrog Films* presumably will settle the First Amendment validity of the existing USIA regulations as applied to imports as well as exports.[418]

e. *Regulation of foreign »political propaganda« under the Foreign Agents Registration Act*

One statute squarely aimed at information flowing into the United States from foreign sources is the Foreign Agents Registration Act (FARA),[419] which regulates such information as »political propaganda.«[420] FARA dates from 1938 and 1942, times of world war and of fear that »foreign agents« and »foreign propaganda« could undermine America's resolve.[421] The Act requires every »agent of a foreign principal« to register with the U.S. Justice Department and to file supplemental registration statements every six months.[422] A »foreign principal« is defined as any foreign government, foreign political party, foreign corporation or »person outside the United States« who is not a citizen and domiciliary of the United States.[423] Exemptions are provided for diplomats, persons engaged in private business and certain other classes of people who otherwise would be required to register as agents under the Act.[424]

FARA imposes on registered agents several requirements with respect to any »political propaganda« they distribute in the United States. »Political propaganda« is defined, for the most part neutrally, as any communication intended to »influence a recipient ... with reference to the political or public interests, policies, or relations of a government of a foreign country

417 *See* Lamont v. Postmaster General, 381 U.S. 301, 307–08 (1965) (Brennan, J., concurring); Kleindienst v. Mandel, 408 U.S. 753, 762 (1972). *But see* Note, *State Laws Restricting Land Purchase by Aliens*, 21 COLUM J. TRANSNAT'L L. 135, 155 (1982). In any event, a would-be importer could have an agent in the United States who was injured by the impact of the USIA regulations on importation of the films and who thus would have standing to sue. *Cf.* Block v. Meese, 793 F.2d 1303, 1308 (D.C. Cir. 1986), *cert. denied*, 106 S. Ct. 3335 (1986).

418 If the regulations are struck down in their application to exports, the Agency surely will not attempt to preserve them for imports, where a U.S. audience would be affected. *See* Lamont v. Postmaster General, 381 U.S. 301 (1965).

419 22 U.S.C. §§ 611–21 (1982 & Supp. II 1982).

420 *See* 22 U.S.C. §§ 611(j), 614(a), (b); *infra* notes 425–30 and accompanying text.

421 Act of June 8, 1938, ch. 327, 52 Stat. 631; Act of Apr. 29, 1942, ch. 263, 56 Stat. 248. The House Report on the 1938 Act stated that »the spotlight of pitiless publicity will serve as a deterrent to the spread of pernicious propaganda.« H.R. REP. NO. 1381, 75th Cong., 1st Sess. 2 (1937). *See also infra* note 459.

422 22 U.S.C. § 612.

423 22 U.S.C. § 611(b).

424 22 U.S.C. § 613(a), (d); *see also id.* §§ 613, 611(d), 612(f).

... or with reference to the foreign policies of the United States.«[425] Registered agents are required to place on public file with the Justice Department copies of any »political propaganda« they transmit within the United States.[426] They are required to report publicly to the Department of Justice on the places, the times and the extent of each transmittal,[427] and they are required to label conspicuously each piece of propaganda they transmit.[428] The prescribed label for a film, for example, includes the names of the agent and the foreign principal, a statement that dissemination reports on the film are available for public inspection at the Justice Department, and a statement that »[r]egistration does not indicate approval of the contents of this material by the United States Government.«[429] The prescribed label does not include the word »propaganda.«[430]

While FARA had been held constitutional insofar as it required the registration of foreign agents,[431] two recent cases, one reaching the Supreme Court, challenged the Act's »political propaganda« requirements for the first time.[432] Both cases involved the same three documentary films – one on nuclear war, *If You Love This Planet*, and two on acid rain, *Acid from Heaven* and *Acid Rain: Requiem or Recovery*. All three films were produced by the National Film Board of Canada (Film Board) and distributed in the United States by the Film Board's New York office. The Film Board was an agency of the Canadian government, and its New York office accordingly was a registered foreign agent under FARA. In June 1982, the Film Board submitted to the Justice Department, along with its semi-annual registration statement, a list of sixty-two new film titles for distribution in the United States. In January 1983, the Justice Department, after screening five

425 22 U.S.C. § 611(j). The definition is not entirely neutral. It includes, among other things, communications intended to »promote in the United States racial, religious, or social dissensions.« *Id.*

426 22 U.S.C. § 614(a).

427 22 U.S.C. § 614(a); 28 C.F.R. § 5.401(a), (b); Report Form CRM-159 (1985).

428 22 U.S.C. § 614(b); 28 C.F.R. § 5.402(a).

429 22 U.S.C. § 614(b); 28 C.F.R. § 5.402(e); Report Form CRM 159; *see also* 28 C.F.R. § 5.400(c).

430 *See id.*

431 *E.g.*, Attorney General v. The Irish People, 684 F.2d 928 (D.C. Cir. 1982), *cert. denied*, 459 U.S. 1172 (1982).

432 Keene v. Meese, 569 F. Supp. 1513 (E.D. Cal. 1983), 619 F. Supp. 1111 (E.D. Cal. 1985), *probable jurisdiction noted*, 106 S.Ct. 1632 (1986); Block v. Meese, 793 F.2d 1303 (D.C. Cir. 1986), *cert. denied*, 106 S.Ct. 3335 (1986). The author was of counsel in the Supreme Court for appellee Keene in *Meese v. Keene*. The case was decided April 28, 1987. *See infra* note 470.

of the films, notified the Film Board that the three named films constituted »political propaganda« under FARA.[433]

Two lawsuits followed. *Block v. Meese*[434] was brought by the U.S. distributor of one of the films, together with libraries and other groups wishing to exhibit the films. The would-be exhibitors claimed that they were deterred from showing the films by the fact that their names would be publicly reported as exhibitors of »political propaganda.«[435] The distributor claimed that he lost income as a result of the exhibitors' reluctance to rent or buy the films.[436] The other case, *Keene v. Meese,*[437] was brought by a California state senator who wanted to exhibit the films to stimulate public debate on the issues they addressed. He claimed he was deterred from showing the films by the harm that would result to his political and personal reputation when it became known that he had shown a film officially designated by the U.S. government as foreign »political propaganda.«[438]

In both cases the U.S. government took the position, surprisingly, that while FARA required the foreign agent to put the statutory label on the film, the person exhibiting the film was free to remove it.[439] As a result, the courts in both cases ruled that the plaintiffs could not complain about the labeling requirement.[440]

In *Keene*, the federal district court in California first ruled that the threat to Keene's reputation gave him standing to challenge the Act's designation of the films as »political propaganda.«[441] The court then held that the Act violated Keene's First Amendment rights.[442] »Propaganda« as used in ordinary speech is a »word of reproach,« the court said, and »whoever disseminates materials officially found to be ›political propaganda‹ runs the risk

433 *See* Block v. Meese, 793 F.2d at 1306–07; Keene v. Meese, 569 F. Supp. at 1516. *See generally* Note, *Neutral Propaganda: Three Films »Made in Canada« and the Foreign Agents Registration Act*, 7 COMM/ENT L.J. 435 (1985).

434 Block v. Meese, 793 F.2d 1303.

435 *See* 793 F.2d at 1308. In the case of a film, the prescribed Dissemination Report must include the names of organizations showing the film. *See* 28 C.F.R. § 5.401(a), (b); Report Form CRM-159 (1985).

436 *See* 793 F.2d at 1308.

437 Keene v. Meese, 619 F. Supp. 1111. *See infra* note 445.

438 619 F. Supp. at 1120.

439 Block v. Smith, 583 F. Supp. 1288, 1291 (D.D.C. 1984); Block v. Meese, 793 F.2d at 1307 n.1; Keene v. Meese, 569 F. Supp. at 1519 & n.2.

440 793 F.2d at 1307 n. 1, 569 F. Supp. at 1519 & n. 2. The district court in *Keene* remarked that »[s]ince the chief importance of the labelling requirement is obviously to inform viewers of the origins of the film, it is frankly surprising to learn that exhibitors of material covered by the Act may, with impunity, frustrate Congressional intent.« *Id.*

441 619 F. Supp. at 1119.

442 *Id.* at 1124–25.

of being held in a negative light by members of the public.«[443] Thus Congress had put Keene to the impermissible choice of foregoing his First Amendment right to show the films or suffering harm to his reputation.[444]

The district court's ruling in *Keene* was appealed directly to the U.S. Supreme Court, where the case was argued in December 1986.[445]

Meanwhile, in *Block*, the U.S. Court of Appeals for the District of Columbia Circuit held that the distributor had standing to challenge the Act, since he would lose money as a result of the reluctance of others to exhibit the films.[446] But Judge Antonin Scalia, writing for the court, went on to reject the constitutional challenge. The Act's own definition of »propaganda« was neutral, the court said. If the word had a derogatory meaning in common usage, this did not signify that the U.S. government in using the word was disparaging the speech described by the word but rather that the public looked unfavorably on the objective phenomenon described by the word (political speech designed to persuade). The court held that, in any event, the government itself has the right to speak, and this includes the right to criticize other people's speech.[447]

The Supreme Court declined to review *Block*,[448] leaving *Keene* as the only challenge to FARA before the Court.

The Supreme Court conceivably could rule in *Keene*, as the government has urged,[449] that Keene lacked standing to challenge FARA because the alleged effect on his reputation was too speculative. Such a ruling, however, would seem evasive and unfair in view of the Court's refusal to review *Block*, in which the court of appeals found that standing did exist.[450]

443 *Id.* at 1121, 1124.

444 *Id.* at 1125–26.

445 No. 85–1180, argued Dec. 2, 1986. The case was decided Apr. 28, 1987. *See infra* note 470.

446 793 F.2d at 1307–09.

447 *Id.* at 1310–14.

448 Certiorari was denied in *Block* on July 7, 1986 (106 S.Ct. 3335), two and one-half months after the Court had noted probable jurisdiction in *Keene* (106 S.Ct. 1632, April 21, 1986). *Block*, decided by the court of appeals on June 18, 1986, had been argued more than sixteen month previously in that court on Feb. 12, 1985. *See* 793 F.2d at 1303. It seems possible that the Supreme Court would have agreed to review *Block* if the case had not been delayed in the court of appeals and thus had reached the Supreme Court before the decision to review *Keene*.

449 Brief for the Appellants, Meese v. Keene, No. 85–1180, at 10–18; Reply Brief for the Appellants, No. 85–1180, at 2–8.

450 793 F.2d at 1307–09; *see supra* text accompanying note 446.

Block established that *somebody* was hurt by FARA's treatment of foreign-source speech as »political propaganda« and further that the injury resulted from the Act's effect of deterring the dissemination of such speech in the United States.

Moreover, there are other parties, not before the court in either case but particularly relevant here, who are even more directly affected by the »political propaganda« requirements of FARA. These are the foreign agents and their foreign principals. Unlike the *Keene* and *Block* plaintiffs, who are discouraged from disseminating the speech of foreign agents in the United States by the requirements of the Act, the foreign agents are directly required to file, report and label any »political propaganda« they disseminate.[451]

The impact of these requirements on the foreign agents could not readily be challenged in either *Block* or *Keene*. The Canadian Film Board had decided for political reasons not to join the litigation,[452] and the rules of standing generally limit a party to complaining about injuries he himself has suffered.[453] If a suit were brought by a foreign agent, however, or if the rights of a foreign agent were allowed to be raised by other parties,[454] the direct impact of FARA's requirements on the foreign agent would eliminate any question about standing.[455] Moreover, the effect of those requirements in burdening and »chilling« the foreign agent's speech

451 The foreign agent is not allowed to remove the label (*see* 22 U.S.C. § 614(b); 28 C.F.R. § 5.402(e)) and is thus compelled to communicate the government's message. In a series of cases, the Supreme Court has established a First Amendment right »not to speak,« holding that the government may not compel persons to communicate messages with which they disagree. *E.g.*, Pacific Gas & Elec. Co. v. Public Utilities Comm'n of California, 106 S.Ct. 903 (1986); Wooley v. Maynard, 430 U.S. 705 (1977).

452 A. Kenneth Shere, who was U.S. general manager of the National Film Board of Canada at the time the *Block* and *Keene* cases arose, stated that he was asked to join as a plaintiff in *Block* but refused. He explained:

> As an agency of the Government of Canada, we have no business suing the United States. Our business is to deal government-to-government. [It is] to obey U.S. laws, not to challenge them. Besides we have other fish to fry right now in our relations with the United States.

Telephone Interview with A. Kennth Shere (Jan. 8, 1987).

453 *See, e.g.*, Valley Forge Christian College v. Americans United for Separation of Church and State, Inc., 454 U.S. 464, 472 (1982); Warth v. Seldin, 422 U.S. 490, 498 (1975).

454 The rule against raising another party's rights has exceptions, as where another party confronts »some genuine obstacle« to asserting his own rights. Singleton v. Wulff, 428 U.S. 106, 116 (1976); *see* G. GUNTHER, CONSTITUTIONAL LAW 1148 (11th ed. 1985). The natural political reluctance of the Canadian government to sue the U.S. government, *see supra* note 452, should bring this case under the exception.

455 *See, e.g.*, Lamont v. Postmaster General, 381 U.S. 301, 307 (1965); United States v. SCRAP, 412 U.S. 669, 689 n.14 (1973).

would present a strong First Amendment case on the merits, probably stronger than in either *Block* or *Keene*.[456]

The reluctance of the Canadian government to sue the U.S. government in these cases thus should not obscure the burdens that the »political propaganda« requirements of FARA directly impose on foreign agents and on the speech they disseminate in the United States.

Does FARA offend the First Amendment rights of those engaged in disseminating foreign-source speech? The parties in *Block* and *Keene* fought a battle of dictionaries and usage experts over whether »propaganda« is a disparaging word.[457] The Department of Justice, however, had effectively conceded that it was. The Department told a congressional committee in 1983 that it would »support the use of a more neutral term like political ›advocacy‹ or ›information‹ to denominate information that must be labeled.«[458] Moreover, the original purpose of Congress in adopting FARA rather plainly embodied a negative attitude toward »propaganda.«[459]

But even if »propaganda« is not held to be a disparaging term, the Act's labeling, reporting and filing requirements are imposed only on foreign-source speech, not on domestic speech. Foreign material thus is singled out for special disclosure requirements. This is done, moreover, on the premise that foreign material is less objective and less trustworthy than domestic material. As two Supreme Court Justices stated in a 1943 dissenting opinion (with which the Court's majority did not appear to disagree on this point), FARA was »intended to label information of foreign origin so that hearers and readers may not be deceived by the belief that the information comes from

456 *See, e.g.*, Lamont v. Postmaster General, 381 U.S. 301; Joint Anti-Fascist Refugee Committee v. McGrath, 341 U.S. 123 (1951); Buckley v. Valeo, 424 U.S. 1, 64–66 (1976). It apparently would not matter whether the foreign agent were a U.S. citizen, since »[f]reedom of speech and of press is accorded aliens residing in this country.« Bridges v. Wixon, 326 U.S. 135, 148 (1945); *see also* Yick Wo v. Hopkins, 118 U.S. 356, 369 (1886).

457 *See* 793 F.2d at 1311–12; 569 F. Supp. at 1520–22.

458 Letter from Deputy Attorney General Edward S. Schmults to Chairman Robert W. Kastenmeier, Subcommittee on Courts, Civil Liberties and the Administration of Justice, House Judiciary Committee, Aug. 8, 1983 *reprinted in* Joint Appendix in Meese v. Keene, *supra* note 445, No. 85–1180, at 118.

459 *See supra* note 421. *See also, e.g.*, the Justice Department's statement, in proposing the 1942 amendments adding the »political propaganda« provisions to FARA, that the amendments were designed to strengthen the Act, »[i]n view of the increased attempts by foreign agents at the systematic manipulation of mass attitudes on national and international questions, by adding requirements to keep our Government and people informed of the nature, source, and extent of political propaganda distributed in the United States.« *Amending Act Requiring Registration of Foreign Agents: Hearings on H.R. 6045 Before Subcomm. No. 4 of the House Comm. on the Judiciary*, 77th Cong., 1st Sess. 25 (1941) (statement of L.M.C. Smith).

a disinterested source.«[460] While the two Justices thought that »[s]uch legislation implements rather than detracts from the prized freedoms guaranteed by the First Amendment,«[461] the assumption that foreign material is less trustworthy than domestic material – less likely to come from »a disinterested source« – would seem to involve content discrimination of a kind now recognized as inconsistent with the First Amendment.[462]

To be sure, discrimination based on source is not necessarily the same thing as discrimination based on content or point of view. But source discrimination itself appears to be constitutionally suspect.[463] Moreover, requirements of source disclosure, even when applied to all speech of a given kind, have been viewed critically by the Supreme Court.[464] When such requirements are imposed on political speech from some sources (foreign) but not from other sources (domestic), they would seem to be especially vulnerable.

Source and content merge in another way. In today's interdependent world, a great many political, economic and environmental issues possess international as well as domestic dimensions. Further, international issues involving the United States often present disagreements between the U.S. government and foreign governments, political parties or other entities abroad.

Acid rain, one of the issues addressed by the Canadian films, is a good example. It involves a bilateral controversy between the governments of the United States and Canada.[465] The effect of FARA with respect to the Canadian films on acid rain is that speech on this issue financed by the Canadian government, when distributed in the United States, must be filed, labeled and reported as »political propaganda.« Meanwhile the U.S. government's speech on the issue bears no such badge of untrustworthiness. On this and other international issues, FARA's discrimination

460 Viereck v. United States, 318 U.S. 236, 251 (1943) (Black, J., joined by Douglas, J., dissenting); *see id.* at 236-___ (majority opinion).

461 *Id.* at ___ (Black, J., dissenting).

462 *See, e.g.*, Police Department of Chicago v. Mosley, 408 U.S. 92, 96 (1972); First National Bank of Boston v. Bellotti, 435 U.S. 765, 777 (1978).

463 See First National Bank of Boston v. Bellotti, 435 U.S. 765, 777 (1978); Posadas de Puerto Rico Associates v. Tourism Co. of Puerto Rico, 106 S. Ct. 2968, 2927 n.9 (1986); *id.* at 2986–87 (Stevens, J., dissenting).

464 *E.g.*, Buckley v. Valeo, 424 U.S. 1, 64–66 (1976); Talley v. California, 362 U.S. 60 (1960).

465 *See, e.g., U.S.-Canadian Relations Take a Testy New Turn*, N.Y. Times, Feb. 26, 1983, at 3, col. 5 (»The neighbors remain far apart on the issue of acid rain«).

against foreign-source speech becomes discrimination against views that are opposed to the views of the U.S. government.[466]

FARA probably also deters foreign-source speech in the United States by deterring »foreign principals« from having U.S. agents in the first place. The cumbersome and continuous requirements that FARA imposes on foreign agents with respect to their distribution of »political propaganda« may discourage some foreign entities from using agents to distribute their material in the United States.[467] Foreign-source material can be distributed in the United States without using a »foreign agent,« but often not as effectively.[468] If foreign sources are discouraged from using such agents, the likely effect is to reduce the access of the American public to foreign-source speech.

FARA's regulation of foreign-source speech as »political propaganda« thus burdens that speech not only if »propaganda« is considered a disparaging word but also if the term is considered a neutral one.[469]

Finally, the question is not simply one of First Amendment law. If the United States courts eventually reject the First Amendment challenge to FARA, domestic and international objections to this statute will remain. FARA's singling out of foreign-source speech for regulation as »political

466 *Cf.* First National Bank of Boston v. Bellotti, 435 U.S. at 785 (»suggests an attempt to give one side of a debatable public question an advantage in expressing its views to the people«).

467 There is an intended stigma attached to being a foreign agent. *See* the statement by one of the House managers at the time FARA was amended, in 1966, to broaden the exemption for persons engaged in commercial activities: »While there is no disgrace in being registered as a ›foreign agent,‹ there is a stigma that should not be unnecessarily extended.« 112 CONG. REC. 10,536 (1966) (Rep. Poff).

468 Foreign material, political or otherwise, can be sent directly to recipients in the United States by mail or other means, in which case it is not subject to FARA. *See* Note, *supra* note 433, at 440 & n.36; *cf.* Lamont v. Postmaster General, 381 U.S. 301. Also, when foreign-source material is distributed in the United States by someone who is not an agent of the foreign source, FARA does not apply. *See, e.g., Capitalist Edition of Pravda for U.S.*, N.Y. Times, Nov. 30, 1986, at 43, cols. 1–2 (private U.S. citizen publishing a daily edition of *Pravda* in English for distribution in the United States, without contact with the Soviet publishers). In such a case, however, the U.S. distributor must have his own incentives for distributing the material, and the foreign source lacks control (copyright aside) over whether and how the distribution is done.

469 Also questionable under the First Amendment is the way FARA requires government functionaries to sit in judgment on protected speech to determine whether it meets the Act's vague definition of »political propaganda.« Broad as that definition is, see *supra* text accompanying note 425, the Justice Department in *Keene* and *Block* found that only three of sixty-two Canadian films met it. *See supra* text accompanying notes 431–33. Meanwhile the record in *Keene* disclosed that the Soviet films *Alexander Nevsky, Potemkin* and *Crime and Punishment* had been deemed »political propaganda« under FARA. Joint Appendix, *supra* note 458, at 63. The vagueness involved in identifying »political propaganda« under FARA seems constitutionally unacceptable under decisions of the Supreme Court. *E.g.*, Coates v. City of Cincinnati, 402 U.S. 611, 614 (1971).

propaganda« will continue to bc not only a relic of wartime fearfulness but also an emblem of unwillingness on the part of the United States to let foreign and domestic ideas compete on level ground within its border.[470]

470 The Supreme Court decided Meese v. Keene on April 28, 1987, 107 S. Ct. 1862 (1987). By the vote of 5 to 3, the Court reversed the district court and upheld the constitutionality of FARA's »political propaganda« provisions.

The majority opinion, by Justice Stevens, first held that Keene had standing to challenge the statute. The Court explained that Keene had submitted detailed, uncontradicted affidavits supporting the conclusion »that his exhibition of films that have been classified as ›political propaganda‹ by the Department of Justice would substantially harm his chances for reelection and would adversely affect his reputation in the community.« *Id.* at 1868. At best, Keene »would have to take affirmative steps at each film showing to prevent public formation of an association between ›political propaganda‹ and his reputation,« and in any event those steps »would be ineffective among those citizens who shun the films as ›political propaganda.‹« *Id.* at 1868–69.

On the merits, the Court began by noting that »the term ›political propaganda‹ has two meanings.« one disparaging and one neutral. *Id.* at 1869. The Court further noted that FARA's definition of the term »includes misleading advocacy« as well as accurate, respected advocacy. *Id.* The Court read the statutory definition, however, as »broad« and »neutral.« *Id.* at 1870.

The Court then held that the district court had erred in ruling that FARA's use of the term »political propaganda« placed unconstitutional burdens on Keene's speech.

First, FARA »does not pose any obstacles to appellee's access to the materials he wishes to exhibit.« the Court said. *Id.* at 1871. Rather, »Congress simply required the disseminators of such material to make additional disclosures that would better enable the public to evaluate the import of the propaganda.« *Id.* True, prospective viewers of the films might »harbor an unreasoning prejudice against arguments that have been identified as the ›political propaganda‹ of foreign principlals and their agents.« *Id.* But FARA »allows appellee to combat any such bias simply by explaining ... that Canada's interest in the consequences of nuclear war and acid rain does not necessarily undermine the integrity or the persuasiveness of its advocacy.« *Id.*

Second, the Court found the reasoning of the district court to be »contradicted by history.« *Id.* at 1872. With FARA's »political propaganda« provisions more than four decades old, »it seems obvious that if the fear of misunderstanding had actually interfered with the exhibition of a significant number of foreign-made films, that effect would be disclosed in the record.« *Id.* at 1872–73. There was no evidence that any public suspicion engendered by the word »propaganda« had »had the effect of Government censorship,« the Court said. *Id.* at 1873.

Finally, the Court invoked »the respect we normally owe to the Legislature's power to define the terms that it uses in legislation.« *Id.*

The Court's opinion is unpersuasive in several respects. It is notable, in general, for its narrow concentration on the arguments made by the district court and its failure at any point to respond to the dissenting opinion.

Specifically, in relying repeatedly on the asserted neutrality of the statute's definition of »political propaganda,« the Court ignored what Justice Blackmun in dissent called »the realities of public reaction to the designation.« *Id.* at 1874 (Blackmun, J., dissenting). The Court itself had recognized those realities in its discussion of standing, noting, for example, that Keene would have to take affirmative steps at each film showing to prevent harm to his reputation. *See id.* at 1868–69.

In claiming neutrality for the statute, the Court also failed to mention recent statements by high Justice Department officials acknowledging its non-neutrality. *See id.* at 1879 (Blackmun, J. dissenting). The Court also passed over statements from the legislative history showing a

f. Restrictions on foreign production of communicative materials: the »manufacturing clause« of the Copyright Act

The flow of communicative materials into a country may be affected by restrictions on foreign production of those materials. To the extent that materials must be produced within the United States, their importation

congressional purpose to limit the spread of »political propaganda.« *See supra* notes 421, 459; 107 S. Ct. at 1871 & nn. 1, 2 (Blackmun, J., dissenting).

Of broader significance, the Court's opinion does casual violence to First Amendment doctrines. In stressing that FARA did not have »the effect of Government censorship« (*id.* at 1873), the Court ignored many decisions holding that government can violate the First Amendment not only by prohibiting or censoring speech but also by inhibiting or deterring speech. *See id.* at 1876 (Blackmun, J., dissenting) (*citing, e.g.,* Bantam Books, Inc. v. Sullivan, 372 U.S. 58 (1963)). In defending FARA on the ground that it »simply requires ... additional disclosures« (*id.* at 1871), the Court ignored many decisions striking down disclosure requirements because they had a deterrent effect on speech. *See id.* at 1877 (Blackmun, J., dissenting) (*citing, e.g.*, Talley v. California, 362 U.S. 60 (1960)).

Particularly relevant here are the implications of the instant case for the position of the United States on transborder speech. The Court quoted approvingly the 1943 dissent of Justices Black and Douglas in Viereck v. United States, 318 U.S. 236, 251; *see supra* text accompanying note 460. The opinion described FARA as »intended to label information of foreign origin so that hearers and readers may not be deceived by the belief that the information comes from a disinterested source.« 318 U.S. at 251 (Black, J., dissenting), *quoted at* 107 S. Ct. 1871 n. 15.

The Court in *Meese v. Keene* did not merely uphold the statute so described; it expressed no doubt about the contemporary validity of the wartime premise that information of foreign origin is less reliable – less likely to come from »a disinterested source« – than domestic information. The Court thus found it constitutionally sufficient, when the views of the Canadian government about acid rain are treated as »political propaganda« under FARA, that the Act allows the film's exhibitor »to combat any [resulting] bias simply by explaining« that Canada's interest in the subject »does not necessarily undermine the integrity or the persuasiveness of its advocacy.« *Id.* at 1871 Meanwhile, no such treatment, and no such defensive combat, is required for the views about acid rain held by the United States government or by any other domestic speaker.

Strikingly, the Court avoided confronting the issue of FARA's discrimination against foreign-source speech. While recognizing that Keene had raised the issue, the Court simply noted that the district court had rejected Keene's argument, and the Court itself gave no consideration to the argument. *Id.* at 1870. This silent treatment was particularly noteworthy in an opinion by Justice Stevens. A year before, he had dissented from the Court's upholding of a statute that, in his view, discriminated between media inside and outside of Puerto Rico. Posadas de Puerto Rico Associates v. Tourism Co. of Puerto Rico, 106 S. Ct. 2968, 2986 (1986) (Stevens, J., dissenting); *see also id.* at 2979 n.9 (majority in response denies such discrimination). In ducking the issue in *Meese v. Keene,* the Court may have wished to avoid an express constitutional endorsement of FARA's discrimination against foreign speech.

In the wake of *Meese v. Keene,* the burden rests on Congress to amend or repeal FARA. Only in that way can the United States remove the deterrence that FARA's regulatory requirements must impose on the circulation of foreign-source speech by actual and potential foreign agents in the United States. *See supra* note 467. Only in that way can the United States show its willingness to let foreign speech compete on equal terms with domestic speech within U.S. borders.

obviously is barred. Whether a requirement of domestic production reduces the volume of communicative materials available in the U.S., and whether it reduces the foreign content of the materials available, will depend on the kind of materials involved.

The »manufacturing clause« of the United States Copyright Act,[471] which expired in 1986, was a classic restriction on foreign production of communicative materials. Dating from 1891,[472] the clause required that nondramatic literary works in the English language, if authored by domiciliaries of the United States,[473] be printed in the United States or Canada in order to qualify for the infringement remedies provided by U.S. copyright law.[474] The clause included various exceptions: for the first 2,000 copies of any work; for works imported for personal use or scholarly libraries; for books in Braille; and others.[475] The purpose of the clause was purely protectionist – »to protect the American printing industry from the competition of foreign printers.«[476]

In 1972, reacting against protectionism, Congress set the manufacturing clause to expire in 1982.[477] In 1982, beset by protectionist pressure, Congress extended the clause, over President Reagan's veto, for another four years.[478] On June 30, 1986, the clause expired, despite a 7–6 vote to renew it and make it permanent by a House of Representatives subcommittee four days earlier.[479] The closeness of the congressional results in 1982 and 1986 suggests that, while the clause is now dead, it could be revived if protectionist sentiment should increase.

Since the requirement of U.S. or Canadian manufacture applied only to books in the English language by domiciliaries of the United States, the impact of the manufacturing clause on the flow of »information« into the

471 17 U.S.C. § 601(a) (1985) [expired 1986].

472 *See* H.R. REP. NO. 94–1476, Copyright Law Revision, 94th Cong., 2d Sess. 164 (1976).

473 The clause applied prima facie to authors who were domiciliaries *or citizens* of the United States. *See* 17 U.S.C. § 601(b)(1) (1985). But it excluded U.S. nationals who were domiciled outside the United States for at least one year immediately preceding the importation of the book, 17 U.S.C. § 601(b)(1) (1985), and thus effectively applied only to domiciliaries of the United States. *See* 2 M. NIMMER, NIMMER ON COPYRIGHT § 7.22[A], at 7-155 (1986).

474 17 U.S.C. § 601(b) (1985).

475 *Id.*

476 Stonehill Communications, Inc. v. Martuge, 512 F. Supp. 349, 351 (S.D.N.Y. 1981).

477 17 U.S.C. § 601(a) (1985).

478 Pub. L. No. 97–215, Act of July 13, 1982; 17 U.S.C. § 601(a) (1985); *see* 32 PAT. TRADEMARK & COPYRIGHT J. (BNA) 227 (1986).

479 *See id.* (vote of House Subcommittee on Courts, Civil Liberties and the Administration of Justice on H.R. 4696, June 26, 1986).

United States from abroad would seem to have been small. The clause applied not to the content of the book but to its place of printing. When an English-language book by an author domiciled in the United States is printed abroad, the importation of that book normally brings into the United States no foreign content, i.e., no communication from a foreign source.

On the other hand, because the costs of printing are higher in the United States than in some foreign countries – the *raison d'être* of the manufacturing clause – the ban on foreign printing may have prevented some books from being printed at all. The manufacturing clause was challenged on this ground as inconsistent with the First Amendment and upheld in a 1986 decision of the U.S. Court of Appeals for the Second Circuit.[480] The court's majority saw no constitutional problem, because the clause did not prevent an author from importing his foreign-printed book but only deprived him of full copyright protection if he did.[481] A concurring judge more perceptively thought the clause could raise a First Amendment problem if it inhibited the publication of a book, but he concluded that this danger had not been established, especially in view of the clause's various exceptions.[482]

In any event, if the manufacturing clause did prevent some books from being published, they would have been English-language books by authors domiciled in the United States. Regrettable as the loss to the United States public might have been, it would not have been a loss of communicative content from abroad.

As a precedent, however, the manufacturing clause could have a wider impact. It was a precedent for legislation requiring that communicative materials disseminated in the United States, at least if authored by domiciliaries of the United States, be produced in the United States. The model could be invoked to support a requirement that a certain proportion of programs on U.S. television be produced in the United States. Such a requirement is not unthinkable. As one writer has observed, if the time were to come when »the United States ha[d] lost its preeminent position in the packaging and export of information and entertainment« and »the volume of programming from abroad increased substantially,« legislation might well be proposed or enacted in the United States, as it has been in other

480 Authors League of America, Inc. v. Oman, 790 F.2d 220 (2d Cir. 1986).
481 *Id.* at 222.
482 *Id.* at 225 (Oakes, J., concurring).

countries,[483] to limit the amount of foreign-produced programming on domestic television.[484]

If some requirement of domestic production of television programs were adopted, the impact would be more closely related to communicative content than it was with respect to books under the manufacturing clause. Requiring television programs to be produced in the United States would not mean that the same content by the same author, domiciled in the United States, would simply be »manufactured« in the United States rather than abroad. Program production is a collaborative enterprise that involves many people and that often reflects the place of production. Program production in the United States rather than abroad would mean that fewer foreigners would participate and that a program's content would embody fewer foreign ideas, cultures, values and points of view.

The fact remains that the manufacturing clause, after existing in United States law for almost a century, was allowed to expire in 1986. This congressional decision must be counted as an important move by the United States away from protectionism in the realm of communicative materials.

g. *Restrictions on importing copyrighted works produced abroad*

While the manufacturing clause has expired, another provision that restrains the importation of communicative materials lives on in United States copyright law. Section 602 of the Copyright Act[485] allows a copyright owner to block the import into the United States of copies of his work that were produced abroad, even if their production were lawful and even if the copyrighted work be not otherwise available in the United States.

United States copyright law gives a copyright owner the exclusive right to

483 *See, e.g.*, the proposal of the Commission of the European Communities for a Council directive concerning broadcast activities, submitted to the Council of the European Communities on April 30, 1986. The proposal would require member-states to reserve at least 30% of their television time – apart from news, sports, game shows and advertising – for works produced by nationals of member-states and would raise the percentage to at least 60% three years after the proposal went into effect. 29 O.J. EUR. COMM. (NO. C 179) 4 (1986); arts. 2, 4, 22.

484 Price, *supra* note 18, at 887–88 (1976). The Federal Communications Commission, in adopting its »prime time access rule« that bans programming produced by U.S. television networks from one hour of prime time each evening, showed sympathy for the argument that the rule »discriminates against American producers and favors foreign producers.« Prime Time Access Rule, 50 F.C.C.2d 829, 838 (1975). But the Commission noted »the reduced role which foreign product plays in access programming this year« and said that action to repeal or change the rule to aid U.S. producers was therefore not necessary. *Id.*

485 17 U.S.C. § 602 (1985).

sell, rent or otherwise distribute copies or phonorecords of his work.[486] This right, however, normally is subject to the »first-sale doctrine.« The first-sale doctrine provides that once a particular copy or phonorecord has been lawfully made, the owner of that copy or phonorecord is entitled to sell it, or otherwise transfer it, without further authority from the copyright owner.[487]

Section 602 is an exception, in turn, to the first-sale doctrine. It allows a copyright owner to prohibit the importation into the United States of copies or phonorecords of his work that »have been acquired outside the United States,«[488] even if they were lawfully made and acquired and thus otherwise would be protected by the first-sale doctrine.[489]

Section 602 applies to two separate situations. The first involves »pirate« copies or records – ones produced without any authority from the copyright owner but in a country where their production was nonetheless lawful (typically because the country had no copyright relations with the United States, and hence the work was in the public domain there).[490] The second situation involves copies or records lawfully produced abroad *with* the authority of the copyright owner and otherwise in full compliance with U.S. copyright law.[491] In either situation, under section 602, »the mere act of importation ... would constitute an act of infringement and could be enjoined.«[492]

Section 602 itself has exceptions, but these are limited (more limited than were the exceptions to the manufacturing clause).[493] Section 602 does not apply to copies or records imported by the United States government or by a U.S. state government, except for »use in schools.«[494] It does not apply to the importation of one copy or record at a time for the private use of the importer; to copies or records carried into the United States in a traveler's personal baggage; or to importation by educational or scholarly organi-

486 17 U.S.C. § 106(3) (1985).

487 17 U.S.C. § 109(a) (1985) (»Notwithstanding the provisions of section 106(3), the owner of a particular copy or phonorecord lawfully made under this title ... is entitled, without the authority of the copyright owner, to sell or otherwise dispose of that copy or phonorecord«).

488 17 U.S.C. § 602(a) (1985) (»Importation into the United States, without the authority of the owner of copyright under this title, of copies or phonorecords of a work that have been acquired outside the United States is an infringement of the exclusive right to distribute copies or phonorecords under section 106 ...«)

489 *See id.*; H.R. REP. NO. 94–1476, Copyright Law Revision, 94th Cong., 2d Sess. 170 (1976).

490 *Id.*

491 *Id.*

492 *Id.*

493 *See supra* note 475 and accompanying text.

494 17 U.S.C. § 602(a)(1) (1985).

zations of one copy of an audiovisual work for archival purposes, or five copies of other works for archival or library lending purposes.[495] Section 602 reportedly is employed by record companies to block the import of recordings of popular music, even if those recordings are out of print or otherwise not available in the U.S.[496]

In addition to use of the statute by record companies holding sound-recording copyrights in recorded music, publishers, composers and songwriters holding composition copyrights in the underlying musical works were seeking, by way of a test case pending in late 1986, to establish *their* right under section 602 to block importation of recordings of the music.[497] This claim could have a much broader impact than the claims of record companies. The claims of record companies are limited to records made since 1972, when copyright protection for sound recordings began in the United States.[498] The claims of the music publishers apply to music released up to seventy-five years ago.[499] Moreover, while the sound recordings on a single record or tape usually have a single owner, an album of ten songs might have ten different composition copyrights; all ten owners would have to give permission for the album to be imported.[500] Yet, under the language and scheme of the Copyright Act, it would appear that the music publishers have a reasonable chance of establishing their claim.[501]

The congressional reports on section 602 offer no reasons for creating this

495 17 U.S.C. § 602(a)(2), (3) (1985).

496 A *New York Times* article in December 1986 reported that a number of recordings of popular music could be purchased abroad but not in the United States, because the copyright owners had blocked import under section 602. Some of the recordings had gone out of print in the United States; others included »many compact discs released in Europe and Japan [that] ... have not yet found American release.« »You have to be very careful about what you import,« one record seller reportedly said. »[I]t's hard to explain to someone why we can't sell them a 12-inch of Springsteen's ›Incident on 57th Street.‹ If it's good enough to be heard in England, why can't an American hear it?« N.Y. Times, Dec. 31, 1986 at C9, col. 1; *see also U.S. Law Spells Bad News for Import Fans*, San Francisco Chronicle, Jan. 1, 1987, at 43, cols. 1–4 (N.Y. Times dispatch).

497 *See* N.Y. Times, *supra* note 496 (case reportedly pending before U.S. District Court in New Jersey).

498 Pub. L. No. 92–140, 85 Stat. 391 (1971); *see* H.R. REP. NO. 94–1476, 94th Cong., 2d Sess. 55 (1976); 1 M NIMMER, NIMMER ON COPYRIGHT § 4.06 [A][1], at 4–34 (1986).

499 *See* 17 U.S.C. § 304(a), (b) (1985).

500 *See* N.Y. Times, *supra* note 496. The owner of a nationwide record-store chain reportedly said, »If the publisher wins, it would stop us importing all kinds of things because there's no way to bookkeep it all.« *Id.*

501 *See* 17 U.S.C. §§ 102, 106 (1985); H.R. REP. NO. 94–1476, 94th Cong., 2d Sess. 53 (1976) (stating that a literary work can be embodied in a phonorecord, which implies that a musical work also can be, and hence can be infringed by unauthorized distribution of the phonorecord).

exception to the first-sale doctrine.[502] The provision seems defensible as applied to »pirate« copies. These were produced abroad without authority from the copyright owner, and their importation at cheap prices would compete unfairly with authorized copies. A ban on importing »pirate« copies existed as well in the 1909 Copyright Act, the predecessor to the present 1976 Act.[503]

Section 602 is hard to defend, however, as applied to copies made abroad *with* the authority of the copyright owner, a provision new in the 1976 Act.[504] The defense offered by record companies – that »[p]arallel imports are an unfair and illicit disruption of the marketplace«[505] – is simply an objection to competition. The first-sale doctrine is designed to protect competition by preventing copyright owners from controlling the »marketplace« for copies of their works once those copies have been sold with the copyright owner's permission.[506] To create an exception for imported copies, as section 602 does, is inconsistent with principles of international free trade and with a free flow of communicative materials across national borders.

Section 602 might be challenged under the First Amendment, but probably without success. A United States resident seeking to import a record or book unavailable in the United States, and blocked from doing so under section 602, might invoke the First Amendment right to receive information from abroad that the Supreme Court has recognized in *Kleindienst v. Mandel*[507] and *Lamont v. Postmaster General*.[508] It would probably be an adequate answer, however, that section 602 does allow the importation of one copy at a time for the private use of the importer, and of five copies of a book or record for library lending purposes.[509]

It is true that, by prohibiting wholesale importation, Section 602 also restricts the ability both of would-be importers to distribute the work in the United States and of many members of the U.S. public to receive the

502 *See* H.R. REP. NO. 94–1476, 94th Cong., 2d Sess. 169–71 (1976); S. REP. NO. 94–473, 94th Cong., 1st Sess. 151–52 (1975); H.R. REP. NO. 94–1733, Conference Report, 94th Cong., 2d Sess. *passim* (1976).

503 1909 Copyright Act, 17 U.S.C. § 107 (1977); *see* H.R. REP. NO. 94–1476, 94th Cong., 2d Sess. 170 (1976).

504 *See id.; compare* 17 U.S.C. § 602 (1985) *with* 1909 Copyright Act, 17 U.S.C. § 109.

505 N.Y. Times, *supra* note 486.

506 *See* 2 M. NIMMER, NIMMER ON COPYRIGHT § 8.12[B], at 8–117, 8–118 (1986); Bobbs-Merrill Co. v. Straus, 210 U.S. 339 (1908).

507 408 U.S. 753 (1972); *see supra* text accompanying notes 314–18.

508 381 U.S. 301 (1965); *see supra* text accompanying notes 308–13.

509 17 U.S.C. § 602(a)(2), (3); *cf.* Authors League of America, Inc. v. Oman, 790 F.2d 220, 225 (2d Cir. 1986) (Oakes, J., concurring); *see supra* note 495 and accompanying text.

work.[510] But the power granted by section 602 is, after all, part of the exclusive rights of the copyright owner under the U.S. copyright law.[511] These rights are authorized by the Constitution[512] and in general are consistent with the First Amendment.[513] For example, a copyrigth owner has the right, without offending the First Amendment, to prevent *any* publication or distribution of his work[514] or to prevent the use of too many quotations from his work in news accounts.[515]

Similarly, although the first-sale doctrine enhances public access to published works, the doctrine probably is not required by the First Amendment. Congress probably could have given copyright owners the right to control all distribution, including all resale, of copies of their works.[516] Section 602 does less than that, lifting the first-sale doctrine only to block the import of copies from abroad.

Does this »discrimination« against foreign copies itself present a constitutional problem? The court of appeals decision upholding the manufacturing clause,[517] which also discriminated against foreign production, suggests not. Moreover, while the manufacturing clause arguably restrained the ability of U.S. authors to publish their works,[518] section 602 gives authors *greater* rights than they otherwise would have under the first-sale doctrine. Section 602 does not hurt U.S. authors but would-be distributors and receivers of the work in the United States.[519] This impact on distributors and receivers seems too slight to overcome the authority of Congress to indulge

510 *Cf. supra* notes 450–56 and accompanying text.

511 *See* 17 U.S.C. §§ 106, 602 (1985).

512 U.S. CONST., art. I, sec. 8, cl. 8.

513 *See, e.g.*, Harper & Row Publishers, Inc. v. Nation Enterprises, 105 S. Ct. 2218, 2229–30 (1985); 1 M. NIMMER, NIMMER ON COPYRIGHT § 1.10 [A, B], at 1–62 – 1–78.2 (1986).

514 *See* Harper & Row Publishers v. Nation Enterprises, 105 S. Ct. at 2230; Estate of Hemingway v. Random House, 23 N.Y.2d 341, 348, 296 N.Y.S.2d 771, 776, 244 N.E.2d 250, 255 (1968).

515 Harper & Row Publishers v. Nation Enterprises, 105 S. Ct. 2218.

516 *Cf. id.* at 2230 (finding sufficient First Amendment protection embodied in Copyright Act's distinction between expression on the one hand and facts or ideas on the other, and in doctrine of fair use).

517 Authors League of America, Inc. v. Oman, 790 F.2d 220 (2d Cir. 1986).

518 *See id.* at 225 (Oakes, J., concurring).

519 Section 602 does hurt the *foreign* authors of *sound recordings* of the works, by allowing the copyright owner to block importation of those recordings into the United States. Although the statute is not phrased in terms of foreign authorship, but rather of phonorecords »acquired outside the United States« (17 U.S.C. § 602(a); *see supra* note 488), it has a disproportionately injurious impact on foreign authors of sound recordings. It may be argued that this discrimination violates the obligation of »national treatment« imposed on the United States by the Universal Copyright Convention. Universal Copyright Convention, Sept. 6, 1952, art. II, 6 U.S.T. 2731, T.I.A.S. No. 3324; revised July 24, 1971, 25 U.S.T. 1341, T.I.A.S. No. 7868.

in a form of protectionism by giving copyright owners special protection against foreign-made copies.[520]

Section 602 thus remains an objectionable provision of United States law, inimical both to free trade and a free flow of information. However, it probably does not offend the First Amendment.

3. *Summary Concerning U.S. Regulation of Incoming Information Flow in General*

The legal stance of the United States toward information flow from abroad bears deep marks of ambivalence. On the one hand, there is support for a »free flow« into the United States, represented most notably by the holding in *Lamont*[521] and by the First Amendment right to receive information from abroad recognized in both *Lamont* and *Mandel.*[522] On the other hand, there are the several statutes that restrict incoming information flow and the court decisions mostly upholding them.

In support of the free-flow commitment, it can be noted that the only cases involving government restrictions on »pure« speech entering the country are *Lamont* and the cases under the Foreign Agents Registration Act. In *Lamont*, the Supreme Court struck down the restriction,[523] and the FARA case, *Meese v. Keene*, at this writing is still before the Supreme Court.[524] The other statutes inhibiting the flow of information do not involve »pure« speech but speech mixed with the entry of aliens, with travel, with the entry of objects or goods or with the rights of copyright owners.[525] The non-speech activities regulated by these statutes not only are traditional subjects of government regulation but also often involve considerations of national security, foreign policy or border control. The Supreme Court long has given special deference to the executive and legislative branches in these areas.[526]

Still, it is hard to deny that the visa restrictions of the McCarran-Walter Act, though based on the government's power to exclude aliens, are designed to prevent dissemination in the United States of unwelcome ideas from

520 *But see supra* note 519.
521 381 U.S. 301 (1965); *see supra* text accompanying notes 308–13.
522 *See supra* notes 308–18 and accompanying text.
523 *See supra* notes 308–13 and accompanying text.
524 *See supra* note 445 and accompanying text. *But see supra* note 470.
525 *See supra* notes 337–418, 471–520 and accompanying text.
526 *See supra* notes 351–53, 383–89 and accompanying text.

abroad.[527] The Foreign Agents Registration Act is similarly designed. While FARA does not by its terms *exclude* any speech from the United States, it requires that political speech disseminated by agents of foreign entities be filed, reported and labeled as »political propaganda,« on the premise that foreign speech is less trustworthy than domestic speech.[528] The McCarran-Walter Act and FARA both betray an unwillingness on the part of the United States to allow foreign speech to enter the country and compete an equal terms with domestic speech. While these statutes stand, the allegiance of the United States to the free-flow principle remains compromised.

B. *Regulation of Incoming Electronic Media Flow*

This section reviews the provisions of United States law that relate specifically to incoming broadcasts or other transmissions of radio or television programming. There are several reasons for treating electronic media separately. First, broadcasting traditionally *has been* treated separately under U.S. law and subjected to greater regulation than other media.[529] Second, special government regulation or control of broadcasting exists in most other countries as well.[530] Separate consideration of the electronic media in the U.S. therefore facilitates international comparisons.

Third, regardless of whether all these characterizations are valid and whether they justify the special regulation of broadcasting under U.S. law, the broadcast media may be said to have a number of special characteristics. There is the alleged scarcity of broadcast frequencies, which has provided the traditional rationale for the limited First Amendment protection

527 *See supra* notes 354–58 and accompanying text.

528 *See supra* notes 459–62 and accompanying text.

529 *See* FCC v. League of Women Voters, 468 U.S. 364, 376–78 (1984); FCC v. National Citizens Committee for Broadcasting, 436 U.S. 775, 799 (1978); FCC v. Pacifica Foundation, 438 U.S. 726, 748 (1978); 15 U.S.C. § 1335 (1973) (prohibiting cigarette advertising »on any medium of electronic communication subject to the jurisdiction of the Federal Communications Commission«).

530 *See, e.g.*, B. PAULU, RADIO AND TELEVISION BROADCASTING ON THE EUROPEAN CONTINENT (1967); *International Control of Broadcast Programming in Western Europe*, in THE INTERNATIONAL LAW OF COMMUNICATIONS, ch. 5 (E. McWhinney ed. 1971); C. DEBBASCH, TRAITÉ DU DROIT DE LA RADIODIFFUSION RADIO ET TÉLÉVISION 15–50, 291–317 (1967).

afforded to broadcasting.[531] There is the »uniquely pervasive presence« of the broadcast media »in the lives of all Americans,« particularly in the privacy of their homes.[532] There is broadcasting's unique accessibility to children, including those too young to read.[533] And there is – perhaps the best explanation for the special government controls on broadcasting – the unique popularity, persuasiveness and influence of the medium.[534] Broadcasting's power as a vehicle of news and political communication,[535] as a source of entertainment and acculturation[536] and as a mode of advertising[537] probably goes far to explain the concern of almost all governments to keep this medium under special control.

There is a further reason for treating electronic media separately in a study of U.S. regulation of *transborder* media flows. »Since radio and television signals obviously do not stop at international borders,«[538] they pose special problems for nations wishing to control their international passage. The transborder flow of television transmissions cannot be controlled, as can other kinds of media flows, through traditional methods of government

531 *See* Red Lion Broadcasting Co. v. FCC, 395 U.S. 367, 388 (1969); National Broadcasting Co. v. United States 319 U.S. 190, 226 (1943). *But cf.* FCC v. League of Women Voters, 468 U.S. 364, 376 n. 11 (suggesting Court may reconsider the »prevailing rationale for broadcast regulation based on spectrum scarcity«).

532 FCC v. Pacifica Foundation, 438 U.S. 726, 748 (1978).

533 *Id.* at 749.

534 *See, e.g.*, Columbia Broadcasting System, Inc. v. Democratic National Committee, 412 U.S. 94, 195 (Brennan, J., dissenting) (»the public's prime source of information«); M. FRANKLIN, MASS MEDIA LAW 760 (3d ed. 1987) (quoting 1980 *New York Times* column by Tom Wicker to the effect that television has become »the principal instrument of American politics«); Gorove, *supra* note 18, at 8 (1985) (reporting view expressed by Soviet delegate to United Nations that »television is the most powerful means of mass communication available«). United States courts, however, would have difficulty in approving the notion that the very persuasiveness of a medium limits its constitutional protection. *See, e.g.*, Stewart, *supra* note 33; Blasi, *supra* note 31.

535 *See e.g.*, M. FRANKLIN, *supra* note 534, at 742. The power of television to move public opinion may come in part from the *simultaneity* of the viewing. When many millions of people each know that millions of others are watching the same broadcast at the same time, they may be more readily moved in their common reactions and resulting public attitudes than when they read newspapers atomistically and alone.

536 *See, e.g.*, Price, *supra* note 18, at 887–90; de Sola Pool, *Direct Broadcast Satellites and the Integrity of National Cultures*, in ASPEN INSTITUTE PROGRAM ON COMMUNICATIONS AND SOCIETY, CONTROL OF THE DIRECT BROADCAST SATELLITE; VALUES IN CONFLICT 27 (1974); Magraw, *supra* note 18, at 27, 29.

537 *See, e.g.*, Banzhaf v. Federal Communications Commission, 405 F.2d 1082, 1100–01 (D.C. Cir. 1968), *cert. denied*, 396 U.S. 842 (1969) (»[i]t is difficult to calculate the subliminal impact of this pervasive propaganda ... but it may reasonably be thought greater than the impact of the written word«); 15 U.S.C. 1335 (1973), *supra* note 529; Capital Broadcasting Co. v. Mitchell, 333 F. Supp. 582 (D.D.C. 1971), *aff'd*, 405 U.S. 1000 (1972).

538 M. FRANKLIN, *supra* note 534, at 716.

border control addressed to immigration, to foreign travel or to objects or mail entering the country.

Moreover, the advent of communications satellites means that it is no longer just »neighboring countries« from which unwanted broadcasts may come.[539] As the national concerns and the international debate over DBS make clear,[540] the allotment and regulation of terrestrial broadcast frequencies no longer can assure a nation that it will not be invaded by undesired broadcasts from abroad. The increasingly international nature of electronic media transmission, and the special difficulties their transmissions pose for government attempts to corral them within national frontiers, call for special treatment of electronic media in a study of regulation of transborder media flows.

The provisions of U.S. law that address incoming electronic media flows are divided in this section into three kinds: (1) restrictions on foreign production of media content or on foreign ownership of U.S. communications facilities; (2) restrictions on terrestrial broadcasts into the United States; and (3) restrictions on the reception or retransmission in the United States of program-carrying signals from foreign satellites.

1. *Restrictions on Foreign Production of Media Content or Foreign Ownership of Communications Facilities*

a. *No limits on foreign production of programming*

The United States to date has placed no legal limits on the amount of U.S. radio or television programming that may be produced or originated abroad. The reason may well lie, not in principle, but in the fact that the United States has had no cause for imposing any such limit. For non-legal reasons, »the percentage of externally produced presentations on the American screen is among the lowest in the world.«[541] Unlike other countries, the United States has not »felt the sting of unwanted foreign programming.«[542] It has had no need to protect its cultural, economic or political values against a massive invasion of foreign material.

If this situation were to change, pressures to limit foreign programming

539 *Id.*
540 *See supra* notes 17–19 and accompanying text.
541 Price, *supra* note 18, at 887.
542 *Id.*

might develop.[543] As has been noted, the manufacturing clause of the Copyright Act, though now expired, could provide a precedent for such measures.[544] Another precedent could be found in the FCC's »prime time access rule.«[545] This rule bars programming produced by the three U.S. television networks from one hour of prime time each evening, »in order that the voices of other persons might be heard.«[546] If the FCC can impose such a restriction in order to reduce the programming sway of the U.S. networks and promote a diversity of programming sources,[547] there is little reason to doubt that the FCC or Congress could take comparable measures to reduce a perceived excess of foreign programming and encourage U.S. program sources. The fact remains that no such measures exist or are now being considered.

b. *Restrictions on foreign ownership of U.S. broadcast stations*

While the United States has no restrictions on foreign ownership of its print media[548] or on foreign production of its broadcast programming,[549] it does limit foreign ownership of its broadcast stations. Section 310 of the Federal Communications Act of 1934 provides that no broadcast license may be held by a foreign government, an alien, a foreign corporation or a corporation whose capital is more than twenty percent foreign.[550]
These provisions date back to the Radio Acts of 1912 and 1927,[551] the predecessors of the present statute. They were intended to protect the national security in wartime. As the secretary of the Navy stated in 1934:

543 *See supra* notes 483–84 and accompanying text.
544 17 U.S.C. § 601 (1985); *see supra* text accompanying notes 483–84.
545 Prime Time Access Rule, 50 F.C.C.2d at 847.
546 *Id.*
547 *See* (basically upholding the rule) Mt. Mansfield Television, Inc. v. FCC, 442 F.2d 470, 477, 483 (2d Cir. 1971); NAITPD v. FCC, 516 F.2d 526, 534 (2d Cir. 1975). *Compare* Krattenmaker, *The Prime Access Rule: Six Commandments for Inept Regulation*, 7 COMM/ENT L.J. 19 (1984).
548 *See supra* notes 327–31 and accompanying text.
549 *See supra* notes 483–84 and accompanying text.
550 47 U.S.C. § 310(a), (b) (1985). For corporation holding broadcast licenses indirectly (holding companies), the statute limits foreign ownership or board-of-directors membership to twenty-five percent, with discretion in the FCC to approve deviations. 47 U.S.C. § 310(b)(4). *See generally* Watkins, *Alien Ownership and the Communications Act*, 38 FED. COMM. L.J. 1 (1980).
551 (1912 Radio Act) Pub. L. No. 62–264, 37 Stat. 302 (1912); (1927 Radio Act) Pub. L. No. 70–632, 44 Stat. 1162 (1927). Section 2 of the 1912 Act required broadcast licensees to be U.S. citizens or domestic corporations; section 12 of the 1927 Act further prohibited foreign stock holdings in U.S. corporations that held licenses. *See* Watkins, *supra* note 550, at 4–6.

»[T]he lessons ... learned from the foreign dominance of the cables and dangers from espionage and propaganda disseminated through foreign-owned radio stations in the United States prior to and during the [First World] War brought about the passage of the Radio Act of 1927, which was intended to preclude any foreign dominance in American radio ...«[552] Thus the FCC has declared: »The alien ownership restriction ... is primarily and uniquely fashioned to curb alien activities against the United States in time of war.«[553]

The ban on foreign ownership of broadcast stations was not adopted without misgivings. Even in 1934, some argued that a flat ban was unnecessarily broad, given the president's emergency powers in wartime, and that the rule would unduly restrict international trade in peacetime.[554] In 1985, the ban gained public notice when it led Rupert Murdoch to acquire U.S. citizenship in order to buy broadcast properties in the United States.[555] A major U.S. newspaper commented that »the xenophobia of this rule is half a century out of date.«[556]

The U.S.-citizenship requirement for broadcast licensees apparently has not been challenged on constitutional grounds, but it could be. In other areas, the Supreme Court has treated alienage as a »suspect classification« that must be justified by a compelling state interest.[557] The Court thus has struck down state laws barring resident aliens from becoming engineers[558] or lawyers.[559] On the other hand, the Court has upheld laws barring aliens from becoming public functionaries, such as police, probation officers or school teachers.[560]

Broadcasting is not a public function in the United States.[561] Moreover, broadcasting involves the exercise of First Amendment rights,[562] a fact that argues further against the validity of a law flatly prohibiting resident

552 Watkins, *supra* note 550, at 5, *quoting Hearings on H.R. 8301 Before the House Comm. on Interstate and Foreign Commerce*, 73d Cong., 2d Sess. 26 (1934)

553 Attribution of Ownership Interests, 97 F.C.C.2d 997, 1009 (1984); *see* Noe v. FCC, 260 F.2d 739 (1958), *cert. denied*, 359 U.S. 924 (1959).

554 *See* Watkins, *supra* note 550, at 6 f.

555 *See e.g.*, Wall St. J., May 9, 1985, at 28 (editorial).

556 *Id.*

557 *See infra* notes 558–60 and accompanying text.

558 Examining Board v. de Otero, 426 U.S. 572 (1976).

559 *In re* Griffiths, 413 U.S. 717 (1973).

560 *E.g.*, Ambach v. Norwick, 441 U.S. 68 (1979).

561 *See* CBS v. Democratic Nat'l Comm., 412 U.S. 94, 119 (1973).

562 *E.g.*, FCC v. League of Women Voters, 468 U.S. 364 (1984).

aliens[563] from engaging in the activity.[564] On the other hand, most of the cases striking down U.S. citizenship requirements have dealt with state laws, not federal ones,[565] and the federal government has wide latitude to make policy regarding aliens.[566]

As unnecessary and xenophobic as the ban on alien ownership appears to be, the original »national security« justification probably would still be viewed as a sufficient governmental interest for constitutional purposes. Communications facilities in general are no less important to national security now than they were during the First World War.[567] Moreover, there may well be an international custom of keeping such facilities out of foreign hands.[568] Beyond that, the deference shown by the Supreme Court for legislative judgments in areas of national security and foreign policy indicates that section 310 of the Communication Act would be upheld.[569]

It is therefore worth considering how far the rationale underlying section 310 might extend. One scholar has written that if section 310 is constitutional, and »if it owes its validity to national security considerations,« then »significant implications arise for the power of the United States to regulate incoming signals originating abroad,« such as those from direct-broadcast satellites.[570] He continues: »The federal government could take equivalent steps to protect national security by regulating direct broadcast messages. Under this analysis, an American licensing procedure would be warranted.«[571]

Those implications do not necessarily follow. The FCC indeed has imposed the U.S.-citizenship requirement of section 310 on domestic licensees of direct-broadcast satellites (DBS).[572] However, it has declined to impose

563 Resident aliens are protected by the First Amendment. *See* Bridges v. Wixon, 326 U.S. 135, 148 (1945).

564 *Cf.* FCC v. National Citizens Committee for Broadcasting, 436 U.S. 775, 800 (1978) (rule against newspaper-broadcast cross-ownership in same city upheld, the Court noting that newspapers remain free to own broadcast stations in other cities).

565 *See, e.g.,* cases cited *supra* notes 558–59.

566 *See, e.g.,* Kleindienst v. Mandel, 408 U.S. 753, 765–67 (1972); Toll v. Moreno, 458 U.S. 1 (1982); Mathews v. Diaz, 426 U.S. 67 (1976); Note, 31 STAN. L. REV. 1069 (1979).

567 Witness the apparent targets of Soviet espionage efforts in the United States in the mid-1980s. *See, e.g.,* N. Y. Times, June 11, 1985, at B5, cols. 3–6 (national ed.).

568 The bilateral trade and investment treaties between the United States and its major trading partners typically exclude »communications« from their provisions assuring reciprocal rights of investment. *See* Note, 72 MICH. L. REV. 551, 568–71 (1974); *supra* note 331 and accompanying text.

569 *See* text at notes 383–89 *supra*.

570 Price, *supra* note 18, at 900.

571 *Id.*

572 47 C.F.R. § 100.11 (1985); *see* note 814 *infra* and accompanying text.

that requirement on entities that lease space on domestic satellites, whether to distribute programming to cable systems in the U.S. or to provide satellite-to-home service (with scrambled signals decodable by paying customers).[573]

Is there a relevant difference? The FCC has explained that a DBS licensee, like a conventional-broadcast licensee, controls »the facility's power or transmissions,«[574] as distinguished from providing programming over a facility controlled by someone else. In this view it is control of the facility itself – »the operational aspects of a valuable communications facility«[575] – that invokes the national-security considerations thought to justify the ban on foreign ownership. At least historically, the view has merit. The perceived danger of foreign ownership lay in the totality of what foreigners might do with the facility in wartime, not simply in their ability to reach the U.S. public with broadcast messages.[576] To be sure, since the operation of a communications facility consists of sending messages, the difference may be only a matter of degree, but the U.S.-citizenship requirement of section 310 rests basically on concerns about media structure, not media content.

Still, the requirement does have implications for other aspects of broadcast regulation. It suggests that other kinds of regulation may be more readily applied to foreign than to domestic broadcasts.[577] Further, section 310, by excluding foreigners from control of U.S. broadcast facilities, »surely results in some reduction in the diversity of voices within the United States.«[578] While its original intent and its constitutional justification are rooted in concerns of national security, particularly in times of war, section 310 inevitably has the continuing peacetime effect of reducing the »foreign content« of U.S. radio and television programming. Section 310 thus constitutes a subordination of the »free flow« principle to concerns of national security, concerns that may well be antiquated.

c. *Restrictions on foreign ownership of DBS licenses*

In its 1982 decision authorizing service by direct-broadcast satellites (DBS)

573 Satellite Business Systems, 95 F.C.C.2d 866, 873 & n.7 (1983).
574 *Id.* at 873 (*quoting* 90 F.C.C.2d at 1258).
575 *Id.* at 873 n.7.
576 *See* the 1934 statement of the secretary of the Navy, text accompanying note 552 *supra* (»the foreign dominance of the cables and dangers from espionage and propaganda«).
577 *See* Comment, *Direct Satellite Broadcasting and the First Amendment*, 15 HARV. INT'L L.J. 514, 524 (1974).
578 Price, *supra* note 18, at 900.

in the United States and granting construction permits to eight would-be DBS operators,[579] the FCC extended to DBS operators the U.S.-citizenship requirement prescribed for broadcast licensees by section 310 of the Communications Act.[580] Regardless of whether this action was required by section 310, it was consistent with the national-security concerns underlying that section.[581] If a conventional-broadcast station in foreign hands somehow represents a threat to U.S. national security, a DBS facility in foreign hands – and capable of reaching virtually all the homes in a U.S. time zone[582] – poses at least as great a threat.

d. *No restrictions on foreign ownership of programming entities using U.S. domestic satellites*

While banning foreign ownership of domestic DBS facilities, the FCC, as already noted,[583] has declined to impose the U.S.-citizenship requirement on entities that distribute programming in the United States by leasing space on conventional satellites.[584] The line thus drawn between control of facilities and provision of programming is not always easy to discern.
Thus, the FCC has allowed a domestic satellite operator to lease five transponders for a six-year period, with an option to purchase at any time, to a British company planning to use them to provide direct service to U.S. homes.[585] As the FCC acknowledged, the differences between control of leased transponders for this purpose and control of a DBS satellite were not overwhelming.[586] But the FCC stressed the legal point – perhaps begging the question – that the British company would not need an FCC license for this service,[587] and it noted that »several foreign controlled enti-

579 Direct Broadcast Satellites, 90 F.C.C.2d 676 (1982); STC Decision, 91 F.C.C.2d 953 (1982); *In re* Application of CBS, 92 F.C.C.2d 64 (1982); *see supra* note 291 and accompanying text.
580 90 F.C.C.2d at 723; 47 C.F.R. § 100.11 (1985).
581 *See supra* notes 295–97, 569–70 and accompanying text.
582 Broadcasting, Dec. 10, 1984, at 46.
583 *See supra* text accompanying note 573.
584 *See* Satellite Business Systems, 95 F.C.C.2d at 873 & n.7.
585 Satellite Business Systems, 95 F.C.C.2d at 866 *ff.*
586 The main differences – which do not seem insubstantial – were that the conventional satellite had one-tenth the power of DBS, requiring almost twice as large as receiving dish, and that its signals would be scrambled. *Id.* at 872–73 & n. 6.
587 *Id.* at 873.

ties« already were distributing program services by satellite to U.S. cable systems.[588] Invoking the facilities-programming distinction, the FCC stated that »none of these programming services control the operational aspects of a valuable communications facility,«[589] so that subjecting the foreign entities to foreign-ownership restrictions »would not seem to serve the purposes of Section 310 (b).«[590]

e. *No restrictions on foreign ownership of U.S. cable systems*

In contrast to the U.S.-citizenship requirement for control of conventional-broadcast stations and of DBS facilities, efforts to restrict foreign ownership of cable television systems in the United States have been rejected by both the FCC and the Congress. In 1976 the FCC declined to act against foreign ownership of cable, explaining (a) that the limited foreign investment in U.S. cable systems posed no threat to the national security, and (b) that cable operators lack the »totality« of control over program content possessed by broadcasters.[591] The Commission likened cable instead to nonbroadcast media:

> Alien ownership restrictions do not apply to communicators generally, to newspapers, wire news services, non-license radio and television networks, film and television producers, cable system networks and channel lessees, and it is not clear that they should apply to a system operator solely because of his potential ability to influence, through his program origination efforts, the ideas and attitudes of cable subscribers.[592]

In 1980, as foreign investment in U.S. cable increased, the FCC reconsidered, but adhered to, its position.[593] The Commission refused to interpret section 310 of the Communications Act »as reflecting a general policy against foreign investments in communications enterprises in the United States.«[594] Congress also has declined to move against foreign owner-

588 In addition, other foreign-controlled entities »sell foreign programming to U.S.-owned programming services,« which in trun distribute the programming to cable systems. *Id.* at 873 n. 7.
589 *Id.*
590 *Id.*
591 Cable Television Citizenship Requirements, 59 F.C.C.2d 723, 726 ff. (1976). *See generally* Note, 10 SYRACUSE J. INT'L L. & COM. 113 (1983)
592 59 F.C.C.2d at 727.
593 Foreign Ownership of CATV Systems, 77 F.C.C.2d 73, 81 (1980).
594 *Id.*

ship of U.S. cable systems, except in the most tentative way.[595]

There is an obvious inconsistency between the FCC's position on foreign ownership of cable and its positions on foreign ownership of broadcast stations, DBS facilities and program providers. Broadcasters and DBS operators have been subjected to U.S.-citizenship requirements, while program providers have not been, on the theory that it is physical control of the facility, not influence over program content, that warrants a ban on foreign ownership.[596] With respect to cable television systems, however, control of the facility is overlooked. It is overlooked although a cable operator may control 50 or 100 channels, in contrast to a broadcaster's single channel, and although normally there will be no other cable operator in the city (or a given part of the city).[597] Ignoring this impressive amount of facility control, the FCC creates and rejects the argument that foreign ownership of U.S. cable should be banned »solely because of« the systems operator's »potential ability to influence, through his program origination efforts, the ideas and attitudes of cable subscribers.«[598]

One explanation for the inconsistency lies in the jurisdictional fact that cable systems are not licensed by the FCC, as broadcasters and DBS operators are, but by local or state governments.[599] (Program providers are not licensed at all.) The FCC thus had no ready vehicle for imposing foreign-ownership restrictions on cable.[600]

595 Congress's main concern has been that Canada, the source of almost all the foreign ownership of U.S. cable, did not reciprocate by letting U.S. citizens own Canadian cable systems. *See* Foreign Ownership of CATV Systems, 77 F.C.C.2d at 78; Note, *supra* note 591, at 113–15, 118. A cable bill approved by the Senate Commerce Committee in 1982 authorized the FCC to make rules barring ownership of U.S. cable systems by nationals of countries that did not grant reciprocal rights to U.S. citizens. S. 2172, 97th Cong., 2d Sess., section 605(b); *see* S. REP. NO. 97–518, 97th Cong., 2d Sess. 15(1982); *see also* S. 66, 98th Cong., 1st Sess., section 605(b) (authorizing FCC only to »conduct inquiries« on the subject); S. REP. NO. 98–67, 98th Cong., 1st Sess. 20 (1983). In the Cable Communications Policy Act as finally passed in 1984, however, Congress stopped well short of that. It created a Telecommunications Policy Study Commission for the apparent purpose, among others, of looking into the problem and perhaps exerting pressure on the Canadian government. Cable Communications Policy Act of 1984, 47 U.S.C. § 611 (1985); *see* 130 CONG. REC. S. 14,285 (Oct. 11, 1984) (statement of Senator Packwood).

596 *See supra* notes 574–75 and accompanying text.

597 *See, e.g.*, Omega Satellite Products v. City of Indianapolis, 694 F.2d 119, 126 (7th Cir. 1982); H.R. REP. NO. 934, 98th Cong., 2d Sess. 23 (1984).

598 59 F.C.C.2d at 727; *see supra* text accompanying note 592.

599 *See, e.g.*, Cable Franchise Policy and Communications Act of 1984, H.R. REP. NO. 934, 98th Cong., 2d Sess. 23 (1984).

600 To be sure, the FCC has imposed some ownership restrictions on cable, banning ownership by local television broadcasters, television networks and telephone companies. *See* 47 C.F.R. §§ 63.54, 76.501 (1985). But broadcasters, telephone companies and (effectively) television networks are themselves licensed by the FCC.

Another explanation lies in the fact that the foreign ownership of U.S. cable is virtually all from one country, Canada, which is a friend and neighbor of the United States.[601] Both the FCC and the Congress, in their refusal to restrict foreign ownership of cable, apparently were influenced by the »close and friendly ties« between the United States and Canada.[602] It would be unrealistic to ignore the cushion this factor provides for the tolerant position the U.S. has taken on foreign ownership of its cable systems.

2. *Restrictions on Terrestrial Broadcasts into the United States*

a. *Frequency allotments by treaty*

Conventional broadcasts capable of reaching into the United States from neighboring countries are limited by the allotment of frequencies for the broadcast stations. The AM radio allotments are governed by multilateral treaties on broadcasting in the North American Region signed in 1937 and 1950.[603] According to Dean Monroe Price, the allocations between the U.S. and Mexico in the 1937 Agreement, as well as those between the United States and Canada, »leave the implication that clear channel authorization was distributed so that the strongest Mexican and Canadian stations (in terms of geographical reach) were spaced away from the common border.«[604] Dean Price remarks that, in this way, without violating the First Amendment, »some classes of foreign broadcasts can be practically prevented from penetrating American borders.«[605] Whatever was true of the 1937 Agreement, it is not clear that the same policies control the U.S.-Mexico allocations prevailing today.[606]

601 *See* 77 F.C.C.2d at 80; Note, *supra* note 591, at 118.

602 77 F.C.C.2d at 80–81, 82 (opinion of Commissioner Washburn); id. at 77.

603 North American Regional Broadcasting Agreement, Dec. 13, 1937, 55 Stat. 1005 (1941), T.S. No. 962; North American Regional Broadcasting Agreement, Nov. 15, 1950, 11 U.S.T. 413; *see* FEDERAL COMMUNICATIONS COMMISSION, ANNUAL REPORT FISCAL YEAR 1982, at 29–30.

604 Price, *supra* note 18, at 898 f. (*citing*, with respect to Mexico, C.B. ROSE, NATIONAL POLICY FOR RADIO BROADCASTING 241 (1940)).

605 Price, *supra* note 18, at 898 f.

606 Although Mexico was not a party to the 1950 Regional Agreement, a separate agreement was subsequently reached between the U.S. and Mexico generally paralleling the 1950 Agreement. *See* FEDERAL COMMUNICATIONS COMMISSION, *supra* note 603, at 30.

b. *Regulation of programming transmitted from the United States for broadcast back into the United States*

One provision of United States law imposes U.S. regulation, indirectly, on programming broadcast into the United States from another country. Section 325(b) of the Federal Communications Act requires an FCC permit for the transmission of material from the United States »to a radio station in a foreign country« for the purpose of broadcasting the material back into the United States.[607] The provision derives from attempts in the 1930s by some stations that were denied U.S. radio licenses to move their transmitters to Mexico and receive American programming there for broadcast back into the United States.[608] Congress's theory was that »[t]he United States cannot control such transmitting apparatus, but it can at least place difficulties in the way of securing American [program] talent.«[609]

Where section 325(b) applies,[610] it reflects an aggressive U.S. concern for the content of broadcasts into the United States from another country. In a 1935 case, the FCC denied the required permit on the basis that »[t]he character of the programs likely to be arranged and transmitted from the proposed studio [in the United States] does not appear to be such as would promote better international relations or serve the public interest.«[611] Thus, the focus there was limited to the programs to be transmitted from the United States for retransmission back into the U.S.

In a 1957 case, the FCC took a similarly restrained approach, granting the permit because it found nothing wrong with the U.S.-originated programs. The FCC said it lacked jurisdiction »to make determinations with respect to the programming of the Mexican station.«[612] The court of appeals, however, reversed.[613] The court said that while the FCC lacked power »to prevent [the Mexican station] from broadcasting to San Diego locally originated programs which are objectionable by American standards,« it did have power »to refrain from issuing a permit which would give those pro-

607 47 U.S.C. § 325(b) (1985).
608 Price, *supra* note 18, at 898.
609 C.B. ROSE, *supra* note 604, at 240.
610 The provision was held not to apply where the programming was conveyed from the United States to Mexico by the physical delivery of recorded programs instead of by radio transmission. Baker v. United States, 93 F.2d 332 (5th Cir. 1937), *cert. denied*, 303 U.S. 642 (1938).
611 *In re* Yount, 2 F.C.C. 200, 207 (1935).
612 *See* Wrather-Alvarez Broadcasting, Inc. v. FCC, 248 F.2d 646, 650 (D.C. Cir. 1957).
613 *Id.*

grams a larger American audience.«[614] The court held that the FCC, in deciding whether to grant the permit, was required to consider the total programming of the Mexican station to determine whether it had »such serious defects ... as would affect the public interest.«[615]
Used in this manner, section 325(b) would seek to employ programming supplied from the United States as a lever to regulate all the programming of foreign stations broadcasting into the United States. While the provision thus has broad implications, it appears to have been used rarely and to have had little practical impact. After fifty years, the two cases noted appear to be the only ones in which section 325(b) has been applied.

c. *Prohibition of »pirate« broadcasting into the United States*

The United States prohibits unlicensed radio broadcasting – »pirate« broadcasting[616] – from ships offshore into the United States. Thus in *United States v. McIntire*,[617] the government, relying on both section 301 of the Communications Act[618] (prohibiting the use of radio without an FCC license) and the International Telecommunication Convention of 1959,[619] succeeded in enjoining broadcasts from a ship three and one-half miles off the coast of New Jersey. Citing the national interest in preventing interference with the use of duly licensed frequencies and also »the adverse effects of defendants' unlicensed broadcasts upon the public interest,« the court upheld »the power of the United States to restrict and regulate radio broadcasts originating beyond territorial limits.«[620]
The concept of pirate broadcasts into a nation from beyond its boundaries, and without its authorization,[621] can cover not only the traditional pirate transmitters on the high seas but also the new possibility of unauthorized broadcasts into a nation's territory from a satellite. There is a tension between condemning pirate broadcasts from an offshore ship and insisting that nations tolerate a »free flow« of incoming broadcasts from satellites.[622]

614 *Id.* at 651.
615 *Id.*
616 A »pirate« broadcaster has been defined as »one who transmits into the territory of a nation from beyond that nation's territorial boundaries and without its authorization.« Smith, *Pirate Broadcasting*, 41 S. CAL. L. REV. 769, 770 (1968).
617 370 F. Supp. 1301 (D.N.J. 1974).
618 47 U.S.C. § 301 (1985).
619 International Telecommunication Convention (1959), art. VII, para. 1(1), 12 U.S.T. 2377, 2480.
620 370 F. Supp. at 1302 f.
621 *See supra* note 616.
622 *See* Hagelin, *supra* note 18, at 219 n. 55; *supra* notes 17–19 and accompanying text.

Meanwhile, if an offshore, foreign or satellite station succeeds in broadcasting into the United States, even in violation of U.S. law, members of the U.S. public apparently are entitled to receive the broadcasts. Section 705 (formerly section 605) of the Federal Communications Act,[623] which prohibits the unauthorized reception of radio communications, probably does not apply at all to reception with the consent of the sender.[624] In any event, section 705 contains a proviso exempting »any radio communication which is transmitted by any station for the use of the general public,«[625] a provision that would appear to protect reception of pirate broadcasts. In addition, the First Amendment's »right to receive« might well prevent government interference with reception by U.S. residents of broadcasts transmitted to them.[626] Also possibly relevant is section 326 of the Federal Communications Act, which prohibits the FCC from interfering »with the right of free speech by means of radio communications.«[627]

d. *U.S. retaliation against advertising by U.S. firms on Canadian stations with U.S. audiences*

United States television stations located near the Canadian border are widely received in Canada, thanks to the high penetration of cable in the major Canadian cities along the border.[628] The television interchange between the United State and Canada thus flows largely in one direction, with some fifty-four percent of prime time viewing in Canada devoted to programs produced in the United States.[629]

Since so many Canadians watch U.S. television, U.S. stations became good media for Canadian advertisers. In 1974 the Canadian government estimated that Canadian advertisers were spending $20 million per year at bordering U.S. television stations, or about ten percent of the total television advertising revenues in Canada.[630]

This outflow of advertising dollars dismayed the Canadian government, especially in light of its potential impact on cultural policy objectives for

623 47 U.S.C. § 705 (formerly § 605) (1985).

624 *See infra* notes 693–700 and accompanying text.

625 47 U.S.C. § 705(a) (1985).

626 *See* Lamont v. Postmaster General, 381 U.S. at 301 ff.; *cf.* Stanley v. Georgia, 394 U.S. 447 (1969).

627 47 U.S.C. § 326 (1985).

628 *See* Stoler, *The Border Broadcasting Dispute: A Unique Case Under Section 301*, 6 INT'L TRADE L.J. 39, 40–41 (1981). The cable penetration in major Canadian markets was estimated in 1978 at seventy percent. *Id.* at 40.

629 *Id.* at 41.

630 *Id.*

Canadian television.[631] Hence in 1976 Canada adopted a tax law denying to Canadian advertisers a business-expense deduction for advertising placed on U.S. broadcast stations and directed primarily to a Canadian audience.[632] Owners of the U.S. broadcast stations near the border protested, claiming that their advertising revenues from Canadian sources had dropped by more than fifty percent as a result of the law.[633]

At the behest of these »border broadcasters,« Congress in 1984 passed legislation responding in kind.[634] The »Canadian Mirror Act« denies a tax deduction to U.S. advertisers for the expenses of advertising »carried by a foreign broadcast undertaking and directed primarily to a market in the United States,« where the foreign country denies the reciprocal deduction to its advertisers.[635]

Such tit-for-tat retaliation between friendly neighbors represents an unfortunate resolution of a trade dispute. But President Carter, in recommending the legislation to Congress, rejected four apparently stronger proposals by the U.S. border broadcasters for economic retaliation against Canada.[636] Regardless of whether the U.S. legislation was a reasonable response to the Canadian move, it clearly was a response and not a U.S. initiative. The burden imposed by the twin U.S. and Canadian enactments on the flow of broadcast advertising between the U.S. and Canada is essentially the work of Canada, albeit resulting from felt economic and cultural needs.

That burden, in any event, has little impact on media content. If U.S. advertisers use U.S. stations instead of Canadian stations to reach the U.S. audience, the content of neither the advertising nor the programs is likely

631 *Id.*

632 Act of Sept. 22, 1976, Bill C-58, § 3 (presented by the minister of finance to the First Session of the Thirtieth Canadian Parliament, Apr. 19, 1975); *see* Stoler, *supra* note 628, at 42–43; Broadcasting, Oct. 15, 1984, at 64; Nov. 5, 1984, at 46.

633 Stoler, *supra* note 628, at 43.

634 Trade and Tariff Act, Pub. L. No. 98–573, 98 Stat. 2991 (1984) (amending section 162 of Internal Revenue Code of 1954); *see* Stoler, *supra* note 628, at 46–53.

635 Pub. L. No. 98–573, 98 Stat. 2991 (1984).

636 Stoler, *supra* note 628, at 51. The other proposals were: (i) special duties on all Canadian feature films and records imported to the U.S.; (2) quantitative restrictions on imports of Canadian feature films and records to the U.S.; (3) continuation of the provision of U.S. tax law limiting deductions for expenses incurred attending conventions abroad; and (4) taking account of the »unreasonable« nature of the Canadian law »when dealing with Canada on matters of mutual concern.« *Id.*

to change much.[637] Somewhat like the now-expired manufacturing clause of the U.S. Copyright Act, this restraint addresses the place of origination rather than the content of the material communicated.[638]

e. *Carriage of foreign broadcast signals by U.S. cable systems*

The FCC in its regulation of cable television does not treat cable carriage of foreign broadcast stations much differently from cable carriage of domestic stations. The FCC rules define a television broadcast station as including »any television station licensed by a foreign government,«[639] and they make it clear that foreign stations »may ... be carried« by U.S. cable systems if consistent with the rules.[640]

The rules do provide that foreign stations, unlike domestic ones, *need* not be carried. Foreign stations may not assert a claim to compulsory carriage, or to program exclusivity, against U.S. cable systems.[641] The FCC's »must carry« and program-exclusivity rules were designed to protect local broadcast stations against cable competition, in support of the »localism« policy embedded in the FCC's licensing scheme.[642] It does not seem unreason-

637 The same is probably true if Canadian advertisers use Canadian stations instead of U.S. stations to reach the Canadian audience. There is, however, a potential indirect effect on program content if the Canadian stations use the additional revenues to produce programming. In this respect, the Canadian legislation may function as a tax levied on Canadian advertisers – and on U.S. stations – to subsidize the production of Canadian programming.

638 *See supra* notes 479–80 and accompanying text.

639 47 C.F.R. § 76.5 (1985).

640 47 C.F.R. § 76.5 (1985). The equal treatment of foreign stations when cable systems choose to carry them was illustrated in Kiro, Inc. v. FCC, 631 F.2d 900 (D.C. Cir. 1980). There, a television station in Seattle, Washington, affiliated with the CBS network, complained about competition from Seattle cable systems carrying Canadian stations, since those stations offered CBS network programming before that programming was available on CBS affiliates in the U.S. The FCC denied relief, applying its usual standard of whether the complaining station had shown substantial economic harm from the cable competition, and the court of appeals affirmed. The fact that the alleged harm arose from carriage of *foreign* stations by the U.S. cable systems was not accorded any significance.

641 47 C.F.R. § 76.5 (1985).

642 *See* M. FRANKLIN, *supra* note 534, at 915, 918; United States v. Southwestern Cable Co., 392 U.S. 157, 166 (1968). The program-exclusivity rule was terminated in 1980. *See* M. FRANKLIN, *supra* note 534, at 915; *In re* Cable Television Syndicated Program Exclusivity Rules (Docket No. 20988), *In re* Inquiry Into the Economic Relationship Between Television Broadcasting and Cable television (Docket No. 21284), 82 F.C.C.2d 375 (1980). The must-carry rule, as then drafted, was held to violate the First Amendment in Quincy Cable TV, Inc. v. FCC, 768 F.2d 1434 (D.C. Cir. 1985), *cert. denied*, 106 S. Ct. 2889 (1986).

able to deny this protection to foreign stations that are not licensed by the FCC.

FCC regulation aside, there is one notable way in which U.S. law discourages cable carriage of foreign stations. The 1976 Copyright Act establishes a compulsory copyright license for cable carriage of »distant signals,« enabling cable systems to carry nonlocal stations on payment of government-prescribed royalties.[643] This compulsory license expressly covers signals of Canadian and Mexican stations.[644] It does so, however, only for carriage of those signals by U.S. cable systems located near the Canadian or Mexican border – specifically, within 150 miles of the Canadian border or within »off-air« reception range of stations in Mexico.[645]

Microwave or satellite facilities are capable of transmitting Canadian or Mexican signals – or signals from more distant countries – to cable systems anywhere in the United States.[646] One may ask, therefore, why foreign signals were not treated the same as U.S. signals insofar as the compulsory license was concerned. To be sure, in the view of Congress the hard decision was to bring *any* carriage of Canadian or Mexican signals under the compulsory license.[647] Moreover, cable systems near the border were, by and large, the ones already carrying Canadian or Mexican signals.[648] But if a U.S. cable system remote from the border wants to carry a foreign signal – if, for example, a system in central California or northern New Mexico, where there are many Mexican-Americans, wants to carry a signal from

643 17 U.S.C. § 111(c)(1), (4) (1985).

644 17 U.S.C. § 111(c)(4).

645 17 U.S.C. § 111(c)(4); *see infra* notes 654–59 and accompanying text. Cable systems north of the 42d parallel but more than 150 miles from the Canadian border may also carry Canadian signals under the compulsory license. 17 U.S.C. § 111(c)(4).

646 *See, e.g.,* M. FRANKLIN, *supra* note 534, at 914; Brotman, *Cable Television and Copyright: Legislation and the Marketplace Model*, 2 COMM/ENT L.J. 477, 481 (1979–1980) (television »superstations« distributed nationwide by satellite).

647 The Senate bill would have made »the carriage of any foreign signals by a cable system ... subject to full copyright liability, because the compulsory license was limited to the retransmission of broadcast stations licensed by the FCC.« H.R. REP. NO. 94–1476, 94th Cong., 2d Sess. 94 (1976) (»House Report«). The House Committee, and eventually the Congress, decided not to go that far, recognizing »that cable systems primarily along the northern and southern border have received authorization from the FCC to carry broadcast signals of certain Canadian and Mexican stations.« *Id.*

648 *Id.* To take further account »of those cable systems that are presently carrying or are specifically authorized to carry Canadian or Mexican signals,« the House Committee, and the Congress, »grandfathered« under the compulsory license any Canadian or Mexican signals already carried at the time of the Act, even if the cable systems were outside the prescribed zones along the border. *Id.* at 95; *see* 17 U.S.C. § 111(c)(4).

Mexico – why should it not be entitled to do so under the compulsory license?[649]

The foreign stations left out of the compulsory license, and the owners of the copyrights on the programs transmitted by those stations, presumably are delighted by this result. They thus are given full copyright protection against U.S. cable systems remote from the border.[650] This protection enables them, at least in theory, to negotiate their own royalties for carriage by those systems.[651]

The interests of copyright owners, however, are not the paramount considerations where the compulsory license is concerned. The compulsory license subordinates the interests of copyright owners in order both to enable cable systems to carry the programs of distant stations and to enable the public to receive those programs.[652] Given this purpose, it seems unlikely that Con-

649 Congress suggested no good reason. That broadcast stations in the United States are »licensed by the FCC« (House Report, *supra* note 647, at 94), while stations abroad are not, has little relevance. Unlike the compulsory-carriage and program-exclusivity rules (*see supra* note 642 and accompanying text), the compulsory license is not a benefit for the stations carried but a restriction imposed on them. While the House Committee saw the issue as raising »important international questions of the protection to be accorded foreign copyrighted works in the United States« (House Report, *supra* note 647, at 94), it did not say what those questions were. The international obligation of the United States is only to give foreign works the same protection accorded to domestic works. Universal Copyright Convention, *supra* note 519, at art. II. The House Committee further stated:

> While the Committee has established a general compulsory licensing scheme for the retransmission of copyrighted works of U.S. nationals, a broad compulsory license scheme for all foreign works does not appear warranted or justified. Thus, for example, if in the future the signal of a British, French, or Japanese station were transmitted in the United States by a cable system, full copyright liability would apply.

House Report, *supra* note 647, at 94. The Committee did not explain why it would not be »warranted or justified« to treat foreign signals the same as U.S. signals insofar as the compulsory license was concerned. *See* text accompanying notes 654–59 *infra*.

650 *See* 17 U.S.C. § 111 (1985); Universal Copyright Convention, *supra* note 519.

651 In practice, one may wonder whether the compulsory license is not a net advantage for foreign stations. By enabling U.S. cable systems to carry their signals without prior negotiation, it may produce carriage by systems that otherwise would not make the effort. At the same time, the license enables the station and the copyright owners to collect royalties automatically from the Copyright Royalty Tribunal (*see* 17 U.S.C. §§ 111(d), 801–10 (1985)).
The desirability of the compulsory license is suggested by the vehement complaints of U.S. copyright owners against Canada for not reciprocating by providing them with comparable compensation for carriage of their programs by Canadian cable systems. *See International Copyright/Communications Policies: Hearings Before the Subcomm. on Patents, Copyrights and Trademarks of the Senate Comm. on the Judiciary*, 98th Cong., 1st Sess. 1–2 (1983) (»1983 Hearings«); *see also* Broadcasting, Oct. 13, 1986, at 104 (»sense of the Senate« resolution). Of course, what the U.S. copyright owners want from Canada is a compulsory license instead of *no* compensation for their signals, whereas Canadian and Mexican stations left out of the compulsory license by U.S. copyright law are consequently entitled to *full* compensation. It may be, however, because of the difficulties of negotiating individual royalties, that in practice the choice is between compulsory carriage and no carriage.

652 *See, e.g.*, House Report, *supra* note 647, at 89; M. FRANKLIN, *supra* note 534, at 916.

gress left most foreign stations out of the compulsory license, while including all domestic stations, in order to benefit the foreign stations and their program-copyright owners. It seems more likely that Congress, in declining to extend the compulsory license to Mexican and Canadian signals generally (or to all foreign signals), determined that it was less important for the U.S. cable audience to have access to foreign programs than to domestic programs. It is not clear why the choice between domestic and foreign programs should not have been left to the U.S. viewing public, with the compulsory license applying to all signals once it applied to any.[653] Such equal treatment of domestic and foreign media would have been more consistent with the »free flow« principle.

Other congressional judgments about foreign programming and U.S. audiences are embodied in the particular lines drawn by Congress in applying the compulsory license to Canadian and Mexican signals. With respect to Canadian signals, Congress made the license applicable to U.S. cable systems located within 150 miles of the border (or north of the 42d parallel, where that is a greater distance).[654] »Thus the cities of Detroit, Pittsburgh, Cleveland, Green Bay and Seattle would be included within the compulsory license area, while cities such as New York, Philadelphia, Chicago, and San Francisco would be located outside the area.«[655] One may ask why the viewing public in New York, Philadelphia, Chicago and San Francisco, rather than the Congress, should not judge the desirability of receiving Canadian signals in those cities.

With respect to Mexico, instead of specifying a distance from the border, Congress made the compulsory license applicable where U.S. cable systems receive the Mexican signals »off the air« rather than by microwave or satellite.[656] To receive adequately a Mexican signal off the air, a U.S. cable system normally would have to be within 100 miles of the transmitter.[657] Thus a cable system in a U.S. border city such as San Diego presumably could receive under the compulsory license a station from the Mexican border city of Tijuana.[658] But cable systems in central California or north-

653 *See supra* notes 643–47 and accompanying text.
654 17 U.S.C. § 111(c)(4).
655 House Report, *supra* note 647, at 94.
656 17 U.S.C. § 111(c)(4).
657 Although the distance for good off-the-air reception varies with the terrain, the height of the transmitter and other factors, normally it is under 100 miles. Telephone conversation with Brian James, engineer, National Cable Television Association, Washington, D.C. (Apr. 20, 1987).
658 *Cf.* BROADCASTING/CABLECASTING YEARBOOK 1985, at C-1983 (list of television stations in San Diego market includes Tijuana station).

ern New Mexico apparently could not receive Mexican signals under the compulsory license. Neither could a cable system in Los Angeles, which is beyond the off-the-air distance from Mexico.[659]

Since these and other areas of the United States distant from the Mexican border have large Mexican-American populations, the congressional judgment excluding such areas from the compulsory license may operate to deny Mexican programming to cable audiences that would wish to receive it.

The off-the-air test for bringing Mexican signals under the compulsory license has the further result of discriminating not only among cable audiences in the United States but also among stations in Mexico. It means that U.S. cable systems can carry under the compulsory license only stations located in Mexico's border cities – and not, for example, a station in Mexico City, whose signal could reach the border only by microwave or satellite. As a result, the Mexican stations received in the United States are likely to reflect the U.S. cultural influence that is pronounced along the border, instead of the most authentic Mexican culture represented by stations deeper inside the country.

3. *U.S. Restrictions on Reception or Retransmission of Signals from Foreign Satellites*

As of December 1984, some eighty active telecommunications satellites were revolving in geostationary orbit above the equator.[660] Approximately fifteen of them belonged to the International Telecommunications Satellite Organi-

659 *See supra* note 657. Los Angeles is approximately 110 miles from Tijuana.

660 Smith, *Space WARC 1985: The Quest for Equitable Access*, 3 B.U. INT'L L.J. 229, 231 n.9 (1985) (*citing* Second Report of the Advisory Committee for the ITU World Administrative Conference on the Use of the Geostationary-Satellite Orbit and the Planning of the Space Services Utilizing It, Jan. 1985, at 2). Geostationary orbit exists 22,300 miles above the equator. A satellite in that orbit revolves at the same speed as the earth and thereby remains »stationary« over a given point on the earth. *See* Cryan & Crane, *International Telecommunications Pirates: Protecting U.S. Satellite Signals From Unauthorized Reception Abroad*, 17 N.Y.U. J. INT'L L. & POL. 851, 851–52 & authorities cited (1985). A geostationary satellite's signal is receivable over a large area, or »footprint.« Hence it is »an almost ideal method of distributing programming, either as an intermediary to local broadcast stations or cable systems, or as a direct transmitter in what is known as DBS (direct broadcast satellite) transmission service.« 1983 Hearings, *supra* note 651, at 17 (statement of David Ladd). The discussion in this section is limited to non-DBS satellites; DBS is discussed in the text accompanying notes 810–57 *infra*.

zation (INTELSAT).[661] Approximately twenty-five were domestic satellites of the United States.[662] The remaining forty or so were domestic or regional satellites of other countries, including Canada, Australia, Mexico, Brazil, Indonesia and the Soviet Union.[663] In the United States, and probably other countries, »it is virtually impossible to watch television or listen to the radio without soon seeing or hearing something that ... at some point pass[ed] through a satellite transponder.«[664]

Given the large and growing role of satellites in distributing television programming throughout the world, national restrictions on the reception or retransmission of signals from foreign satellites may constitute important barriers to incoming media flow. This section examines the extent to which such restrictions exist in United States law.

a. *Reception without consent of originator*

Reception in the United States of a program-carrying signal from a foreign satellite – other than a DBS satellite[665] – without the consent of the originator[666] may violate several provisions of United States law. The most readily applicable prohibition is found in section 705(a) (formerly section 605)

661 INTELSAT Report 1985–86, at 1. INTELSAT is an international consortium that operates a system of communications satellites and earth receiving stations serving more than 165 nations, dependencies and territories. *Id.* In 1984 INTELSAT had 63 signatories to its treaty and revenues of more than $411 million. *See* Separate Systems, 101 F.C.C.2d 1046 (1985). *See generally* L. HENKIN, INTERNATIONAL LAW: CASES AND MATERIALS 1056–58 (2d ed. 1980). INTELSAT was established by the »Interim Agreements« in 1964. T.I.A.S. No. 5646. The »Definitive Agreement« (Agreement) went into effect Feb. 12, 1973. 23 U.S.T. 3813, T.I.A.S. No. 7532.

662 Staple, *The New World Satellite Order: A Report from Geneva*, 80 AM. J. INT'L L. 699, 701 (1986) (*citing* Memorandum Opinion & Order, 50 Fed. Reg. 35,228 (1985) (1985 U.S. Orbital Assignment Plan)).

663 Staple, *supra* note 662, at 701 (*citing* D. DEMAC, G. CODDING, H. HUDSON, & R. JAKHU, EQUITY IN ORBIT: THE 1985 SPACE WARC, Ann. B. (International Institute of Communications, 1985).

664 Broadcasting, July 8, 1985, at 43.

665 As already noted, this section is concerned with conventional, »fixed service« satellites that transmit programming to broadcast stations, cable systems or other distributors, and not with direct-broadcast satellites (DBS) that in the future may broadcast directly to homes *See supra* note 660; Hagelin, *supra* note 18, at 265. In any event, reception from a DBS satellite presumably would not be without the consent of the originator. *See infra* notes 691–700 and accompanying text; *supra* notes 623–24 and accompanying text.

666 References to the consent of the »originator« include the consent not only of the entity that transmits the signal carried by the satellite but also of the owners of the copyrights on the programs carried by the signal.

of the Federal Communications Act.[667] The second and third sentences of section 705(a) provide:

> No person not being authorized by the sender shall intercept any radio communication and divulge or publish the existence, contents, substance, purport, effect, or meaning of such intercepted communication to any person. No person not being entitled thereto shall receive or assist in receiving any interstate or foreign communication by radio and use such communication (or any information therein contained) for his own benefit or for the benefit of another not entitled thereto.[668]

At least one of these provisions apparently would apply to prohibit reception of satellite signals without the consent of the originator.[669]

There are, however, at least two possible defenses under section 705. First, a 1984 amendment exempts the reception »for private viewing« of »satellite cable programming,« if the signal is not scrambled and if a market mechanism has not been established to let people pay to receive the signal.[670] Second, the proviso to section 705(a) exempts from the section's coverage »any radio communication which is transmitted by any station for the use of the general public.«[671] These possible defenses, together with others based on the Constitution, will be discussed shortly in considering the legal status of particular examples of foreign satellite reception in the U.S.[672]

In addition to section 705, reception of a signal from a foreign satellite without the consent of the originator, if done by a cable system that retrans-

667 47 U.S.C. § 705(a) (1985). *See* 130 CONG. REC. 14,286, Oct. 11, 1984, Explanation of Section 705 as Redesignated and Amended by H.R. 4103 (statement of Sen. Packwood) (sec. 705 »provides protection against the unauthorized reception of subscription television (STV), multi-point distribution services (MDS), and satellite communications«).

668 47 U.S.C. § 705(a) (1985).

669 The second sentence, expressly covering any person »not being authorized by the sender,« presumably would apply whenever the person receiving the satellite signal »divulge[s] or publish[es]« the programming to any other person – that is, lets anyone else view it. Even if the person receiving the signal views the programming in hermit-like isolation, he probably has »receive[d]« it without »being entitled thereto« and used it »for his own benefit,« in violation of the third sentence. On the applicability of section 705(a) to the unauthorized reception of satellite signals, see, e.g., 130 CONG. REC. S14,286 (daily ed. Oct. 11, 1984) (statement of Sen. Packwood); Regulation of Domestic Receive-Only Satellite Earth Stations, 74 F.C.C.2d 205, 215–16 (1979); Rice, *Calling Offensive Signals Against Unauthorized Showing of Blacked-Out Football Games: Can the Communications Act Carry the Ball?*, 11 COLUM-VLA J.L. & ARTS 413, 424, 426 (1987). On the applicability of the third sentence of section 705(a) to a person who views the programs for his own enjoyment without financial gain, see, e.g., Movie Systems v. Heller, 710 F.2d 492, 494 & n.5 (8th Cir. 1983); Rice, *supra*, at 421–22 & n.56.

670 47 U.S.C. § 705(b) (1985); *see infra* notes 704–22 and accompanying text.

671 47 U.S.C. § 705(a); *see supra* note 625, *infra* note 696, and accompanying text.

672 *See infra* text accompanying notes 704–58.

mitted the signal, would produce a violation of U.S. copyright law.[673] It also could constitute an invasion of privacy under applicable state law.[674] Further, failure by the United States to take measures against unauthorized reception of foreign-satellite signals could violate treaty obligations of the U.S. It might violate article 17 of the International Radio Regulations, in which the member-states of the International Telecommunication Union agree to prohibit and prevent »the unauthorized interception of radio communications not intended for the general use of the public.«[675] A refusal by the U.S. government to act against unauthorized »distribution« of satellite signals also might violate the Brussels Satellite Convention, which obligates each of its signatories »to take adequate measures to prevent the distribution on or from its territory of any program-carrying signal by any distributor for whom the signal emitted to or passing through the satellite is not intended.«[676]

b. *Reception with consent of originator*

(i) *The FCC's position: such reception is illegal unless authorized by the FCC*

If someone in the United States receives programming from a foreign satellite[677] *with* the consent of the originator, does the reception violate United States law? The Federal Communications Commission says it does, unless the FCC has given its own consent.

The FCC first took this position in a 1979 decision in which it lifted its regu-

673 *See* 17 U.S.C. § 111(b) (1985).

674 *See* W. PROSSER & P. KEETON, TORTS 850 (5th ed. 1984).

675 International Telecommunication Convention, *supra* note 619, at art. 17. *But cf.* Cryan & Crane, *supra* note 660, at 864 (»the ITU has not sought to regulate airwave piracy, and therefore is not a promising forum for satellite signal carriers seeking to stem signal theft«).

676 Convention Relating to the Distribution of Programme-Carrying Signals Transmitted by Satellite (ratified by United States in October 1984), art. 4(i), (iii), 28 PAT. TRADEMARK & COPYRIGHT (BNA) 723. However, the Convention provides broad exceptions. Member-states need not prohibit unauthorized reception of signals carrying »reports of current events,« used for instructional purposes, quoted in accordance with »fair practice,« or distributed »solely for the purpose of teaching.« *Id.*, art 4(i), (ii), (iii). Ratification of the Brussels Convention was considered by the U.S. Copyright Office and other federal agencies to require no new legislation in the United States; section 705 of the Communications Act, together with the copyright laws, was regarded as adequate implementing legislation. *See* 1983 Hearings, *supra* note 651, at 32–33 (statement of David Ladd). *See generally* Cryan & Crane, *supra* note 660, at 871–74.

677 References to »foreign satellites« mean domestic or regional satellites of foreign nations and do not include INTELSAT satellites. *See supra* notes 660–63 and accompanying text.

lation of receive-only satellite earth stations (i.e., dish antennas).[678] The Commission recounted that domestic satellite service was initiated in the United States at the end of 1973, and by early 1977 its growth had become explosive.[679] Early receive-only earth stations, being very expensive, were installed primarily by common carriers to serve multiple users.[680] But the technology and the equipment market advanced quickly, and in 1975 the FCC first authorized a cable system to construct an earth station for its own private use.[681] A flood of similar applications followed, and the FCC progressively streamlined its procedures. In 1977 it dropped the requirement that earth-station licensees obtain FCC approval to receive specific programming from a domestic satellite.[682] In 1979 the FCC deregulated receive-only earth stations altogether, ruling that a license was no longer necessary to construct and operate one.[683]

But this did not mean, the FCC declared, that an earth-station operator could receive programming from a *foreign* satellite, even with the consent of the originator, without governmental permission. The Commission said that the treaty obligations of the United States under the INTELSAT Agreement stood in the way.[684] Under section XIV(d) of the Agreement, a signatory-nation intending to use satellite-related facilities separate from the INTELSAT system for the purpose of international telecommunications must first notify and consult with INTELSAT, in order to assure technical compatibility and »to avoid significant economic harm to the global system of INTELSAT.«[685] Only after such consultation has taken place, and INTELSAT's Assembly of Parties has responded with its recommendations, may the proposed non-INTELSAT operation go forward.[686] The FCC noted these treaty obligations and continued:

> Thus, any deregulation of receive-only earth stations does not imply permission to receive service from non-U.S. domestic satellites ... Such permission can be

678 Reregulation of Domestic Receive-Only Satellite Earth Stations, 74 F.C.C.2d 205 (1979) (»Earth Stations«); *see also In re* Amendment of Parts 73 and 97 of the Commission's Rules Concerning Rebroadcasts of Transmissions of Non-Broadcast Radio Stations, 101 F.C.C.2d 32, 43 (para. 34) (1985) (»Rebroadcasts«); Transborder Satellite Services, 88 F.C.C.2d 258, 278 n.25 (1981).

679 Earth Stations, *supra* note 678, at 207.

680 *Id.*

681 Florida Cablevision, 54 F.C.C.2d 881 (1975); *see* Earth Stations, *supra* note 678, at 207.

682 Florida Cablevision, 67 F.C.C.2d 339 (1977); *see* Earth Stations, *supra* note 678, at 207–08.

683 Earth Stations, *supra* note 678, at 264.

684 *Id.* at 219 n. 27; *see* T.I.A.S. No. 7532; *see supra* note 661.

685 T.I.A.S. No. 7532; art. XIV(d); Earth Stations, *supra* note 678, at 219 n. 27.

686 T.I.A.S. No. 7532; art. XIV(d); Earth Stations, *supra* note 678, at 219 n. 27.

> provided only after discharge of our treaty obligations to INTELSAT. Therefore, until such permission is granted, any reception of non-U.S. signals is unauthorized and subject to the sanctions of Section 605 [of the Federal Communications Act].[687]

(ii) *Evaluation of the FCC's position*

The FCC's position evidently is respected by earth-station operators. At least one such operator does seek permission from the FCC, subject to the consultation process with INTELSAT, in order to receive programming from a foreign satellite even with the consent of the originator.[688] It is not clear, however, where the FCC gets the legal authority for its position.

The FCC seems to rely basically on the INTELSAT Agreement. Since that Agreement provides that permission to receive international telecommunications service from a non-INTELSAT satellite can be granted »only after discharge of our treaty obligations to INTELSAT,« the FCC reasons that »until such permission is granted, any reception of non-U.S. signals is unauthorized and subject to the sanctions of Section 605.«[689] One must ask whether this reasoning is sound.

Reception of signals from a foreign satellite by a person in the United States, with the consent of the originator but without the permission of the U.S. government pursuant to the INTELSAT Agreement, might indeed violate the obligations *of the United States* under that Agreement. Article XIV(d) requires that the consultation process first be pursued »[t]o the extent that any Party or Signatory *or person within the jurisdiction of a Party«* intends to use non-INTELSAT facilities for international telecommunications.[690] It does not follow, however, that non-INTELSAT reception

687 *Id.* at 219 n.27. *See also* Rebroadcasts, *supra* note 678, at 43 (para. 34) (INTELSAT Agreement »protected in the U.S. through enforcement of Section 705«).

688 *See, e.g., In re* Cable News Network, Inc., Application for authority to construct and operate a receive-only earth station in the Domestic Fixed-Satellite Service, to be located in Atlanta, Georgia, to receive signals from all domestic communications satellites as well as the Soviet Union's GHORIZONT STATIONS 4 and 7 satellites, Memorandum Opinion, Order and Authorization, File No. 907–DSE-L-85, May 14, 1985 [«GHORIZONT«]; Comments of Turner Broadcasting System, *In re* Amendment of Parts 73 and 97 of the Commission's Rules Concerning Rebroadcasts of Transmissions of Non-Broadcast Radio Stations, BC Docket 79–47, RM 2830, 101 F.C.C.2d 32 (1985), filed Oct. 24, 1984, at 4–7 (»Turner Comments«); *see also infra* notes 770–78 and accompanying text.

689 Earth Stations, *supra* note 678, at 219 n. 27.

690 Agreement, *supra* note 661, at art. XIV(d). (emphasis added).

by a person in the United States would violate U.S. domestic law. Article XIV(d) manifests no intention to be self-executing.[691] Indeed, it is doubtful whether a treaty can be self-executing so as to impose criminal sanctions under U.S. law without an implementing act of Congress.[692]

The FCC purports to find such implementing legislation in section 605 (now section 705) of the Communications Act. Reception of non-U.S. satellite signals without official permission given pursuant to the INTELSAT process, the FCC says, »is unauthorized and subject to the sanctions of Section 605.«[693] The FCC appears never to have indicated which provision of section 705 it relies on.[694] It is hard to find anything in section 705 that has the claimed effect. Apparently the FCC reads section 705 as a general prohibition of »unauthorized« reception of radio communications, and it then concludes that reception lacking government approval pursuant to the INTELSAT Agreement is »unauthorized.«[695] But, lengthy and opaque as section 705 is, there is nothing in it that can reasonably be read as prohibit-

691 A treaty is self-executing if it »manifests an intention that its provisions shall be effective under the domestic law of the parties at the time it comes into effect.« RESTATEMENT (SECOND) OF FOREIGN RELATIONS LAW OF THE UNITED STATES, § 154(2) (1965); *see also* Riesenfeld, *The Doctrine of Self-Executing Treaties and U.S. v. Postal: Win at Any Price?*, 74 AM. J. INT'L L. 892, 896–97 (1980) (»whether the treaty aims at the immediate creation of rights and duties of private individuals which are enforceable and to be enforced by domestic tribunals«); *id* at 898 n. 29 (»the treaty must ... be specific enough not to need further concretization by domestic action«).

692 »Treaty regulations that penalize individuals ... are generally considered to require domestic legislation before they are given any effect.« Hopson v. Kreps, 622 F.2d 1375, 1380 (9th Cir. 1980) (*citing* L. HENKIN, FOREIGN AFFAIRS AND THE CONSTITUTION 159 (1972)). *See* RESTATEMENT *supra* note 691, at § 141(3) (1965) (treaty cannot be self-executing to extent it involves »governmental action that under the Constitution can be taken only by the Congress«); Riesenfeld, *The Power of Congress and the President in International Relations: Three Recent Supreme Court Decisions*, 25 CALIF. L. REV. 643, 651 (1937) (listing the appropriation of money and the imposition of penalties for criminal offenses as two examples of such governmental action); The Bello Corrunes, 19 U.S. (6 Wheat.) 151, 171–72 (1821); *see* also United States v. Postal, 589 F.2d 862, 877 & authorities cited (5th Cir. 1979).

693 Earth Stations, *supra* note 678, at 219 n. 27; *see also* Rebroadcasts, *supra* note 678, at 43; Transborder Satellite Services, 88 F.C.C.2d 258, 278 n. 26 (1981).

694 Earth Stations, *supra* note 678, at 219 n. 27; Rebroadcasts, *supra* note 678, at 40.

695 *See* Transborder Satellite Services, 88 F.C.C.2d at 278 n. 25:

> The Communications Act, in Section 605, prohibits the unauthorized interception and disclosure of interstate or foreign radiocommunications except those designated as broadcasts for use by the general public .... After completion of the INTELSAT coordination process, and with the bilateral concurrence of the foreign government, Section 605 will not stand as an impediment to the reception of transborder television programming at U.S. receive-only earth stations.

ing reception with the consent of the sender.[696] Moreover, explicit language would be required since section 705 is a criminal statute, to be strictly construed.[697]

There would also be First Amendment problems in making the reception of a foreign satellite signal illegal where the sender has given consent. In *Lamont*, the Supreme Court struck down a much less onerous burden on incoming speech, namely, the requirement that the addressee send in a postcard request in order to receive mail from abroad.[698] True, the communication there was by mail rather than radio, and the use of radio frequencies traditionally has justified greater regulation.[699] Further, the United States has a substantial interest in complying with its treaty obligations to INTELSAT. On the other hand, the First Amendment interests at stake here could be stronger than in *Lamont* – if, for example, the signals from the foreign satellite carried news coverage and the receiving entity were a news organization wanting to retransmit that news in the United States.[700]

Thus, if the U.S. Congress had passed a law requiring FCC permission for reception of programming from a foreign satellite with the consent of the sender, a substantial constitutional question would be presented. Congress

696 Section 705(a) contains five, quite-wordy sentences, which may be summarized as follows: The first sentence prohibits any person receiving a communication from divulging its contents, »except through authorized channels,« to »any person other than the addressee,« or to a person employed to forward the communication, or on demand of lawful authority. The second sentence provides that »[n]o person not being authorized by the sender shall intercept« any communication and divulge its contents. The third sentence provides: »No person not being entitled thereto shall receive« any communication and use it »for his own benefit or for the benefit of another not entitled thereto.« The fourth sentence provides that »[n]o person having received any intercepted radio communication« shall divulge its contents or use it for his own benefit. The fifth sentence provides that the section shall not apply to »any radio communication which is transmitted by any station for the use of the general public.« 47 U.S.C. § 705(a) (1985).

The FCC conceivably might rely on the third sentence, arguing that a person is not »entitled« to receive a signal from a foreign satellite, although he has the consent of the sender, if he does not also have the permission of the FCC given after compliance with the INTELSAT Agreement. But some specific language should be necessary, especially in a criminal statute, to establish that permission must come from the government and not just the sender. The third sentence seems more reasonably read as the twin of the second sentence – prohibiting reception where the second sentence prohibits interception, in both cases without the consent of the sender.

697 *See* Rathbun v. United States, 355 U.S. 107, 111 (1957); Brandon v. United States, 382 F.2d 607, 611 (10th Cir. 1967); United States v. Hall, 488 F.2d 1983, 195 (9th Cir. 1973).

698 Lamont v. Postmaster General, 381 U.S. 301, 305–07 (1965); *see supra* text accompanying notes 308–11.

699 *See, e.g.*, FCC v. League of Women Voters, 104 S. Ct. 3106, 3116–18 (1984); *supra* note 529 and accompanying text.

700 *See* GHORIZONT, *supra* note 688; *see infra* notes 770–78 and accompanying text.

has not passed such a law, but the FCC interprets section 705 as though it had. This position is untenable.

c. *Examples of U.S. reception of foreign satellite signals*

Against that background, some current examples of foreign-satellite reception in the United States pose interesting legal questions.

(i) *Backyard-dish reception*

By mid-1986 more than 1.5 million homes in the United States had their own earth stations – »backyard dishes« – to receive television programs from satellites.[701] The satellites at which these dishes are pointed include foreign satellites.[702] Since dish owners normally lack the consent of the signal's originator, their reception of satellite signals has been assumed to violate section 705 of the Federal Communications Act, as that section stood prior to the 1984 »satellite cable programming« amendment.[703] The questions arise whether that amendment covers reception of signals from *foreign* satellites and whether other protection for such reception can be found in section 705.

The 1984 amendment provides a specific exemption from section 705 for reception of satellite signals by home earth stations. It exempts the reception of »any satellite cable programming for private viewing« unless the signal is scrambled or, if it is not scrambled, unless there is a »marketing system« through which dish owners can buy the right to view the programming.[704] While most U.S. programmers have responded to the amend-

701 Broadcasting, Oct. 6, 1986, at 74.

702 *See, e.g., Sky's the Limit on Home Sales of Satellite Dishes*, San Francisco Chronicle, June 10, 1985, at 20 (»Programming includes commercial-free feeds from the major networks, foreign broadcasts and even pay-TV channels such as those offering first-run movies«); *Nyetwork TV: America Tunes in Soviet Broadcasts*, Wall St. J., Nov. 18, 1986, at 1, col. 4

703 *See supra* notes 667–69. *See* National Subscription Television v. S & H T.V., 644 F.2d 820 (9th Cir. 1981); Chartwell Communications v. Westbrook, 637 F.2d 459 (6th Cir. 1980); Cryan & Crane, *supra* note 660, at 859; 130 CONG. REC. S14,286, Oct. 11, 1984 (statement of Sen. Packwood on Cable Communications Policy Act of 1984), *quoted supra* note 667. The reception presumably would violate the second and/or third sentence of section 705. *See supra* note 668.

704 47 U.S.C. § 705(b) (1985); Pub. L. No. 98–549, §§ 5(a), 6(a); 98 Stat. 2802, 2804 (Oct. 30, 1984).

ment by scrambling their satellite-carried signals,[705] programmers using foreign satellites may not have done so.[706] If signals carried by foreign satellites are not scrambled, and are not subject to a marketing system,[707] the question remains whether the 1984 amendment protects U.S. dish owners in receiving those signals.

There appears to be nothing in the amendment that precludes its application to foreign satellites. But the programming must be »satellite cable programming,«[708] defined as programming »primarily intended for the direct receipt by cable operators for their retransmission to cable subscribers.«[709] This test apparently would protect the U.S. reception of some signals carried by Canadian satellites, which evidently are transmitted to Canadian »cable operators« similar to cable operators in the United States.[710]

Where the satellites of other countries are concerned, questions arise. Must »cable operators« be private entrepreneurs? Must »cable subscribers« pay separately for the cable service, as distinct from supporting the government that provides the service? An affirmative answer to either question would exclude from the 1984 amendment any programming carried by a foreign satellite to a government-furnished cable system that serves all homes in a given area, as may exist in the Soviet Union and other countries.

There is nothing in the statutory terms »cable operators« or »cable subscribers,« however, that indicates any such limitations.[711] In addition, no reason appears why the purpose of the amendment – to make cable programming available for home-dish reception, unless the signal is scrambled or a marketing plan provided – does not apply to a state-run and state-funded cable operation.

What then if the programming carried by the foreign satellite is distributed, not by cable, but by broadcast stations? In this situation, the 1984 amendment clearly does not apply. It may be suggested, however, that home-dish

705 *See* Broadcasting, Oct. 6, 1986, at 74 (most major cable programmers will have scrambled their satellite feeds by early 1987); Broadcasting, Feb. 2, 1987, at 9 (CBS broadcast network sets July 1987 date to begin scrambling its satellite feed to its affiliates).

706 *See, e.g., infra* text accompanying notes 723–57 (reception of unscrambled Soviet programming).

707 The purpose of the amendment presumably would require that the marketing system be available to viewers in the United States.

708 47 U.S.C. § 705(b) (1985).

709 47 U.S.C. § 705(c)(1) (1985).

710 *See* 1983 Hearings, *supra* note 651, at 20 (statement of David Ladd, Register of Copyrights).

711 »[C]able operators« easily includes a government cable operation. »[C]able subscribers« can mean separately paying subscribers, but can just as well mean more generally the people who receive, and are entitled to receive, the cable service.

reception now is protected by the proviso to section 705, which exempts reception of »any radio communication which is transmitted by any station for the use of the general public.«[712] The argument would be that since broadcasting is defined by the Communications Act as radio communications »intended to be received by the public,«[713] satellite transmissions that result in conventional broadcasts are »for the use of the general public« under the proviso.[714]

In support of the argument, it can be said that nothing in the statutory language prevents treating the broadcast-bound satellite signal as a transmission »for the use of the general public,« especially when the broadcast proceeds simultaneously with reception of the signal by the broadcast station. Further, broadcast networks, like cable networks, are able to protect their satellite signals by scrambling them.[715] If they fail to do so, why shouldn't their signals be fair game in the open sky for home dishes?[716]

Still further, the Communications Act, through its definition of »broadcasting« and its exemption for signals transmitted »for the use of the general public,« arguably embodies a policy of enabling members of the public to have access somehow to broadcast programming. This policy may be offended if members of the U.S. public are prohibited from receiving at their home earth stations, for private viewing, broadcast-bound programs from foreign satellites, when satellite reception is the *only* way those programs can be received in the United States.[717]

712 47 U.S.C. § 705(a) (1985).

713 47 U.S.C. § 153(o) (1985); *see* National Subscription Television v. S & H T.V., 644 F.2d 820, 823 (9th Cir. 1981); Chartwell Communications v. Westbrook, 637 F.2d 459, 465 (6th Cir. 1980).

714 Conventional broadcasts are distinguishable in this respect from subscription broadcasts (STV) intended only for paying subscribers. *See, e.g., id.* It may further be argued with respect to some countries that satellite transmissions destined for cable or other nonbroadcast distribution are likewise »for the use of the general public.« *See infra* note 736.

715 *See supra* note 287.

716 The argument can claim inferential policy support in the Electronic Communications Privacy Act of 1986, Pub. L. No. 99–508, 100 Stat. 4573 (Oct. 21, 1986). This act, while amending the federal anti-wiretapping laws to reach unauthorized interception of new communications technologies, excludes from its coverage the interception of an unscrambled satellite signal »transmitted ... to a broadcasting station for purposes of retransmission to the general public,« provided that the interception is not »for the purposes of direct or indirect commercial advantage or private financial gain.« *Id.* § 101(d)(2), 100 Stat. 4577 (Oct. 21, 1986). The legislative history makes clear, however, that the Act does not authorize any conduct that violates section 705(a) of the Communications Act. *See* H.R. REP. NO. 647, 99th Cong., 2d Sess. 43–44 (1986); 132 CONG. REC. S14,452–53 (daily ed. Oct. 2, 1986) (statement of Sen Mathias); Rice, *supra* note 669, at 437–38.

717 One may reply, however, that if U.S. viewers are too remote to receive the foreign broadcasts, they are not within the »public« that was intended to have access to those broadcasts under either the definition of »broadcasting« or the section 705 proviso.

But the argument confronts major problems. The home earth station receives the signal *from the satellite*. At that point the signal is not being broadcast but is being transmitted point-to-point to the broadcast station. Point-to-point transmission, as distinct from broadcasting, probably was intended to be outside the section 705 proviso.[718] Moreover, the argument would have to apply also to reception of broadcast-network programming from United States domestic satellites. Such an interpretation of the proviso, making it applicable to »satellite broadcast programming,« would seem contrary to the limited congressional intent behind the 1984 »satellite cable programming« amendment.[719] This is especially so because the satellite feeds of the major U.S. broadcast networks lack the commercials that the local stations insert in the programming.[720] Reception of the program signals directly from the satellite thus would undermine the broadcast marketing scheme, a result Congress did not intend.[721]
For these reasons, the argument that the section 705 proviso protects home-dish reception of broadcast-bound programming, whether received from foreign or from U.S. domestic satellites, must be rejected.[722]

(ii) *Reception for academic purposes*

Legally questionable reception of foreign satellite signals is also found increasingly at U.S. universities. According to a 1984 report, »Columbia

718 *See* Cryan & Crane, *supra* note 660, at 859 (section 705, with limited exemption for reception of satellite cable programming, »covers theft of ... ›point-to-point‹ radio messages«). In 1979 the FCC held, and a federal district court agreed, that transmissions by amateur radio operators were not as a general rule »for the use of the general public« under the proviso, in large part because they were point-to-point transmissions. James Reston, Jr., 72 F.C.C.2d 662, 667–68 (1979); Reston v. FCC, 492 F. Supp. 697, 701 n.3, 702 (D.D.C. 1980). As a result section 605 was amended in 1982 to make clear that reception of amateur transmissions is within the proviso: »any radio communication which is transmitted by any station for the use of the general public, which relates to ships, aircraft, vehicles, or persons in distress, or which is transmitted by an amateur radio station operator or by a citizens band radio operator.« 47 U.S.C. § 705(a); *see* Communications Amendments Act of 1982, Pub. L. No. 97–259, Sept. 13, 1982; S. REP. NO. 97–191, 97th Cong., 2d Sess. 8–10 (1981); HOUSE CONFERENCE REPORT NO. 97–765, 97th Cong., 2d Sess. 59–60 (1982).

719 *See* 130 CONG. REC 14,286, 14,287 (Sen. Packwood) (»This authorization is carefully designed as a specific, limited exception to the general liability associated with unauthorized use«); Rice, *supra* note 669, at 426, 433, 438–39.

720 *See* San Francisco Chronicle, June 10, 1985, at 20, *quoted supra* note 702; Rice, *supra* note 669, at 434–35.

721 *Cf.* National Subscription Television v. S & H T.V., 644 F.2d 820, 825 (9th Cir. 1981) (decoding of STV signals would undermine STV marketing scheme).

722 The possibility of a First Amendment right to receive satellite programming is considered in the text accompanying notes 739–54 *infra*.

University has announced that it is receiving up to 15 hours a day of live television programs broadcast internally in Russia.«[723] Having installed an eleven-foot rooftop dish antenna to receive signals from four domestic satellites of the Soviet Union, Columbia reportedly was using the programs for research and teaching purposes.[724] According to a *Wall Street Journal* article in November 1986, a growing number of U.S. universities, cable systems, U.S. government officials and private individuals were receiving Soviet programming.[725] So far as appears, neither Columbia University nor any of the other recipients, with one exception, had obtained the consent of the Soviet originators.[726]

University reception of foreign satellite programming differs from home earth-station reception in at least two legal respects. First, the universities are engaged in an educational and scientific endeavor. If Columbia University were sued by the Soviets for copyright infringement in receiving the satellite programming and if the Soviets otherwise had a good claim under the U.S. copyright law, the educational, scientific and nonprofit nature of Columbia's activity might well provide a »fair use« defense.[727] It is doubtful, however, that the Soviets would have a good claim in the first place. The Copyright Act exempts the »public reception« of a television transmission »on a single receiving apparatus of a kind commonly used in private homes.«[728] Notwithstanding the technical sophistication of the antenna used by Columbia to receive the Soviet programming,[729] the receiving sets

723 Broadcasting, Nov. 5, 1984, at 79.

724 *Id.*

725 *Nyetwork TV, supra* note 702, at 1, col. 4. The article reported that five small companies had been formed »to build and market Soviet TV reception stations and the software to run them.« Some fifteen universities already had the receivers (which sold from $10,000 to $100,000); a dozen more universities planned to buy them in 1987; and »[p]romoters claim no fashionable campus will be without Moscow TV in a few more years.« The United States Information Agency began receiving the signals in June 1986. Meanwhile ten cable companies in large cities, including New York, were planning to carry one week of Soviet programming to test the market. *Id.*

726 The *Wall Street Journal* article reported that one earth-station operator asked the Soviets for permission and received it, in return for arranging a study of U.S. reactions to Soviet television. *Id.*

727 *See* 17 U.S.C. § 107(1), (4) (1985); 17 U.S.C. § 110(2) (exemption for transmission of a work as part of »the systematic instructional activities of a ... nonprofit educational institution,« but limited to nondramatic works). *See also* Harper & Row, Publishers, Inc. v. Nation Enterprises, 105 S. Ct. 2218, 2225–27 (1985).

728 17 U.S.C. § 110(5) (1985); *see* H.R. REP. NO. 94–1476, 94th Cong., 2d Sess. 86–87 (1976); Twentieth Century Music Corp. v. Aiken, 422 U.S. 151, 157 (1975).

729 *See Nyetwork TV, supra* note 702.

on which the programs are shown may well be of a kind commonly used in private homes.[730]

If the Soviets were to have no case against Columbia under the Copyright Act, what about the private action they might bring for violation of section 705 of the Communications Act?[731] Here a second difference between Columbia and the home earth station cuts *against* the university. To the extent that the Soviet programming is distributed to viewers in the U.S.S.R. by cable systems, home earth-station owners in the U.S. probably are protected in receiving the satellite signals by the 1984 amendment to section 705.[732] A university, however, could not claim this protection. The amendment is limited to »private viewing,« defined as viewing for private use »in an individual's dwelling unit.«[733]

Reception of Soviet signals by a U.S. university without consent thus would seem to violate section 705, unless it could find protection in the »use of the general public« proviso.[734] As indicated earlier, that proviso probably does not protect the reception of signals being transmitted point-to-point but only those being broadcast.[735] Hence, even if the signals ultimately are distributed to the Soviet public by broadcasting, the university's reception of them from the Soviet satellite, without the consent of the originator, would still appear to violate section 705.[736]

730 It might also be argued that any performance at Columbia is not »public« (*see* 17 U.S.C. § 106(4)). But the argument would seem precluded by the Act's definition of »publicly« as »at a place open to the public or at any place where a substantial number of persons outside of a normal circle of a family and its social acquaintances is gathered.« 17 U.S.C. § 101.

731 *See* 47 U.S.C. § 705(d)(3) (1985). The U.S. government might also bring a civil or criminal action against Columbia for violating section 705. *See* 47 U.S.C. § 705(d)(1).

732 47 U.S.C. § 705(b), (c) (1985); *see supra* text accompanying notes 286–88.

733 47 U.S.C. § 705(b), (c)(4) (1985).

734 47 U.S.C. § 705(a), (1985); *see supra* note 671 and accompanying text.

735 *See supra* text accompanying notes 717–21.

736 *See supra* note 722 and accompanying text. *If* the reception of satellite signals were within the proviso when the signals ultimately are distributed to the public by broadcasting, one might argue, in the context of Soviet signals, that the proviso should apply regardless of the mode of distribution. In the U.S. context, only broadcasting is considered to be »for the use of the general public,« while cable and other distribution modes are considered commercial, subscriber-supported, limited-audience enterprises. *See* 47 U.S.C. § 153(o); National Subscription Television v. S & H T.V., 644 F.2d 820, 823 (9th Cir. 1981); statement of Senator Packwood, 130 CONG. REC. 14,286, *supra* note 667. In the Soviet Union, however, it may be that all modes of program distribution are state provided and available generally to the public in the area served. If so, any programming transmitted by a Soviet satellite would be »for the use of the general public.« This theory would protect reception not only by universities but also by anyone in the United States. (Cable systems that retransmitted the Soviet programs would remain liable for copyright infringement. *See* 17 U.S.C. § 111(c).) The theory still founders, however, on the likely inapplicability of the section 705 proviso to signals being transmitted point-to-point. *See supra* notes 717–21 and accompanying text.

Are there any other defenses for the university? Perhaps the First Amendment provides a right of access to unscrambled satellite signals, when those signals carry the basic television programming of a nation and when that programming otherwise would be inaccessible for study in the United States.[737] Regardless of whether the »free flow« principle supports a right to broadcast into a country without that country's consent,[738] it may support a right, protected against the U.S. government by the First Amendment, to *receive* from any country television programming transmitted to the public there.[739]

But the claim seems too broad, vague and novel to stand independently on a First Amendment foundation. There is no satisfactory way to define and limit the programming to which the right of access would apply.[740] There is no stopping place short of an unfettered right to receive from any satellite any unscrambled signal carrying »programming.«[741] Programmers indeed can scramble their signals,[742] and the day may come when unscrambled satellite signals are viewed as being in the public domain. It is hard to believe, however, that the First Amendment already goes so far.

The First Amendment interest in university reception of Soviet programming might be accommodated, however, in another, more flexible way. If the educational and nonprofit character of the university's use of the programs would support a fair-use defense to a Soviet claim of copyright infringe-

737 *Cf.* Richmond Newspapers, Inc. v. Virginia, 448 U.S. 555 (1980) (First Amendment right of access to criminal trials); *id.* at 583 (Stevens, J., concurring) (describes decision as holding that »an arbitrary interference with access to important information« abridges First Amendment).

738 *See supra* text accompanying notes 16–19.

739 As one indication of international norms, the Brussels Satellite Convention, *supra* note 676, obligates each signatory to take action against »the *distribution* on or from its territory of any program-carrying signal by any *distributor* for whom the signal emitted to or passing through the satellite is not intended.« Brussels Satellite Convention, art. 2 (emphasis added). The Convention apparently contemplates no action against the simple reception of satellite signals by home viewers.

740 One may ask whether satellite-carried *cable* programming, if unscrambled, would thus be made available by the First Amendment for *nonprivate* viewing, overriding section 705. 47 U.S.C. § 705(a), (b), (c); *see supra* notes 286–88 and accompanying text. Or whether reception of the unscrambled satellite feeds of the U.S. broadcast networks, free of local commercials, would thus become a constitutional right. *See supra* notes 720–21 and accompanying text. Attractive as the latter idea may be, it is hard to find support for it yet in the First Amendment.

741 Indeed, if unscrambled satellite signals are in the public domain, it is hard to see how the right of access can be limited to »programming« and prevented from reaching telephone conversations and other »private« communications.

742 *See supra* note 705 and accompanying text.

ment,[743] a fair-use defense might be read into section 705 as well.[744] Just as the fair-use defense to copyright infringement reflects First Amendment interests,[745] a fair-use defense under section 705 could vindicate the interest in access to a nation's television programming.[746] Fair use could provide a suitably flexible vehicle under section 705, just as it does in copyright law. It could protect reception of satellite programming for »nonprofit, educational purposes« but not reception »of a commercial nature.«[747] It could take into account the effect of the signal reception on the »potential market« for the programming.[748] On this basis the reception of Soviet programming, distributed free across an entire nation, might be protected, while liability was retained for reception of programming distributed by cable systems or other market-based modes.[749]

There is, however, a substantial obstacle to reading a fair-use defense into section 705. Congress has expressly included in section 705 two »fair use« provisions – for »private viewing« of »satellite cable programming,«[750] and for reception of signals transmitted »for the use of the general public.«[751] Especially since the section was amended in this context as recently as 1984,[752] it is a fair inference that no further exceptions were intended.[753] Thus, while the question is debatable, respect for congres-

743 *See supra* note 727 and accompanying text.

744 The fair-use defense originally was read into copyright law by the courts. *See* Harper & Row Publishers, Inc. v. Nation Enterprises, 105 S. Ct. 2218, 2225 (1985). It is true that section 705 is not limited to copyright considerations. It is aimed not simply at the taking of the material but at the way it is taken: by intercepting a communication without the consent of the sender. *See* 47 U.S.C. § 705(a). One would not want to give a wiretapper a fair-use defense under section 705 based on his educational, nonprofit use of the material overheard. In the case of unscrambled signals received from a satellite, however, the element of eavesdropping is much more attenuated. With more than 1.5 million satellite dishes operating in the United States alone, *see supra* note 701 and accompanying text, the reasonable expectation of privacy for an unscrambled signal would seem quite limited. *Cf.* United States v. Ramsey, 431 U.S. 606 (1977) (no justified expectation of privacy as against border search).

745 *See* Harper & Row Publishers, Inc. v. Nation Enterprises, 105 S. Ct. 2218, 2230 (1985):

746 *See supra* notes 737–39 and accompanying text.

747 17 U.S.C. § 107(1) (1982 and Supp. III 1985).

748 17 U.S.C. § 107(4) (1982 and Supp. III 1985).

749 The Brussels Satellite Convention takes a fair-use approach to the unauthorized reception of satellite signals. It provides exemptions for reception of satellite signals carrying »reports of current events,« or used for instructional purposes, or distributed »solely for the purpose of teaching.« Brussels Satellite Convention, *supra* note 676, at art. 4(i), (iii); *see supra* notes 704–17 and accompanying text.

750 47 U.S.C. § 705(b) (1985); *see supra* note 670 and accompanying text.

751 47 U.S.C. § 705(a) (1985); *see supra* note 671 and accompanying text.

752 Pub. L. No. 98–549, §§ 5(a), 6(a), 98 Stat. 2802, 2804 (Oct. 30, 1984); *see supra* notes 284–86 and accompanying text.

753 *See* statement of Senator Packwood, *quoted supra* note 667, concerning the 1984 amendment, 130 CONG. REC. 14,286, 14,287.

sional intent should restrain the courts from reading a fair-use defense into section 705.

Still, a fair-use defense would represent sound public policy. University reception of Soviet programming for educational purposes should not violate United States law. Congress therefore should amend section 705. The amendment might extend the exception already created for »private viewing« of »satellite cable programming«[754] to cover private or educational viewing of any satellite-carried programming, if unscrambled. Alternatively, Congress might simply authorize the courts to apply to the reception of unscrambled satellite signals under section 705 the same principles of fair use that are applied to copyright infringement.

Another possible solution for U.S. universities desiring to receive Soviet programming is to ask the Soviets for permission. In one reported instance where this was done, permission was granted.[755] However, the Federal Communications Commission apparently would take the position that the universities were violating section 705 even if they had the Soviets' permission, as long as they did not also have the FCC's permission pursuant to the INTELSAT consultation process.[756] This FCC interpretation of section 705, erroneous in any event,[757] seems especially inappropriate here. While it stands, however, the FCC's condemnation of even consented-to reception of foreign satellite signals, absent the FCC's own permission, underlines the need for congressional action to establish that reception without consent for appropriate purposes does not violate U.S. law.

(iii) *Reception for retransmission as news*

A third current example of U.S. reception of foreign satellite signals involves reception by a news organization for the purpose of retransmitting the material as news within the United States. This problem will be considered after examining cases in which the reception of foreign satellite signals is specifically permitted by U.S. law.[758]

d. *Permitted reception of foreign satellite signals under U.S. law*

In some situations the FCC has authorized the reception in the United

754 47 U.S.C. § 705(b) (1985); *see supra* note 670 and accompanying text.
755 *See Nyetwork TV, supra* note 702.
756 *See supra* notes 684–87 and accompanying text.
757 *See supra* notes 688–97 and accompanying text.
758 *See infra* notes 770–78 and accompanying text.

States of programming from foreign domestic satellites. Three examples are the FCC's *Transborder* policy; FCC permission given to Cable News Network for continuing reception of Soviet signals; and grants of special temporary authority to Cable News Network for coverage of international news events.

(i) *The FCC's* Transborder *decision*

In its 1981 *Transborder* decision,[759] the FCC permitted owners of earth stations in the United States to receive programming from Canadian domestic satellites (and simultaneously permitted U.S. domestic satellite carriers to provide programming to reception points in Canada, as well as in Central America and the Caribbean). At least some of the proposed reception services,[760] if not all of them,[761] had the consent of the originators.[762]
The FCC determined that the proposed use of U.S. earth stations for international service from a nearby country would be consistent with U.S. law – in particular, the Communications Satellite Act of 1962[763] – and with the U.S. commitment to INTELSAT and its global satellite system.[764] As suggested by the U.S. State Department, the FCC applied two tests for determining whether use of non-INTELSAT facilities for an international service should be approved: (1) whether the INTELSAT global system could

759 Transborder Satellite Video Services, 88 F.C.C.2d 258 (1981).

760 *See id.* at 262, 263.

761 The FCC did not discuss the consent question, possibly implying that consent was present in all cases. *See*, however, the FCC's 1985 final order approving the services, which states that it »does not include the video programming of superstations (WGN, WOR, and WTBS) and other premium pay services (i.e. Showtime etc.) because of copyright concerns.« 220 Television, No. 318-DSE-ML-78, Nov. 22, 1985, para. 4, n.2.

762 The FCC here reiterated its position that reception by a U.S. earth station of a signal from a foreign satellite, even with the consent of the sender, would be »unauthorized,« in violation of section 705 of the Communications Act, if it did not also have the permission of the FCC after the INTELSAT consultation process. 88 F.C.C.2d at 278 & n.26; *see supra* notes 684–87 and accompanying text. This time the FCC sought to bolster the position by relying also on the International Radio Regulations (I.R.R.), in which the members of the International Telecommunication Union agree to prevent »the unauthorized interception of radiocommunication not intended for the general use of the public.« 88 F.C.C.2d at 278 & n.26; ch. VI, Administrative Provisions for Stations, ITU Radio Regulations, Art. 23(a) (1982). But the I.R.R. share with the INTELSAT Agreement a lack of apparent intent, and probably of legal capacity, to impose self-executing criminal sanctions on persons in the U.S. *See supra* notes 691–92 and accompanying text. Moreover, the I.R.R. fall short even of the INTELSAT Agreement in lacking any suggestion that an interception is »unauthorized« when it has the consent of the sender but lacks the permission of the government. *Compare supra* text accompanying note 690.

763 47 U.S.C. §§ 701–44 (1985).

764 88 F.C.C.2d at 271–76.

not provide the service, or (2) whether it would be clearly uneconomical or impractical for that service to use the INTELSAT system.[765] The Commission found that INTELSAT was technically able to provide the transborder services over its satellites but that the use of INTELSAT facilities for these services would be »uneconomical, ... impractical and undesirable.«[766] The FCC's decision was not final; it required that the consultation process under article XIV(d) of the INTELSAT Agreement be pursued before the transborder service could begin.[767] This process took four years, reaching completion (and approval) at the October 1985 meeting of the INTELSAT Assembly of Parties.[768] In November 1985, the FCC issued final grants of authority for the transborder services.[769]

(ii) *FCC approval for continuing reception from Soviet satellites*

In another approval of foreign satellite reception, the FCC permitted a U.S. news organization, Cable News Network, to receive signals from Soviet satellites. In February 1985, CNN sought FCC permission to receive at its Atlanta (Georgia) earth station, located within the footprint of one of the Soviet Union's GHORIZONT satellites, news programming transmitted on the satellite by the Soviet-bloc news agency, Intervision.[770] With Intervision's consent, CNN planned to extract segments for insertion into its own news programming.[771] A few months later, CNN signed a two-year agreement with the U.S.S.R.'s State Committee for Television and Radio (Gostelradio) to exchange news, entertainment and sports programming.[772]

In May 1985, the FCC, applying its *Transborder* standards, approved CNN's request.[773] The approval was conditioned on consultation by the U.S. with INTELSAT pursuant to article XIV(d) of the INTELSAT Agreement.[774] It was also made subject to: (a) possible modification »as a result of consultation with the Secretary of State on foreign, political and related matters«; and (b) »express immediate revocation without hearing«

765 *Id.* at 279–81.
766 *Id.* at 280–81.
767 *Id.* at 284.
768 *See* 220 Television, No. 318-DSE-ML-78, Nov. 22, 1985, para. 1.
769 *See id.*, paras. 1, 3, 4. The FCC previously had issued some authorizations based on the January 1985 INTELSAT meeting. *Id.*
770 GHORIZONT, *supra* note 688, at paras. 1, 3.
771 *Id.* at para. 3.
772 Broadcasting, June 3, 1985, at 129.
773 GHORIZONT, *supra* note 688, at paras. 6–10; *see supra* notes 759–69 and accompanying test.
774 GHORIZONT, *supra* note 688, at para. 11.

if the FCC, in consultation with the Secretary of State, should determine that revocation was »in the public and national interest.«[775]

In October 1985, the INTELSAT Assembly of Parties approved the CNN proposal.[776] Meanwhile the State Department had also given approval, subject to two added conditions: (a) that CNN be required to submit to the FCC and the State Department »a report covering the first five months of usage of the Soviet signal in terms of CNN air time and CNN's understanding of any Soviet use of CNN news programming«; and (b) that the license be granted for only six months, »with renewal requiring a favorable foreign policy finding made by the Department of State.«[777]

In November 1985, the FCC, though noting that the six-month term would be »considerably shorter than the term that can be granted under the Communications Act,« decided to »defer to the State Department because of the important foreign policy considerations that are involved here.« It thus gave final approval to CNN's application on the conditions proposed by the State Department.[778]

(iii) *Special temporary approvals for news coverage*

The FCC also has sometimes granted »special temporary authority« (STA) to receive a foreign satellite signal for the purpose of news coverage of a particular event. In 1984 the Commission granted an STA to Turner Broadcasting System (parent of Cable News Network) to receive from Canada's Anik B satellite coverage of the Pope's visit to Canada.[779] In this and other cases involving Canada, the FCC found that no further steps were necessary. Bilateral coordination was provided by a 1982 exchange of letters between the U.S. and Canada governing the transborder use of U.S. and Canadian domestic satellites, and INTELSAT coordination was pro-

775 *Id.*

776 *See In re* Cable News Network, File No. 907-DSE-L-85, Nov. 15, 1985, para. 3.

777 *Id.* at para. 3. The State Department's determination would be based in part on CNN's report. *Id.*

778 *Id.* at paras. 4–10. Subsequently, CNN asked the FCC for a six-month extension of the license, explaining that the earth station had not yet been contructed because the planned site had proved unavailable. In September 1986, the FCC granted the extension. *In re* Cable News Network, Inc., File No. 907-DSE-L-85, Sept. 22, 1986. In doing so, it noted, and adopted, the State Department's further stipulation that CNN's report on its use of Soviet programming and Soviet use of its programming must be submitted prior to any renewal of the license. *Id.* at para. 5. *See supra* note 777 and accompanying text.

779 *See* Turner Comments, *supra* note 688, at 6.

vided by INTELSAT's approval in 1982 of U.S.-Canada transborder services.[780]

Also in 1984, the FCC granted Turner an STA to receive from a Soviet satellite coverage of the Soviet bloc's »Friendship Games.«[781] This time it could not be said that INTELSAT coordination had been accomplished in advance. But the FCC, stressing the immediacy of the need and the limited duration of the use, nonetheless made the STA effective immediately, without going through the INTELSAT process.[782] In 1985 the FCC granted Turner an STA to receive from a Soviet satellite coverage of the Soviet Union's 40th anniversary celebration of the end of the Second World War, again without waiting for the INTELSAT coordination process.[783]

These STA grants have made INTELSAT increasingly unhappy. INTELSAT charges that the FCC, by its willingness to bypass the coordination process, demonstrates its lack of understanding of U.S. obligations under the INTELSAT Agreement.[784] In INTELSAT's view, it is not the FCC, but only INTELSAT's Assembly of Parties acting as part of the coordination process, that has authority to determine such questions as economic harm to INTELSAT from the proposed service.[785]

This clash between the FCC and INTELSAT over the granting of STAs illustrates the tension, indeed the fundamental inconsistency, built into this area of U.S. law. A process requiring not only advance approval by the U.S. government but also protracted coordination with INTELSAT cannot be squared with the journalistic demands of reporting news events. Whether such a process can be squared with the First Amendment is considered next.

e. Constitutional problems in the U.S. law governing reception from foreign satellites

There are First Amendment problems in a U.S. legal rule that compels a news organization, such as Cable News Network, to apply to the FCC for permission to carry on-the-scene coverage of particular news events. The need to get a government license in order to report a news event would

780 *See* Turner Comments, *supra* note 688, at 6; *In re* applications of Cable News Network, Inc. for modification of radio station license to add the ANIK-B satellite as a point of communication (»Anik-B Proceeding«), FCC File Nos. 2409-DSE-ML-84, 2410-DSE-ML-84, Dec. 6, 1984, para. 5.

781 *See* Turner Comments, *supra* note 688, at 6 n.2

782 *See id.*

783 Broadcasting, June 3, 1985, at 84.

784 *Id.* (reported statement of INTELSAT deputy director).

785 *Id.*

seem to be a classic »prior restraint« forbidden by the First Amendment.[786]

In 1985 the Turner Broadcasting System urged the FCC to lift the rule. Commenting in an FCC proceeding concerning the rebroadcasting of radio transmissions,[787] Turner sought a ruling »that it does not violate Section 605 to rebroadcast brief excerpts of programming obtained from foreign satellites, without FCC approval, but with the consent of the signal originator.«[788] Turner urged the FCC to conclude that »tapping into« foreign satellite programming, with the consent of the originator, for the purpose of retransmitting brief portions as part of bona fide news programming was a »modified fair use« that did not require INTELSAT coordination at all.[789] Alternatively, Turner said the United States should ask INTELSAT to coordinate such use by news organizations on a »generic« basis »for all present and future non-INTELSAT satellites.«[790]

Turner's argument, which was opposed by the Communications Satellite

786 *See* Near v. Minnesota, 283 U.S. 697, 713–14 (1931); Grosjean v. American Press Co., 297 U.S. 233, 245–50 (1936); Nebraska Press Ass'n v. Stuart, 427 U.S. 539, 590 n.17 (1976) (Brennan, J., concurring). Among the different kinds of prior restraint, this one recalls the licensing scheme of 17th-century England, which the First Amendment was especially intended to repudiate. *See* Emerson, *The Doctrine of Prior Restraint*, 20 LAW & CONTEMP. PROB. 648, 650 (1955); Pittsburgh Press Co. v. Pittsburgh Comm'n on Human Relations, 413 U.S. 376, 390 (1973).
The First Amendment objections become concrete when the government arranges the prior-licensing requirement in the way the FCC did, at the request of the State Department, in ruling on Turner's application for continuing authority to receive programming from Soviet satellites. *See supra* notes 775–78 and accompanying text. When the license term is made as brief as six months, with a report required from the licensee on its use of Soviet programming and Soviet use of its programming, and when renewal is conditioned on »a favorable foreign policy finding made by the Department of State« (*see supra* text accompanying note 777), the licensee is put on notice that its permission to carry such news will not be continued if the arrangement does not satisfy the U.S. government.

787 Rebroadcasts, *supra* note 678.

788 Turner Comments, *supra* note 688, at i (Summary). Turner pointed out that the INTELSAT approval process »can take from one and a half to three years,« and that if Turner bypassed the INTELSAT process it would »risk the sanctions – both civil and criminal – that could be imposed pursuant to Section 605.« *Id.* at 5,7. Acknowledging that there were special facilitating arrangements between the U.S. and Canada, Turner said: »The problem for a U.S. news organization is that news events are fast-breaking and unpredictable and do not all originate in Canada.« *Id.* at 5–6.

789 *Id.* at 7–8. Turner pointed out that in copyright law, »›fair use‹ can be made of copyrighted material even without consent of the copyright holder,« and said it was seeking only the ability to use material from foreign satellites with the consent of the originator but without prior FCC approval. *Id.* at 7. *Cf. supra* text accompanying notes 743–54 (possible fair-use defense under section 705 without consent of originator).

790 Turner Comments, *supra* note 688, at 9 n.3

Corporation (Comsat),[791] failed to engage the FCC. »[T]he issues with respect to United States treaty obligations and international agreements raised in Turner's request are beyond the scope of this proceeding,« the FCC found, refusing to rule on Turner's request.[792] The Commission claimed it was taking no position on the request, but it noted that »once a licensee has obtained clear authority from the Commission to receive and use foreign satellite programming, there is no bar to rebroadcasting such programming.«[793] The implication seemed clear that licensees like Turner were expected to obtain that »clear authority from the Commission.«

Turner's position, however, was well taken. The First Amendment means, the Supreme Court has said, that journalists are »free to seek out sources of information not available to members of the general public,« and that »government cannot restrain the publication of news emanating from such sources.«[794] When a news organization must get the government's permission to use on-the-scene television footage obtained abroad – regardless of whether it must also wait while the government pursues a diplomatic consultation process – the organization's news coverage, if not restrained, is delayed and burdened in a way offensive to the First Amendment.[795]

To be sure, the FCC bases its position on the obligations of the United States under the INTELSAT Agreement.[796] Ratified treaties like the INTELSAT Agreement are law in the United States.[797] In case of con-

791 *See* Rebroadcasts, *supra* note 678, at 43 (para. 34). Comsat argued that Turner's request was inconsistent with the FCC's established position on »blanket authority to intercept foreign satellites,« and further that it introduced questions of »United States treaty obligations and other national and foreign policy interests« that went beyond the specified issues in the FCC's proceeding. *Id.* at 43 (para. 34). (Comsat is the designated U.S. representative to INTELSAT. *See* 100 F.C.C.2d 250 n.5 (1984).)

792 Rebroadcasts, *supra* note 678, at 43–44 (para. 35).

793 *Id.*

794 Pell v. Procunier, 417 U.S. 817, 834 (1974). The amendment prevents government from »limiting the stock of information from which members of the public may draw.« First Nat'l Bank of Boston v. Bellotti, 435 U.S. 765, 783 (1978). *See also* United States v. Associated Press, 52 F. Supp. 362, 372 (S.D.N.Y. 1943), *aff'd*, 326 U.S. 1 (1944) (L. Hand, J.) (»the dissemination of news from as many different sources, and with as many different facets and colors as is possible«). In FCC v. League of Women Voters, 468 U.S. 364 (1984), the Supreme Court struck down a restriction on editorializing by public broadcasters, noting that editorial opinion »lies at the heart of First Amendment protection.« *Id.* at 381. News coverage, whether domestic or foreign, also lies at the heart of First Amendment protection. *See* New York Times Co. v. United States, 403 U.S. 713 (1971).

795 *See, e.g.*, Nebraska Press Ass'n v. Stuart, 427 U.S. 539, 609 & n. 38 (1976) (Brennan, J., concurring); New York Times Co. v. United States, 403 U.S. 713, 715 (1971) (Black, J.) (First Amendment violated by »every moment's continuance« of a restraint on publication that did *not* involve a fast-breaking news story).

796 *See, e.g.*, Earth Stations, *supra* note 678, at 219, n. 27.

797 U.S. CONST., art. VI; United States v. The Schooner Peggy, 1 Cranch. 103, 109–10 (U.S. 1801).

flict, however, they must give way to the Constitution.[798] Such a conflict is presented by the rule requiring FCC permission before a U.S. news organization can obtain news coverage from a foreign satellite, even with the consent of the originator.

f. *The right to rebroadcast programming received from a foreign satellite*

Apart from the right to receive programming from a foreign satellite, there is a separate question about the right to retransmit that programming in the United States – as Cable News Network would do by including excerpts of Soviet news programming in its own news coverage.[799] Until recently, FCC regulations were confusing on the point.[800] But CNN, in its various applications for FCC permission to receive programming from foreign satellites, apparently had never considered it necessary to ask separate permission to retransmit the programming received. Such a requirement might indeed be an impermissible prior restraint, not on the gathering of news, but on its publication.[801]

In any event the answer is now clear. In a 1985 ruling, the FCC stated: »[O]nce a licensee has obtained clear authority from the Commission to receive and use foreign satellite programming, there is no bar to rebroadcasting such programming.«[802] Thus, United States law poses obstacles to the reception of programming from foreign satellites but not to the retransmission of that programming once legally received.

g. *Summary concerning U.S. reception of signals from foreign satellites*

Two points stand out from this examination of U.S. law concerning reception of programming from foreign satellites. First, reception of such programming in the United States, even for private viewing at home or for academic purposes, may well be unlawful under section 705 of the Communications Act if done without the consent of the originator. It appears to be lawful only if the reception is for private viewing and if the programming is distributed in its home country by cable.[803] Beyond that, one can argue (a) that the reception is lawful because the programming is transmitted »for

798 Kinsella v. United States, 361 U.S. 234 (1960).
799 *See supra* text accompanying notes 770–78.
800 *See* 47 C.F.R. § 73.1207(b)(4), (c) (1984); *see also* 47 U.S.C. § 325(a) (1985).
801 *See, e.g.*, New York Times Co. v. United States, 403 U.S. 713 (1971).
802 Rebroadcasts, *supra* note 678, at 43–44 (para. 35).
803 *See supra* text accompanying notes 704–11.

the use of the general public« under the proviso to section 705; or (b) that a »fair use« defense should be read into section 705 for the reception of programming used for nonprofit educational purposes.[804] However, both arguments are likely to fail, and should fail, under section 705 as presently written.[805] A First Amendment right to receive unscrambled satellite signals without the consent of the originator also seems untenable at this time, though one day it may be recognized.[806]

Second, the FCC claimes that reception of foreign satellite signals *with* the consent of the originator is illegal under section 705, unless approved by the FCC pursuant to the INTELSAT Agreement.[807] The FCC takes this position even with respect to reception by a news organization for the purpose of news reporting in the United States.[808] The FCC's claim stands on weak ground, however, both as an interpretation of section 705 and as a restriction of First Amendment speech.[809]

4. *Possible U.S. Restrictions on Foreign DBS Broadcasts into the United States*

There appear to be no existing provisions of United States law that expressly apply to foreign direct-broadcast satellites (DBS) or to the broadcasts they might make into the United States. In addition, no such satellites are as yet in existence. Assuming, however, that a foreign DBS existed and were broadcasting, or claiming the right to broadcast, into the United States, one could ask whether existing U.S. law would be hospitable to those broadcasts or whether it might be invoked against them.

There is a certain hospitality. Section 705 of the Federal Communications Act, which prohibits unauthorized reception of radio communications, exempts »any radio communication which is transmitted by any station for the use of the general public,«[810] a protection that presumably would cover foreign DBS broadcasts.[811] The First Amendment also might pre-

804 *See supra* text accompanying notes 712–21, 743–49.

805 *See supra* text accompanying notes 722, 736, 750–53; *but cf. supra* text accompanying notes 754–57.

806 *See supra* notes 737–42 and accompanying text.

807 *E.g.*, Earth Stations, *supra* note 678, at 219 n.27.

808 *See supra* notes 786–93 and accompanying text.

809 *See supra* notes 794–98 and accompanying text.

810 47 U.S.C. § 705(a) (1985).

811 *See supra* note 714 and accompanying text.

vent the government from restricting reception of such broadcasts.[812] Neither of these protections for broadcast reception, however, necessarily would preclude the U.S. government from taking measures, unilaterally or internationally, to regulate the broadcasts or prevent them from taking place. Various provisions of U.S. law could be invoked to support such measures. Many of these provisions have already been mentioned, but they are collected here with specific reference to foreign DBS.

a. *Restrictions on foreign involvement in U.S. communications*

(i) *Foreign-ownership restrictions*

Section 310 of the Federal Communications Act prohibits ownership of U.S. broadcast stations, or more than twenty-percent control of them, by foreigners or foreign governments.[813] This prohibition has been applied by the FCC to licensees of *domestic* DBS.[814] FCC licensing presumably applies only to frequencies controlled by the United States, so foreign DBS operators presumably would not be subject to section 310 or to the domestic DBS regulatory scheme.[815] But if a foreign DBS were broadcasting into the United States, as it readily could,[816] the policy behind the U.S. ownership restrictions arguably would be undermined by foreign ownership of such a facility.[817] The argument is readily resisted. As noted earlier,[818] the national-security considerations thought to require the banning of foreign ownership of United States communications facilities were based on fears of hostile use in wartime and were concerned with the total capability of those facilities, not simply with their ability to broadcast to a United States audience.[819] Especially when the broadcasts come from »foreign« communications facilities, it might be recognized as beyond the legitimate concern of the United States to insist, or try to insist, that the facilities be under U.S. ownership.

812 *See* Lamont v. Postmaster General, 381 U.S. 301 (1965); *supra* notes 739–42 and accompanying text.
813 47 U.S.C. § 310(a), (b) (1985); *see supra* note 550 and accompanying text.
814 47 C.F.R. § 100.11 (1985); *see supra* notes 572, 579–80 and accompanying text.
815 *See* Comment, *supra* note 577, at 524.
816 *See* Hagelin, *supra* note 18, at 269; Magraw, *supra* note 18, at 29.
817 *See* Price, *supra* note 18, at 900.
818 *See supra* notes 551–56 and accompanying text.
819 *See* Attribution of Ownership Interests, 97 F.C.C.2d 997, 1009 (1984); Note, *supra* note 591, at 116 ff; *supra* note 576 and accompanying text.

(ii) *Foreign »political propaganda«*

The Foreign Agents Registration Act[820] provides that when an »agent of a foreign principal« disseminates material in the United States that is designed to influence its recipients concerning the policies of the United States or a foreign nation, that material is »political propaganda« and must be labeled, filed, and reported to the U.S. government as such.[821] The Justice Department regulations make it clear that FARA applies to material »televised or broadcast« by such an agent.[822] The question thus arises whether a foreign DBS operator broadcasting into the United States would be subject to FARA's requirements.

Under the present statute, the answer seems to be no. The broadcasts would come directly from the satellite to U.S. homes, with no »agent« distributing them in the United States. The DBS operator itself might be an »agent of a foreign principal,« but the DBS operator would not be acting »within the United States,« as the statute requires.[823]

On the other hand, the purpose of FARA – to advise the U.S. public about the source of foreign »political propaganda« disseminated to them[824] – certainly would apply to DBS broadcasts. So if Congress adheres to that purpose, and if FARA survives constitutional attack,[825] the Act might be amended to impose its requirements on foreign DBS broadcasts (and perhaps other broadcasts)[826] into the United States. The impracticality and presumptuousness of such a move, however, might strengthen the case for dismantling FARA's »political propaganda« requirements.[827]

820 22 U.S.C. §§ 611–21 (1985); *see supra* notes 419–70 and accompanying text.

821 22 U.S.C. §§ 611(c), (j), 614(a), (b), (c) (1985).

822 28 C.F.R. § 5.402(d) (1986) (»[p]olitical propaganda ... which is televised or broadcast, or which is caused to be televised or broadcast, by an agent of a foreign pricipal, shall be introduced by a statement which is reasonably adapted to convey to the viewers or listeners thereof such information as is required under section 4(b) of the Act«).

823 22 U.S.C. §§ 611(c)(1), 614(a), (b). *See* Note, *supra* note 433, at 440; Note, *Government Exclusion of Foreign Political Propaganda*, 68 HARV. L. REV. 1393, 1398 (1955); Schwartz & Paul, *Foreign Communist Propaganda in the Mails: A Report on Some Problems of Federal Censorship*, 107 U.PA. L. REV. 621, 626 (1959).

824 *See supra* note 460 and accompanying text.

825 It now has. *See* Meese v. Keene, 107 S. Ct. 1862 (1987), *supra* note 470.

826 There would be no clear reason to limit such an amendment to DBS broadcasts. The same purpose might well apply, for example, to the Soviet programming brought into the United States by Cable News Network (*see supra* notes 770–778 and accompanying text), or, for that matter, to British Broadcasting Corporation (BBC) programs shown on U.S. television.

827 *See supra* notes 457–70 and accompanying text.

b. *Policies underlying the regulation of U.S. broadcasting*

(i) *Effects of a new service on the existing system*

In administering and interpreting the Federal Communications Act, the FCC and the courts have been solicitous of certain values built into the U.S. broadcast system. These values include »local service,«[828] a diversity of program sources[829] and advertiser-supported »free« programming.[830] When cable television began to grow in the 1960s, for example, it was held back by the FCC on the ground that it threatened local broadcasting.[831] Before authorizing domestic DBS service, the FCC weighed the potential benefits of that service against the potential adverse impact on existing licensees, particularly on the ability of existing licensees to provide local service.[832]

It would be at odds with this policy and tradition to allow foreign DBS to broadcast into the United States without first considering the potential effects on the existing U.S. broadcast system.[833] Rather than stand by and let foreign DBS operators threaten the long-nurtured values of that system, the United States could be expected, through international negotiations or other means, to seek limitations or prohibitions on foreign DBS in order to protect those values.

(ii) *Content controls*

Incoming DBS broadcasts also would challenge U.S. restrictions on broadcast content. »Obscenity,« which is not protected by the U.S. Constitution

828 *See, e.g.*, Public Service Responsibility of Broadcast Licensees (»Blue Book«), FCC, 1956 (broadcast station »a sort of mouthpiece on the air for the community it serves,« *quoting* Great Lakes Broadcasting Co., Federal Radio Commission Docket No. 4900, 1928); Sixth Report and Order, Television Allocations, 41 F.C.C. 1967 (1952) (first priority: to provide at least one television service to all parts of the U.S.; second priority: to provide each community with at least one television broadcast station); FCC v. Sanders Brothers Radio Station, 309 U.S. 470, 475 (1940); Carroll Broadcasting Co. v. FCC, 258 F.2d 440 (D.C. Cir. 1958).

829 *See, e.g.*, Multiple Ownership of Standard, FM, and Television Broadcast Stations, 22 F.C.C.2d 306 (1970); on reconsideration, 28 F.C.C.2d 662 (1971). *See generally* R. NOLL, M. PECK & J. MCGOWAN, ECONOMIC ASPECTS OF TELEVISION REGULATION 99 (1973).

830 *See, e.g.*, Subscription Television Service, 15 F.C.C.2d 466 (1968).

831 *See* United States v. Southwestern Cable Co., 392 U.S. 157, 175–77 (1968).

832 Direct Broadcast Satellites, 90 F.C.C.2d 676, 680–83, 684–92 (1982).

833 *See* Hagelin, *supra* note 18, at 290; Price, *supra* note 18, at 892 ff.

in any medium,[834] is prohibited in broadcasting by one U.S. statute[835] and made a ground for FCC license suspension by another.[836] Moreover, the Supreme Court has held that language that is »indecent,« though not »obscene,« may be prohibited in broadcasting, although in other media it has First Amendment protection.[837] Special content controls are justified in broadcasting, the Court has said, by the »pervasiveness« of the medium and its accessibility to children,[838] both attributes that would hold true for foreign DBS broadcasts.

The FCC also has used less formal powers in the name of protecting the public, especially children, from »offensive« programming of various kinds. After the FCC began receiving complaints about »drug-oriented« song lyrics, for example, it warned broadcasters that their public-interest responsibilities required them to pre-screen the lyrics of the songs they broadcast,[839] a warning well calculated to take the offending songs off the air.

United States law thus embodies strong concerns about obscene, indecent or otherwise offensive content in broadcasting. Foreign DBS broadcasts could well carry material unacceptable by U.S. standards.[840] It seems unlikely that the U.S. would remain passive as a »free flow« of offensive programming from a foreign DBS operation washed over the U.S. broadcast audience. The United States could be expected to try to regulate or prevent such broadcasts not only because of their own content but also to protect the integrity and effectiveness of U.S. domestic broadcast regulation. It would be pointless to regulate domestic broadcasting while foreign DBS broadcasts went unrestrained.

(iii) *»Political« obligations*

United States law imposes on broadcasters three major obligations to support public debate and the political process. The »fairness doctrine« requires broadcasters, once they have aired one point of view on a controversial issue of public importance, to give reasonable coverage to opposing

834 Roth v. United States, 354 U.S. 476 (1957).
835 18 U.S.C. § 1464 (1985).
836 47 U.S.C. § 303(m)(1)(D) (1984).
837 FCC v. Pacifica Foundation, 438 U.S. 726 (1978). The Court defined »indecent« as involving »nonconformance with accepted standards of morality.« *Id.* at 740.
838 *Id.* at 748–49.
839 *See* Yale Broadcasting Co. v. FCC, 478 F.2d 594, (D.C. Cir. 1973), *cert. denied*, 414 U.S. 914 (1973) (upholding the FCC action).
840 *See* Price, *supra* note 18, at 900-01.

points of view on that issue.[841] Second, broadcasters must give or sell »reasonable amounts of time« to candidates for federal political office during their campaigns.[842] Third, after providing air time to one candidate for a public office, a broadcaster must give »equal opportunities« to all other candidates for that office.[843]

The significance of these obligations in the U.S. system of broadcast regulation has been underscored in the very context of DBS. In its 1982 decision authorizing domestic DBS,[844] the FCC, in order to minimize the regulatory burden on the new service, declared that the classification of a DBS operator as either »broadcaster« or »common carrier« under the Communications Act would depend on how the operator functioned.[845] If the operator provided its own programming, it probably would be regulated as a broadcaster and thus be subject to the »political« obligations.[846] If the operator leased its transmission facilities to other programmers, it would be regulated as a common carrier and thus be required to lease without discrimination to all comers.[847] In the latter case, the FCC indicated, neither the DBS operator nor the programmer would be treated as a broadcaster and be subject to the »political« obligations of broadcast regulation.[848]

The FCC met a stiff rebuke on this point from the court of appeals.[849] Reversing this part of the Commission's order, the court quoted a statement from the legislative history of the 1927 Radio Act declaring that unless regulatory obligations were imposed on broadcasters, »American thought and American politics will be largely at the mercy of those who operate these stations.«[850] The court emphasized that »DBS, with its power to reach into every home in the United States, has a potential impact far in excess of the limited radio services« with which Congress was originally concerned.[851] Under the FCC's approach, the court continued, a well-funded candidate »could purchase enough time on a broadcast station operated as a common carrier to dominate American thought and

841 Fairness Report, 48 F.C.C.2d 1 (1974) [the FCC repealed the fairness doctrine in August 1987; *see supra* note 146]; *see* Red Lion Broadcasting Co. v. FCC, 395 U.S. 367 (1969).

842 47 U.S.C. § 312(a)(7) (1985); *see* CBS v. FCC, 453 U.S. 367 (1981).

843 47 U.S.C. § 315 (1985).

844 Direct Broadcast Satellites, 90 F.C.C.2d 676 (1982).

845 *Id.* at 708–09.

846 *Id.* at 709.

847 *Id.*

848 *Id.* at 709–11.

849 NAB v. FCC, 740 F.2d 1190 (D.C. Cir. 1984).

850 *Id.* at 1202.

851 *Id.*

American politics without any regulatory restraints.«[852] It was to avoid such a result »that Congress imposed restraints such as the equal opportunity rule upon broadcasters.«[853] Hence the court required the FCC to impose the regulatory obligations of a broadcaster on someone, either the DBS operator or its programmer-customer.[854]

The court's concerns would apply equally to foreign DBS. An unregulated foreign DBS operation could discriminate among candidates for U.S. political office in terms of access, equal opportunities and editorial support, free of any legal obligation to provide reply time. Given the enormous geographic range and the number of channels that DBS could command,[855] the intrusion into the U.S. political process could be substantial. The United States could not readily accept a »free flow« so jarring to the rules it has established for the political process by which the nation governs itself.

c. *Summary concerning foreign DBS*

Foreign DBS broadcasts into the United States, uncontrolled and unregulated by the United States, would pose fundamental challenges to U.S. broadcast regulation and its underlying policies. The United States accordingly could be expected to resist foreign DBS operations or to seek to regulate them.[856] The U.S. interest in preventing or regulating such broadcasts would be reinforced not only by the practical difficulty of preventing reception once the broadcasts took place but also by the likelihood that reception in the United States would be protected by the existing section 705 of the Communications Act and quite possibly by the First Amendment as well.[857]

852 *Id.* at 1203.
853 *Id.*
854 *Id.* at 1205. *See also* United States Satellite Broadcasting Co. v. FCC, 740 F.2d 1177, 1187 (D.C. Cir. 1984).
855 *See* NAB v. FCC, 740 F.2d at 1202.
856 *See*, Hagelin, *supra* note 18, at 290–91; Price, *supra* note 18, at 887; Magraw, *supra* note 18, at 27, 30.
857 *See supra* notes 712–17, 738–39 and accompanying text.

Chapter VI: Regulation of Media Flow Out of the United States

A. *Regulation of Outgoing Information Flow in General*

If there is surprisingly little United States law on the application of the First Amendment to information flowing into the United States,[858] there is even less on information flowing out of the country. There appears to be only one court decision directly in point: the 1986 ruling by a federal district court in *Bullfrog Films, Inc. v. Wick.*[859] In that case, involving the U.S. government's certification of films as »educational« for the purpose of duty-free import to other countries under the Beirut Agreement,[860] the court squarely considered »whether the First Amendment applies with equal force to communications directed toward foreign audiences as it does to domestic communications.«[861]

The U.S. government took the position in *Bullfrog Films* that »the exercise of free speech within foreign nations by Americans is subordinate to significant foreign policy considerations and, as such, subject to reasonable regulation.«[862] The court disagreed. Analyzing *Haig v. Agee*[863] and other Supreme Court »right to travel« cases relied on by the government,[864] the court found that they did not establish a lower level of constitutional protection for speech by Americans abroad than for domestic speech.[865]

However that may be, speech by Americans abroad is not necessarily the same as speech by Americans in the United States to audiences abroad.

858 *See supra* text accompanying notes 786–98.

859 646 F. Supp. 492, 502 (C.D. Cal. 1986), *appeal docketed,* No. 86–6630 (9th Cir.).

860 *See supra* notes 405–18 and accompanying text; *infra* notes 910–35 and accompanying text.

861 646 F. Supp. at 502.

862 *Id.* at 503, Previously, in Haig v. Agee, 453 U.S. 280 (1981), *see supra* text accompanying notes 377–78, the government had told the Supreme Court that the secretary of state could refuse to issue a passport to a U.S. citizen who proposed to go to a foreign nation to denounce U.S. policy toward that nation, since »the freedom of speech that we enjoy domestically may be different from that that we can exercise in this context.« 453 U.S. at 319 n.9 (Brennan, J., dissenting) (quoting oral argument of solicitor general).

863 453 U.S. 280 (1981).

864 *E.g.*, Regan v. Wald, 468 U.S. 222 (1984); Zemel v. Rusk, 381 U.S. 1 (1965); Kent v. Dulles, 357 U.S. 116 (1958).

865 676 F. Supp. at 503–04.

When media content flows from the United States to other countries, what crosses the border is »pure speech,« unencumbered by the movement of persons and by such attendant government powers as the control of foreign travel.[866] When what *enters* the United States is speech alone, like the mail in *Lamont*,[867] the protection afforded by the First Amendment may be substantially stronger than it is, for example, when what enters is live foreign visitors, subject to the government's power to exclude aliens.[868] Similarly, the constitutional protection of outgoing speech may be stronger when the speaker remains in the United States and pure transborder speech is involved.

Still, the audience is foreign, and this fact arguably undercuts the First Amendment claim. If the chief purpose of the First Amendment is to let truth prevail in the marketplace of ideas,[869] and specifically to enable Americans to enlighten themselves in order to govern themselves,[870] these objectives arguably do not apply when the audience is foreign. The government thus contended in *Bullfrog Films*: »the world at large is not a ›First Amendment forum.‹«[871]

The government was wrong. When the audience is foreign, the constitutional protection accorded to speech should not be diminished. In the first place, what the Constitution protects is »freedom of speech.«[872] It would elevate the asserted purpose of the First Amendment over the Amendment itself to deny protection to the speaker or the speech because of the location or nationality of the audience.[873] Second, facilitating the search for truth, political or otherwise, is not the only respected purpose of the First

866 *See, e.g.*, Haig v. Agee, 453 U.S. at 306–09.

867 Lamont v. Postmaster General, 381 U.S. 301; *see supra* text accompanying notes 308–13.

868 *See, e.g.*, Kleindienst v. Mandel, 408 U.S. at 762–65; *supra* text accompanying notes 346–58.

869 *See, e.g.*, Abrams v. United States, 250 U.S. 616, 630 (1919) (Holmes, J. dissenting); T. EMERSON, *supra* note 26, at 6.

870 *See, e.g.*, Whitney v. California, 274 U.S. 357, 375–77 (Brandeis, J., concurring); A. MEIKLEJOHN, *supra* note 28, at 37–39; T. EMERSON, *supra* note 26, at 6–8; Carey v. Brown, 447 U.S. 455, 467 (1980):

871 646 F. Supp, at 503 n.16. The government additionally contended, as stated by the court, »that when United States citizens direct their speech at foreign audiences, the government may regulate such speech on the basis of content; further, that the traditional standards for determining if a law is unconstitutionally vague should be relaxed when foreign audiences are involved, since the government must be permitted to fashion foreign affairs-related regulations in a broad manner.« *Id.* at 503.

872 U.S. CONST. amend. I.

873 As the court in *Bullfrog Films* said with respect to an American speaking abroad: »[T]he government obviously could not constitutionally prohibit, say, an American professor of political science from expressing his or her opinions before an international symposium in Paris on the ground that his or her foreign listeners do not participate in the American political process.« 646 F. Supp. at 506–07.

Amendment. In addition to the social ends served by freedom of expression, »[s]peech is protected not as a means to a collective good but because of the value of the speech conduct to the individual.«[874] This purpose applies regardless of the nationality, the location or perhaps even the existence of the audience.

Third, the world at large *is* a First Amendment forum. The interdependence of nations and the worldwide reach of communications media in today's world make the »marketplace of ideas« no less international than the marketplace of trade. Political, military, economic and other decisions made abroad can affect the United States almost as readily as decisions made in the United States. Speech conveyed from the United States to a foreign audience can have an impact, directly or indirectly, on domestic debate in the United States.[875]

The court in *Bullfrog Films* thus correctly concluded that »in the absence of some overriding governmental interest such as national security, the First Amendment protects communications with foreign audiences to the same extent as communications within our borders.«[876]

Against that background, the following sections review the relatively few pertinent provisions of U.S. law that restrict information flowing out of the country.

1. *Restrictions on International Mail*

Although a U.S. restriction on incoming mail was held to violate the First Amendment in *Lamont v. Postmaster General*,[877] in handling outgoing mail the United States stands ready to enforce restrictions adopted by other countries.

This readiness is found in a provision of the Foreign Agents Registration Act authorizing the U.S. Post Office to block politically inflammatory mail

874 Baker, *supra* note 30, at 966; *see* Whitney v. California, 274 U.S. at 375 (Brandeis, J. concurring); T. EMERSON, *supra* note 26, at 3–11; *Bullfrog Films*, 646 F. Supp. at 507 (»Speech concerning public affairs is more than a tool of self-government; it is also an essential form of self-expression«).

875 *Cf. Bullfrog Films*, 646 F. Supp. at 503 n.16 (»matters occurring abroad, e.g., government ›news leaks‹ to the foreign press, are likely to find their way into this country and become a part of our domestic political debate«). As the *Bullfrog* court further pointed out, inhibition of a U.S. speaker who is addressing a foreign audience may »chill« that speaker's future speech to domestic audiences. *Id.* at 502 n.14.

876 *Id* at 502.

877 381 U.S. 301 (1965); *see supra* notes 308–13 and accompanying text.

sent by a foreign agent in the United States to another »American republic« whose law bars the material.[878]

More broadly, U.S. willingness to block international mail undesired by other countries is reflected in provisions of the Universal Postal Union to which the U.S. has subscribed. The United States has agreed through the Universal Postal Union to refuse to accept for mailing materials that are prohibited by the destination country.[879] A variety of prohibitions are currently listed for various countries: Peru will not accept »Communist propaganda.«[880] Indonesia bars printed matter in the Indonesian language that was printed outside Indonesia, except for educational books approved by the Indonesian Department of Commerce.[881] Iran prohibits fashion newspapers.[882] The Soviet Union excludes toys »of a military nature« or »in the form of a military firearm.«[883]

As Dean Price has observed, these regulations »assume that the United States can constitutionally be party to an international agreement for the exchange of information where one party reserves the right to censor.«[884] The regulations may not be constitutional, at least if the United States itself performs a censoring or blocking function. While the foreign addressees may have no First Amendment right to receive uncensored mail from

878 22 U.S.C. § 618(d) (1979). This section of FARA provides that if an »agent of a foreign principal« offers for mailing to »any other American republic« material that promotes »any racial, social, political, or religious disorder,« forceful conflict, or the forceful overthrow of a government in an American republic, and if the postmaster general is informed by the secretary of state that the diplomatic representative of that republic has declared »that the admission or circulation of such communication or expression in such American republic is prohibited by the laws thereof and has requested in writing that its transmittal thereto be stopped,« the postmaster general may declare the matter to be unmailable.
The material described in section 618(d) falls under clause (2) of FARA's definition of »political propaganda.« *See* 22 U.S.C. § 611(j) (1979). Unlike the rest of FARA, which requires the labeling, filing and reporting of foreign »political propaganda« distributed in the United States (*see* 22 U.S.C. § 614; *supra text* accompanying notes 426–30), this subsection provides for the actual stopping of »political propaganda« on its way out of the United States.

879 United States Postal Service, International Mail Manual (1986) § 131.32 (»Articles which are prohibited by the destination country, are unmailable.«) Moreover, mail containing such materials may be returned or seized by the destination country, »[w]hether or not notice of such prohibition or restriction has been provided to or published by the Postal Service.« *Id.* at § 131.33.

880 *Id.* at App. D.

881 *Id.*

882 *Id.*

883 *Id.*

884 Price, *supra* note 18, at 891 n. 63.

the United States,[885] the sender of the mail is a speaker in the United States who can claim the First Amendment's protection.[886]
Nonetheless, these regulations have been accepted and adopted by the U.S. government and are apparently enforced. They would provide a precedent for agreement by the United States, for example, to an international DBS convention recognizing rights of receiving states to regulate or help shape incoming DBS broadcasts.[887]

2. *Export Restrictions*

The United States has extensive restrictions on the export of information considered to have national-security significance. Under the Arms Export Control Act,[888] the State Department has issued regulations limiting the export of classified information and of unclassified information related to weapons and munitions.[889] Unclassified »technical data« may also require an export license.[890] However, these regulations are subject to a general exemption permitting the export of unclassified information in printed form that is available to the public through newsstands, bookstores, subscriptions or public libraries.[891]
Under the Export Administration Act,[892] the Department of Commerce has issued regulations requiring a license for the export of a large range of advanced technical information.[893] The information covered need not be classified, and its technical applications need not be military.[894]

885 *Cf.* Lamont v. Postmaster General, 381 U.S. at 307–08 (Brennan, J., concurring) (case might be troublesome if it turned on First Amendment rights of foreign senders); Kleindienst v. Mandel, 408 U.S. at 762 (alien speaker has no First Amendment right to enter U.S.).
886 *Cf.* Procunier v. Martinez, 416 U.S. 396, 408–09 (1974) (whatever the merits of prisoner's claim to uncensored correspondence with an outsider, the outsider has First Amendment interest in uncensored correspondence with the prisoner (citing *Lamont*)); Lamont v. Postmaster General, 381 U.S. at 308 (Brennan, J., concurring) (addressees in U.S. have First Amendment right to receive); Kleindienst v. Mandel, 408 U.S. at 762–65 (professors in U.S. may have First Amendment right of access to foreign speaker).
887 *See* Price, *supra* note 18, at 890–91.
888 22 U.S.C. § 2778 (1982).
889 22 C.F.R. §§ 125.1–125.10 (1987).
890 *Id.* at § 125.2.
891 22 C.F.R. § 125.11(a)(1) (1982).
892 50 U.S.C. §§ 2401–20 (Supp. 1987).
893 15 C.F.R. §§ 368.1–399.2 (1987).
894 *See id.*

Under the Atomic Energy Act of 1954,[895] the export of a wide range of information related to nuclear technology is prohibited unless approved by a number of U.S. officials.[896] In *United States v. The Progressive*,[897] the government claimed authority under this act to restrain the publication of unclassified material in the public domain concerning atomic technology, publication of which allegedly threatened »immediate, direct and irreparable harm to the interests of the United States.«[898] The court granted the government's request for an injunction, but the case was withdrawn when it became evident that the material was already publicly known.[899]
Under one or more of these statutes, particularly the Arms Export Control Act, the U.S. Department of Defense claims the right to restrict or cancel the presentation of unclassified research papers at international scientific conferences in the United States.[900]
The extent of U.S. export controls is a controversial subject inside and outside the U.S. government, pitting business interests against asserted national-security interests. In early 1987, the U.S. Commerce Department – which processes some 110,000 export licenses a year[901] – announced a broad proposal to limit the controls, primarily with respect to trade with U.S. allies.[902] The Defense Department was expected to resist at least some of the proposed changes.[903]
The *Progressive* case aside, it does not appear that any of these export restrictions have come under First Amendment attack. If they were to, the government could be expected to argue that the restrictions applied not simply to speech but to actions,[904] in the form of the export of the related goods; and perhaps that they applied only to the »secondary effects« of the speech,[905] in the form of the technological capability that the informa-

895 42 U.S.C. § 2011 (Supp. 1987).
896 10 C.F.R. § 810 (1987).
897 467 F. Supp. 990 (W.D. Wis. 1979), *dismissed mem.*, 610 F.2d 819 (7th Cir. 1979).
898 *Id.* at 991.
899 The Justice Department announced that the publication of similar material had mooted its attempts to block publication of the *Progressive's* article. *See* Kroll, *National Security: The Ultimate Threat to the First Amendment,* 66 MINN. L. REV. 160, 163 n. 15.
900 In 1985, for example, the Department ordered the Society of Photo-Optical Instrumentation Engineers to cancel the presentation of some twelve papers and to restrict the attendance by foreign scientists at the presentation of other papers. N.Y. Times, Apr. 8, 1985, at 11, cols. 5–6 (national ed.).
901 N.Y. Times, Feb. 10, 1987, at 1, col. 4, 41, col. 3 (national ed.).
902 *Id.* at 1, col. 4.
903 *Id.*
904 *See, e.g.*, Haig v. Agee, 453 U.S. 280, 304 (1981); United States v. O'Brien, 391 U.S. 367, 376–77 (1968).
905 *See* City of Renton v. Playtime Theatres, Inc., 106 S. Ct. 925, 929 (1986).

tion could give to U.S. enemies. The analogy of espionage laws, which also prohibit the export of information, might be invoked.[906] Given the grounding of the export controls in national-security considerations[907] and the exemption for unclassified information publicly available,[908] the government's position would probably find a sympathetic judicial reception in any case where the national-security claim were plausible.

3. *Certification of »Educational« Films for Duty-Free Import to Other Countries*

As discussed earlier,[909] under the Beirut Agreement[910] a person seeking duty-free transborder shipment for audiovisual materials must apply for a certificate of their educational, scientific or cultural character from the appropriate agency of the exporting country.[911] The certificate is then submitted to the importing country, which makes its own determination but must give »due consideration« to the exporting country's certification.[912] Under the terms of the Agreement, materials shall be deemed of »educational, scientific or cultural« character:

> (a) When their primary purpose or effect is to instruct or inform through the development of a subject or an aspect of a subject, or when their content is such as to maintain, increase or diffuse knowledge, and augment international understanding and goodwill; and
> (b) When the materials are representative, authentic, and accurate; and
> (c) When the technical quality is such that it does not interfere with the use made of the material.[913]

In the United States, the president has designated the United States Information Agency to administer the Agreement.[914] One of the USIA's imple-

906 18 U.S.C. §§ 791–98 (1985).
907 *Cf.* Haig v. Agee, 453 U.S. 280, 306 (1981).
908 *See supra* note 891 and accompanying text.
909 *See supra* text accompanying notes 405–18.
910 *Supra* note 405.
911 *Id.* at art. IV, para. 2.
912 *Id.* at art. IV, paras. 4–6; *id.* at art. IV, para. 6. On the administration of the Beirut Agreement by the United States with respect to audiovisual materials seeking duty-free import into the United States, *see supra* notes 408–18 and accompanying text.
913 Agreement, *supra* note 405, at art. I.
914 *See* Bullfrog Films, Inc. v. Wick, 646 F. Supp. 492, 495 (C.D. Cal. 1986); Pub. L. No. 89–634, 80 Stat. 879 (1966).

menting regulations,[915] defining the materials the Agency will certify, incorporates word-for-word the definition contained in the Agreement.[916] A second, »interpretive« regulation provides that the Agency will not certify materials »which by special pleading attempt generally to influence opinion, conviction or policy (religious, economic or political propaganda), to espouse a cause, or conversely, when they seem to attack a particular persuasion.«[917] A third regulation, also »interpretive,« provides:

> The Agency does not regard as augmenting international understanding or good will and cannot certify or authenticate any material which may lend itself to misinterpretation, or misrepresentation of the United States or other countries, their peoples or institutions, or which appear to have as their purpose or effect to attack or discredit economic, religious, or political views or practices.[918]

In *Bullfrog Films, Inc. v. Wick*,[919] the owners of seven films that the USIA had declined to certify challenged the USIA regulations as inconsistent with the First Amendment. The films included *In Our Own Backyards: Uranium Mining in the United States, Whatever Happened to Childhood?*, and *From the Ashes: Nicaragua Today*.[920] The USIA had found the films ineligible because they »espouse[d] a cause,« were »inaccurate« or »imbalanced,« or were capable of »being misinterpreted or misunderstood by foreign audiences lacking adequate American points of reference.«[921] While declining to certify these films, the USIA had certified such films as *To Catch a Cloud: A*

915 22 C.F.R. §§ 502.1–502.8 (1985). Under the regulations, applications for certification first are reviewed by an attestation officer; a denial by him may be appealed to a review board; and final Agency review is by the director of USIA. 22 C.F.R. § 502.3(g), 502.5(b), 502.5(c) (1986).

916 22 C.F.R. § 502.6(a)(3).

917 22 C.F.R. § 502.6(b)(3).

918 22 C.F.R. § 502.6(b)(5).

919 646 F. Supp. 492 (C.D. Cal. 1986).

920 *See id.* at 496. *See generally* Note, *supra* note 405.

921 646 F. Supp. at 496. For example, *In Our Own Backyards: Uranium Mining in the United States* was found to »espouse a cause and influence opinion« because it presented »an anti-nuclear message« and had a purpose of »persuad[ing] the audience that all uranium mining should be prevented.« *Id. Whatever Happened to Childhood?* was found not to be »representative« because »the Agency does not find that the youth in the film are typical or representative of all American youth today.« *Id. From the Ashes: Nicaragua Today* was rejected because it led viewers to conclude »that the United States is the primary cause of instability, poverty, and oppression in Nicaragua,« thereby constituting both »an attempt to persuade« and »an attack on the institutions of the United States.« *Id.* at 496–97. The film was also found to be unbalanced because it did not discuss »any of the reasons for the policy adopted by the Government of the United States toward the present or former government of Nicaragua.« *Id.* at 497.

Thoughtful Look at Acid Rain, by the Edison Electrical Institute; *Radiation ... Naturally,* by the Atomic Industrial Forum; and *The Family: God's Pattern for Living,* by the Moody Institute of Science.[922]

Judge Wallace Tashima of the federal district court, ruling in October 1986, first found that the plaintiffs had standing to challenge the USIA certification process.[923] He then concluded that, in the absence of some overriding interest such as national security, »the First Amendment protects communications with foreign audiences to the same extent as communications within our borders.«[924]

Applying the First Amendment, the court held that the USIA's two »interpretive« regulations were unconstitutionally vague.[925] No one could know what was meant by terms such as »special pleading,« or »attempt generally« to influence opinion, or »seem to attack a ... persuasion,« the court said.[926] Further, the two regulations impermissibly »discriminate on the basis of political content.«[927] In particular, the provision rejecting materials that »misrepresent« the United States »places the government in the position of determining what is the ›truth‹ about America, politically and otherwise.«[928] The court held the first interpretive regulation additionally invalid because it prohibited certification of materials that state a point of view, thus impermissibly limiting expressions of opinion on issues of public controversy.[929]

The court also struck down the regulation that adopted verbatim the Agreement's definition of »educational.«[930] The requirements that the material »augment international understanding and goodwill« and be »representative, authentic and accurate« were unduly vague, and the term »accurate« also involved content discrimination and a government determination of

922 *Id.* at 497. The last film was certified under a section of the regulations making materials eligible if »intended for use only in denominational programs or other restricted organizational use in moral and religious education.« 22 C.F.R. § 502.6(b)(3); *see* 646 F. Supp. at 497 n.7.

923 646 F. Supp. at 497–502. Although the plaintiffs remained free to distribute their films anywhere in the world, and simply had to pay whatever customs duties the importing country might require, they had been denied the exporting country's certification, which is »an indispensable prerequisite to obtaining the benefits of the Treaty,« the court said. *Id.* at 501–02.

924 *Id.* at 502; *see supra* note 876 and accompanying text.

925 646 F. Supp. at 505.

926 *Id.* at 505.

927 *Id.* at 506.

928 *Id.* at 506.

929 *Id.* at 506–07.

930 *Id.* at 507–08.

truth, the court said.[931] The court did not strike down the Agreement itself, expressing the belief that regulations could be drafted that would fit within the Agreement's definition of »educational« and still be specific and neutral enough to comply with the United States Constitution.[932] The court ordered the USIA to reconsider the eligibility of each of the plaintiffs' films under proper constitutional standards.[933]

The district court's decision in *Bullfrog Films* – which the government has appealed[934] – is correct. Although denial of a certificate under the Beirut Agreement does not block export of the materials, it burdens their export more substantially than the statute in *Lamont* burdened the import of material through the mails.[935] The Beirut Agreement admittedly requires the U.S. government to determine, somehow, what films are »educational.« Developing neutral and specific standards for this task poses a difficult problem. Perhaps the solution lies not only in drafting better standards but also in delegating the job of applying them to a body insulated from direct government control. In any event, determinations founded on the vague and content-based standards at issue in *Bullfrog Films* cannot coexist with the First Amendment.

B. *Regulation of Outgoing Electronic Media Flow*

1. *Licensing of International Broadcast Stations*

While the USIA regulations in *Bullfrog Films* at least could claim their genesis in a treaty, no such explanation can be offered for the overt content regulation of outgoing media flow found in the FCC's licensing scheme for international broadcast stations. These are stations, licensed to private entities, that broadcast overseas from the U.S. on short-wave frequencies. The applicable regulations require licensees to »render only an international broadcast service which will reflect the culture of this country and which will promote international goodwill, understanding, and cooperation.«[936]

931 *Id.*
932 *Id.* at 510–11.
933 *Id.*
934 No. 86–6630 (9th Cir.).
935 381 U.S. 301 (1965).
936 47 C.F.R. § 73.788(a) (1986).

Although this provision was strongly opposed on its adoption in 1939,[937] it remains in effect 1986 and apparently has not been challenged in the courts.[938]

Another FCC regulation for international radio stations restricts their commercial advertising. Among other things, it requires that commercials »give no more than the name of the sponsor of the program and the name and general character of the commodity, utility or service, or attraction advertised.«[939] This requirement was adopted by the FCC »because it appeared that institutional advertising [as distinct from product advertising] would create a better impression of the United States.«[940]

The private international broadcast service of the United States, while still limited, has grown in recent years.[941] In 1973, the FCC set a flexible ceiling of 100 frequency-hours per day for all U.S. private international broadcasters as a group; each station used varying frequencies and had to apply for daily frequency assignments for each season.[942] At that time, no more than 75 frequency-hours per day were being used.[943] In 1986, U.S. private international broadcasters as a group used about 450 frequency-hours per day.[944]

One constant of private international broadcasting has been the dominance of religious programming. Of the stations operating in 1986, only one clearly did not have a religious format.[945]

The single nonreligious station, which went on the air in 1982, was the first

937 It was met by the »united opposition of the industry and ... attacked in Congress as being an entering wedge for censorship of domestic programs.« C.B. ROSE, *supra* note 604, at 244. But the protests were mooted when the wartime government took over private international broadcasting, and they have not resurfaced. *See* Garay, *WRNO Worldwide: A Case Study in Licensing Private US International Broadcast Stations*, 26 J. BROADCASTING 641, 642 (1982).

938 *See* 47 C.F.R. § 73.788(a) (1986); Price, *supra* note 18, at 897.

939 47 C.F.R. § 73.788(b)(1) (1986). This requirement was waived by the FCC, however, for WRNO, the one clearly commercial international station it has licensed. Telephone conversation with Jonathan David, chief, international negotiations, Mass Media Bureau, FCC, Mar. 27, 1987; *see infra* text accompanying notes 946–51.

940 International Broadcasting Stations, 41 F.C.C.2d 736, 750 (1973).

941 In 1980, only four stations were transmitting. *Garay, supra* note 937, at 641. In 1986, twelve stations were listed as providing private international broadcast service. *See* 1985 BROADCASTING/CABLECASTING YEARBOOK, at B-350 (1986).

942 *See* Garay, *supra* note 937, at 644; 41 F.C.C.2d at ___.

943 Garay, *supra* note 937, at 644.

944 Telephone conversation with Tom Polain, Mass Media Bureau, FCC, Mar. 27, 1987).

945 *See* 1985 BROADCASTING/CABLECASTING YEARBOOK, at B-350-351. An attorney at the FCC's Mass Media bureau explained that the stations are not commercially attractive because of the relatively steep power requirements for international transmission. Telephone conversation with Jonathan David, *supra* note 939.

station licensed in nearly two decades.[946] Its license application met considerable resistance at the FCC, reflecting at least in part an official reluctance to have anyone but the U.S. government broadcasting abroad from the United States.[947] The FCC chairman said of the application:

> I think a ... fundamental issue is: Should we have this type of allocation of frequencies? Why should private entities be broadcasting viewpoints overseas? That's part of the VOA [Voice of America], RFE [Radio Free Europe], or other government entities. Why should foreign policy be determined by a private licensee's view?[948]

The chairman, however, was alone in opposing the application,[949] and his view was at odds with the 1948 Smith-Mundt Act, which created the United States Information Agency.[950] That act prohibits the U.S. government from monopolizing short-wave broadcasting and provides further that the USIA director »shall reduce such Government information activities whenever corresponding private information dissemination is found to be adequate.«[951] On the other hand, the limited scope of private overseas broadcasting from the United States suggests that the FCC chairman's view may better reflect the prevailing reality.

2. *U.S. Government Use of International Broadcast Frequencies*

Despite Congress's directive that the government not monopolize overseas broadcasting,[952] something close to that has happened. In 1973, overseas broadcasting by the Voice of America (VOA), the broadcasting arm of the USIA, had increased to about 440 frequency-hours per day, while private international transmissions had decreased to about 45 frequency-hours per

946 *See generally* Garay, *supra* note 937.
947 *Id.*
948 *See id.* at 649–50.
949 *Id.*
950 United States Information and Educational Exchange Act, 22 U.S.C. § 1462 (1985). The chairman also need not have worried about the foreign-policy predilections of the new licensee. The licensee's programming objective was to »play rock 'n' roll music for the world« and turn a profit in the process. Garay, *supra* note 937, at 652. Confronted with the regulation requiring service that »will reflect the culture of this country,« *see supra* text accompanying note 936, the licensee responded, reasonable enough, that »[t]here's nothing more American in our culture than rock music.« Garay, *supra* note 937, at 654 & n. 56.
951 22 U.S.C. § 1462 (1985).
952 22 U.S.C. § 1462 (1985); *see* International Broadcasting Stations, 41 F.C.C.2d at 737.

day.[953] The FCC at that time set a ceiling of 100 frequency-hours per day for private transmissions, over the protests of VOA that even this was too much.[954] Noting the statutory prohibition of a government monopoly, the FCC remarked that »[t]o set a ceiling on private international broadcasters that would give them less than one-fifth of the frequency-hours used by the U.S.-based stations of VOA borders on being contrary to this mandate.«[955]

By 1986, private international transmissions had increased to about 450 frequency-hours per day. But the 100-frequency-hour »ceiling« has not been formally changed[956] and serves, perhaps, to keep private international broadcasters on notice that they should not expect too much. The deterrent effect on actual and potential broadcasters is difficult to estimate.

The ceiling on private frequency-hours is not the only way the U.S. government discourages private international broadcasting and protects its own position on the international airwaves. By limiting private broadcasters to »institutional« commercials that give no more than »the name and general character« of the article advertised,[957] the FCC makes the service unattractive to potential commercial broadcasters. It is no wonder that, until 1982, all the private international stations had religious formats.[958] As the FCC in 1973 noted, ironically, in justifying its ceiling on frequency-hours, »we may not expect a great rush into international broadcasting since it is not a financially remunerative activity.«[959] Further government efforts to limit the private service were evidenced in the resistance at the FCC to licensing the one commercial station in 1982.[960]

These efforts by the U.S. government to keep international broadcasting mostly for itself not only seem inconsistent with the congressional directive that government information activities be reduced »whenever private information dissemination is found to be adequate,«[961] but they also contradict the FCC's own observation that »[a] credibility gap attaches to governmental broadcasting. Broadcasting by private stations is often more effec-

953 *Id* at 738, 740–41.
954 *Id*. at 739.
955 *Id.*
956 Telephone conversation with Jonathan David, *supra* note 939.
957 47 C.F.R. § 73.788(b)(1) (1985); *see supra* note 939 and accompanying text. *But see supra* note 944.
958 *See supra* note 945 and accompanying text.
959 41 F.C.C.2d at 741.
960 *See generally* Garay, *supra* note 937.
961 22 U.S.C. § 1462 (1985).

tive because it has a greater credibility.«[962] Further, for a nation that gives such a dominant role in its domestic broadcast system to private, commercial broadcasting, this reluctance to show the same face to the world suggests a lack of self-confidence about what goes on at home.
The U.S. government's enthusiasm for its own overseas broadcasting was demonstrated anew in 1985 by the inauguration of a new Voice of America service, called Ratio Marti, broadcasting to Cuba.[963]
As far as the content of the U.S. government's overseas broadcasting is concerned, the Congress has required that Voice of America news broadcasts be »accurate, objective, and comprehensive.«[964] The statute also requires that VOA »present a balanced and comprehensive projection of significant American thought and institutions,« that it »present the policies of the United States clearly and effectively,« and that it »also present responsible discussion and opinion on these policies.«[965] After some debate, Congress made Radio Marti subject to the same standards.[966]
The extent to which VOA broadcasts meet these standards is difficult to gauge from the United States. One reason is a statutory directive that information disseminated abroad by the USIA »shall not be disseminated within the United States,« except that it shall be available on request, »for examination only,« to members of the press, scholars, and members of Congress.[967] While this provision presumably seeks to protect the U.S. public from government propagandizing, it also has the effect of denying to the U.S. public knowledge about the content of the information, or propaganda, disseminated by their government to the rest of the world.

3. *Sale of U.S. Televison Programming Abroad*

There are no direct limits in U.S. law on the sale of U.S. television programming (or other media content) for distribution abroad. Any such limits not

962 41 F.C.C.2d at 739. The policy is not solely the FCC's, however. As the Commission noted, the increased budgets of the Voice of America demonstrate congressional support for VOA's proliferating broadcast activities. *Id.* at 737.
963 Radio Broadcasting to Cuba Act, Pub. L. No. 98–111, Oct. 4, 1983; 22 U.S.C. § 1465 (1985).
964 22 U.S.C. § 1463 (1985).
965 *Id.*
966 22 U.S.C. § 1465(b) (1985).
967 22 U.S.C. § 1461 (1985).

only would be inconsistent with U.S. trade interests but would raise constitutional problems as well.[968]

The foreign market for U.S. television programming is so substantial, however, that the control of this market by the three major U.S. networks has been limited in an attempt to reduce network control over the production of programming in the U.S. The FCC has barred the networks both from syndicating in foreign countries programs of which the network was not the sole producer and from acquiring financial interests in the exhibition or distribution of such programs abroad.[969] In 1983 the FCC proposed to lift these restrictions, along with parallel restrictions governing syndication and financial interests in the U.S.,[970] but opposition from the motion picture industry killed the proposal.[971] In any event, similar restrictions have been imposed on the three networks by consent decrees in antitrust suits brought by the U.S. government.[972] These decrees, which go somewhat farther than the FCC restrictions,[973] will remain in effect, unless modified, until the late 1980s or early 1990s.[974]

The limitations thus imposed on the export of television programming produced by the U.S. networks seem fundamentally different from other U.S. limitations on outgoing media flow. In this case, the regulation of transborder speech serves as an adjunct to a domestic regulatory policy – reducing network dominance – and is not based on reasons peculiar to transborder communications.

4. *Satellite Distribution of U.S. Programming Abroad*

Just as United States law restricts the use of satellites to bring television programming into the United States,[975] companies wishing to send program-

968 *See* Bullfrog Films, Inc. v. Wick, 646 F. Supp. 492 (C.D. Cal. 1986); *supra* notes 872–76 and accompanying text; *cf.* Lamont v. Postmaster General, 381 U.S. 301 (1965).

969 47 C.F.R. § 73. 658 (1984).

970 *See* 94 F.C.C.2d 1019 (1983).

971 *See* Broadcasting, Apr. 1, 1985, at 95; Kintzer, *The Proposed Repeal of the Financial Interest and Syndication Rules: Network Domination or Public Interest Representations?*, 6 COMM/ENT L.J. 513 (1984).

972 *E.g.*, United States v. National Broadcasting Co., 449 F. Supp. 1127 (C.D. Cal. 1978), *aff'd mem.*, No. 77–3381 (9th Cir., Apr. 12, 1978); *see also* 45 Fed. Reg. 34,463, 58,441 (1980).

973 Unlike the FCC regulations, the consent decrees prohibit the networks from procuring the rights to foreign syndication of foreign-produced programming in the same negotiations in which they obtain domestic syndication rights. *See* 94 F.C.C.2d 1019 (para. 19).

974 *See* 45 Fed. Reg. 34,463, 58,441 (1980); 449 F. Supp. at 1132.

975 *See supra* text accompanying notes 810–57.

ming abroad by way of satellite also must contend with U.S. legal requirements.

If U.S. cable networks or other program distributors wish to use even INTELSAT satellites to send their programming abroad, they need the permission of the FCC. FCC permission is required under provisions of the Communications Act regarding new transmission services[976] and also under provisions of the Communications Satellite Act regarding construction and operation of international earth stations.[977] The FCC, however, now readily grants these permissions. In 1984 the Commission liberalized its policy on ownership of U.S. earth stations using the INTELSAT system.[978] It ruled that such stations no longer need be owned by a consortium of carriers, and it said further that applications to provide television services through such stations would be processed »in routine fashion.«[979] Thus in 1985 the Commission granted an application by Turner Teleport, Inc., a subsidiary of Turner Broadcasting System, to transmit television programming through INTELSAT satellites over the Atlantic.[980]

However, signal transmissions by way of satellite are expensive.[981] Therefore, just as receiving stations in the United States seek to receive programming from foreign domestic satellites already carrying the signals – where the »footprint« of the satellite falls on the United States[982] – carriers and programmers seek to distribute programming carried by U.S. domestic satellites to countries abroad in the same manner.

In its 1981 *Transborder* decision,[983] the FCC ruled not only that U.S. earth stations could be used to receive programming from Canadian domestic satellites[984] but also that U.S. domestic satellites could be used to distribute programming to Canada and countries in Central America and the

976 47 U.S.C. § 214, Title III (1982); *see In re* Modification of Policy on Ownership and Operation of U.S. Earth Stations that Operate with the INTELSAT Global Communications Satellite System (Ownership of INTELSAT Earth Stations), 100 F.C.C.2d 250, para. 13 n. 23, paras. 20, 22 (1984).

977 47 U.S.C. § 201(c)(4), (6), (7) (1985); *see* Ownership of INTELSAT Earth Stations, *supra* note 976, paras. 13 n. 23, 20 n. 43, 22.

978 Ownership of INTELSAT Earth Stations, *supra* note 976, at para. 55.

979 *See id.* paras. 3, 21, 23, 24.

980 Turner Teleport, Inc., Nos CSG-85-001-P/L; I-T-C-85-033, Mar. 13, 1985.

981 *See infra* note 989.

982 *See supra* notes 759–85 and accompanying text; Transborder, 88 F.C.C.2d 258 para. 47 (1981). The footprint of a typical U.S. domestic satellite will cover the forty-eight contiguous states, parts of Canada and Mexico, and a substantial part of the Caribbean and Latin America. *See* 1983 Hearings, *supra* note 651, at 17 (statement of David Ladd).

983 88 F.C.C.2d 258; *see supra* notes 759–69 and accompanying text.

984 *See supra* text accompanying notes 759–69.

Caribbean.[985] Since these were non-INTELSAT satellites, the Commission ruled that the consultation process established in the INTELSAT Agreement must be observed.[986] As noted earlier, this requirement could hinder the reception of programming in the United States, including news programming, and thus presents constitutional problems.[987] The requirement may have the same effect on the transmission of news programming *from* the United States and so may present similar problems in the context of outgoing speech.[988]

In more distant lands where the footprints of U.S. domestic satellites do not fall, it has been necessary for U.S. programmers to use INTELSAT satellites to distribute their product abroad. The high price of INTELSAT service may have discouraged such distribution.[989] Currently, however, INTELSAT is losing its monopoly position over international satellite communications from the United States. In 1984 President Reagan determined that the U.S. national interest required separate U.S. systems providing international satellite service, as long as restrictions were imposed to protect the economic health of INTELSAT.[990] The FCC subsequently established policies for authorizing separate systems[991] and conditionally granted six applications, subject to the INTELSAT coordination procedure.[992] The first of these applications was approved by the INTELSAT Assembly of Parties in April 1987.[993]

The FCC initially restricted the separate-system operators to selling their facilities or leasing them for a minimum of one year, in order to protect

985 *See* 88 F.C.C.2d at 263–66.

986 *Id.* at 279–85.

987 *See supra* notes 796–98 and accompanying text.

988 *Cf. supra* notes 876, 886, 924, 968 and accompanying test.

989 At least one U.S. programmer complains that distribution of U.S. programming to distant countries has been impeded by monopoly prices charged by INTELSAT for the use of its satellites. The general counsel of Turner Broadcasting System, parent of Cable News Network, said in 1985 that efforts to »take CNN international« were impeded by INTELSAT's pricing policy. He said that networks in Australia and Japan wanted to receive CNN's news programming, that the reception costs were minimal because the footprint of CNN's INTELSAT satellite fell there, but that INTELSAT's extra charges for down-link points added a prohibitive cost of some $120,000 per receiving country. Telephone interview with Robert Ross, general counsel, Turner Broadcasting System, (Jan. 22, 1985).

990 Presidential Directive No. 85–2, Nov. 28, 1984; *see* 47 U.S.C. §§ 701(d), 721(a) (1985).

991 Establishment of Satellite Systems Providing International Communications (Separate Systems), 101 F.C.C.2d 1046 (1985).

992 *E.g.*, International Satellite, Inc., 101 F.C.C.2d 1201 (1985); Pan American Satellite Corp., 101 F.C.C.2d 1318 (1985); *see* Broadcasting, Jan. 5, 1987, at 144–46.

993 *Id.*

INTELSAT's basic revenues.[994] But the FCC subsequently ruled, reversing its earlier position, that the one-year lease requirement did not preclude contracts of one year or more for »occasional use television service.«[995] This ruling presumably will facilitate the use of the separate system by U.S. television networks and other programmers that do not use the facilities on a full-time basis.

Until recently it could be said, then, that the INTELSAT system posed substantial obstacles, both legal and financial, to the satellite distribution of private U.S. programming abroad – much as the U.S. government's domination of the short-wave frequencies impeded the terrestrial distribution of private U.S. radio programming.[996] The *Transborder* decision and the advent of private international satellite systems, however, may markedly liberate the distribution of U.S. programming by satellite.

C. *Conclusion Concerning Outgoing Media Flow*

United States restrictions on outgoing media flow are less developed than restrictions on incoming flow, largely because the available policy justifications are not as numerous or strong. There is less room to invoke national-security or foreign-policy considerations and no room to rely on the government's power to exclude aliens or on trade protectionism. Hence, there is no restriction on outgoing speech that is nearly as broad as either the regulation of all political speech distributed by »foreign agents« in the United States under the Foreign Agents Registration Act[997] or the facial exclusion under the McCarran-Walter Act of all would-be visitors who have been »communists.«[998]

At the same time, the restrictions on outgoing flow reflect some effort by the U.S. government to shape the content of transborder information. The government appears to acknowledge this objective by its claim in *Bullfrog Films* that »the exercise of free speech within foreign nations by Americans is subordinate to significant foreign policy considerations.«[999] The USIA

994 Separate Systems, 101 F.C.C.2d at 1105–06.

995 Separate Systems Reconsideration Order, CC Docket No. 84–1299 (Apr. 17, 1986); *compare* Separate Systems, 101 F.C.C.2d at 1105–06.

996 *See supra* notes 952-67 and accompanying test.

997 *See supra* text accompanying notes 419–70.

998 *See supra* text accompanying notes 337–72.

999 646 F. Supp. 492, 503 (C.D. Cal. 1986).

regulations struck down in *Bullfrog Films* show an effort by the U.S. to deny duty-free treatment under the Beirut Agreement to films critical of United States positions.[1000] These films appear to be much the same as those that are treated as »political propaganda« under the Foreign Agents Registration Act.[1001] Thus, while not attempting directly to stop the trans-border flow of such films, the U.S. government restricts that flow in both directions. It regulates the films as »propaganda« when they are distributed on behalf of a foreign entity within the United States, and it seeks to prevent the films from circulating duty-free to other countries.

Meanwhile, the U.S. government's domination of the international short-wave frequencies suggests a desire to maximize the government's own speech to the rest of the world at the expense of speech by private U.S. citizens.[1002]

Still, these efforts by the U.S. government to restrict outgoing media flow are quite limited in scope. The overwhelming proportion of that flow is unaffected. Moreover, the U.S. government's decision to license private international satellites outside the INTELSAT system may markedly facilitate the distribution of U.S. television programming to other countries.[1003]

1000 *See supra* 921–33 and accompanying text.
1001 *See supra* notes and accompanying notes 465–70.
1002 *See supra* notes and accompanying notes 952–67.
1003 *See supra* notes 989–96 and accompanying text.

Conclusion

United States regulation of transborder speech reflects pervasively the opposing tendencies noted earlier.[1004] There are First Amendment rights to receive information from abroad and to send information abroad, rights recognized most clearly by the Supreme Court's decision in *Lamont,*[1005] the Court's opinion in *Mandel*[1006] and the district court's decision in *Bullfrog Films.*[1007] But there also are various laws restricting transborder information flows, and these laws generally have been upheld by the courts.[1008]

Particularly hard to reconcile with the »free flow« and First Amendment commitments of the United States are the visa restrictions of the McCarran-Walter Act[1009] and the »political propaganda« provisions of the Foreign Agents Registration Act.[1010] Both statutes show an unwillingness to allow foreign speech to enter the United States and compete on equal terms with domestic speech.

With respect to the electronic media, the most important restrictions on transborder flow are the ban on foreign ownership of U.S. broadcast facilities[1011] and the rules limiting reception of signals from foreign satellites.[1012] The ban on foreign ownership, though antiquated and unnecessary, can claim some historical justification and apparently is consistent with international practice.[1013] It also is balanced by U.S. toleration of foreign ownership in virtually all other media.[1014]

The restriction on the reception of signals from foreign satellites, insofar as it applies (in the view of the FCC) to reception with the consent of the originator, is based on the treaty obligations of the United States to INTELSAT.[1015] On its face, this is a content-neutral consideration. But the

1004 *See supra* text accompanying notes 305–07.

1005 Lamont v. Postmaster General, 381 U.S. 301 (1965); *see supra* notes 308–13 and accompanying text.

1006 Kleindienst v. Mandel, 408 U.S. 753, — (1972); *see supra* notes 346–58 and accompanying text.

1007 Bullfrog Films, Inc. v. Wick, 646 F. Supp 492; *see supra* notes 859–76 and accompanying text.

1008 *See supra* notes 337–520, 548–82, 603–59, 665–802, 810–55, 877–967 and accompanying text.

1009 *See supra* notes 337–72 and accompanying text.

1010 *See supra* notes 419–70 and accompanying text.

1011 47 U.S.C. § 310(a); *see supra* notes 548–78 and accompanying text.

1012 *See supra* notes 660–809 and accompanying test.

1013 *See supra* note 568 and accompanying text.

1014 *See supra* notes 511–47, 583–602 and accompanying text.

1015 *See supra* notes 684–87 and accompanying text.

FCC's position, as applied to incoming signals, harbors strains of content control. Content control is palpable in the FCC's imposition of conditions requested by the U.S. State Department limiting Cable News Network to a six-month license for reception of Soviet programming and stipulating that renewal depends on a »favorable foreign-policy finding.«[1016] Potential content control is inherent in the requirement than CNN or any other U.S. programmer get FCC permission to receive any programming from a foreign satellite, even for coverage of a news event.[1017] It is hard to see why this requirement is not a »prior restraint« inconsistent with the First Amendment.[1018]

Content control and the First Amendment aside, the FCC's insistence on FCC approval for reception of foreign-satellite signals with the consent of the originator is unauthorized. It lacks support in section 705 of the Communications Act or any other provision of U.S. law.[1019]

U.S. law does restrict the reception of foreign-satellite signals without the consent of the originator, even for private viewing at home or for educational viewing at universities.[1020] Present law appears to permit such reception only for *home* viewing of unscrambled signals being transmitted by the satellite to *cable* systems.[1021] This state of the law is difficult to fault on First Amendment grounds.[1022] The law should be amended, however, to legitimize nonprofit viewing of unscrambled foreign (and domestic) signals, preferably on a fair-use rationale.[1023]

Across the range of U.S. regulation of transborder media flows, a number of provisions seem inconsistent with the »free flow« position of the United States, if not with the First Amendment as well. This should not be surprising. The diverse laws brought together in this report were adopted at different times, in different political climates and for different purposes. They have never been systematically considered by the U.S. Congress from the point of view of their impact on transborder speech or their consistence with current U.S. principles concerning such speech. They are overdue for systematic reappraisal from these perspectives, in particular, for testing against the »free flow« commitment and the First Amendment. Lacking such a reappraisal, United States regulation of transborder speech will continue to reflect a wide gap between the nation's law and its principles.

1016 *See supra* note 777 and accompanying text.
1017 *See supra* notes 770–78 and accompanying text.
1018 *See supra* note 786 and accompanying text.
1019 *See supra* notes 693–700 and accompanying text.
1020 *See supra* notes 665–76, 701–57 and accompanying text.
1021 *See supra* notes 284–88, 701–11 and accompanying text.
1022 *See supra* notes 737–40 and accompanying text.
1023 *See supra* notes 743–54 and accompanying text.

NATIONAL REPORT QUESTIONNAIRE*

Part 1: Telephone services

A. Regulation of transborder telephone services

I. Basic regulations of domestic telecommunications law for transborder telephone services[1]

1. Transformation of international regulations into domestic law and practice
   a) Survey of the relevant international law
      aa) Multilateral agreements
      bb) Bilateral agreements
   b) Scope of questions of transborder telephone services reserved for national regulation
   c) Domestic regulatory power to transform international regulations into domestic law and practice
      aa) Power to issue regulations affecting the domestic sphere[2]
         aaa) Legislature
         bbb) Public administration (administrative agencies)
         ccc) Operating companies (providing telephone services)
      bb) Power to issue regulations affecting foreign states[2]
         aaa) Legislature
         bbb) Administrative agencies
         ccc) Operating companies
   d) Contents of the international regulations as transformed into domestic law (including their application and construction)
2. Domestic law unaffected by international law
   a) Regulatory power[2]
      aa) Legislature
      bb) Administrative agencies

* The Questionnaire was prepared by a Work Group at the Max Planck Institute in Hamburg. Under the direction of Prof. E.-J. Mestmäcker, the Group consisted of Thomas Born, Reinhard Ellger, Beate-Katrin Graben and Detlev Witt.

cc) Operating companies

b) Survey of the contents of the domestic law (including application and construction)

II. Legal relations between domestic carriers (networks) providing transborder telephone services and domestic users of those services

1. Use of telephone services
   a) Public networks (common carriers)[3]
      aa) Who operates public networks?
      bb) Legal requirements for establishment and operation of public networks
         aaa) Contents of the requirements
         bbb) Power to regulate the requirements, to license operating companies, etc.
         ccc) Judicial review or other legal recourse against regulatory decisions
      cc) What services may be offered? What services are actually available?
      dd) Requirements for access to and conditions for use of public networks[4,5]
         aaa) Who has access to the networks?[6]
            (1) Ultimate consumers
            (2) »Resellers« of transmission services (lessees of network capacity)
            (3) Power to regulate access to networks
         bbb) Setting of tariffs
            (1) Tariff principles
            (2) Power to regulate tariffs (or market pricing?)
         ccc) Liability (of operating company for malfunction, etc.)
         ddd) Technical standards (especially standards for terminal equipment and its usage)
            (1) Power to regulate standards (source of regulation: international/national, governmental/private?)
            (2) Contents of technical standards
         eee) Judicial review or other legal recourse against regulatory decisions

b) Private networks
   aa) Who operates private networks?
   bb) Legal requirements for establishment and operation of private networks[6]
      aaa) Contents of the requirements[7]
      bbb) Regulatory power[7]
      ccc) Judicial review or other legal recourse[7]
   cc) What services may be offered? What services are actually available?
   dd) Are private network operators allowed to sublease networks? If so, under which conditions?

c) Networks operated by closed user groups
   aa) Who operates closed-user-group networks? (e.g., SITA, SWIFT)
   bb) Legal requirements for establishment and operation of closed-user-group networks[6]
      aaa) Contents of requirements[7]
      bbb) Regulatory power[7]
      ccc) Judicial review or other legal recourse[7]
   cc) What services may be offered? What services are actually available?
   dd) Requirements for access to and terms of usage of closed-user-group networks[6,7]
      aaa) Who can become a member of the »user group« and thereby gain access to the network?
      bbb) Setting of tariffs
         (1) Tariff principles
         (2) Who sets the tariffs?
      ccc) Liability (for errors, malfunction, etc.)
      ddd) Technical standards
      eee) Judicial review or other legal recourse; government supervision

2. Admission of terminal equipment to the network[8,9]
   a) What terminal equipment is part of the network – according to domestic telecommunications law – and therefore subject to the regulatory powers governing the telephone services?
   b) Who regulates the admission of terminal equipment to the network?
      aa) Administrative agencies

bb) Network operators

c) Criteria for admission (e.g., technical compatability)[5]

d) Judicial review or other legal recourse

III. Legal relations between domestic and international or foreign network operators

1. Access of domestic networks to and terms of usage of foreign networks

a) Requirements of domestic telecommunications law[6] for access to the international network[10,11]

aa) Contents of the requirements

aaa) International law (multilateral/bilateral agreements) and domestic implementation thereof

bbb) Domestic law unaffected by international law

bb) Regulatory power

aaa) International organizations

bbb) Bilateral coordination

ccc) Domestic legislature

ddd) Domestic administrative agencies

eee) Operating companies

cc) Judicial review or other legal recourse

b) Requirements of domestic telecommunications law for the use of the international network (to what extent does domestic law influence these requirements?)[12]

aa) Contents of the requirements

aaa) Setting of tariffs, accounting

(1) International framework (multilateral/bilateral) agreements, including their transformation into domestic law)

(2) Domestic law unaffected by international law

bbb) Technical standards

(1) International framework

(2) Domestic law

ccc) Liability (for malfunction, etc.)

bb) Regulatory powers for setting tariffs and technical standards

aaa) International organizations

bbb) Bilateral coordination

ccc) Domestic legislature

ddd) Domestic administrative agencies
eee) Operating companies
cc) Judicial review or other legal recourse

2. Access of foreign networks to and terms of usage of domestic networks
   a) Are several domestic networks accessible from abroad?
   b) Requirements of domestic telecommunications law[6] for access to domestic network(s)
      aa) Contents of the requirements
         aaa) International regulations (including their transformation into domestic law)
         bbb) Domestic law unaffected by international law
      bb) Regulatory powers
         aaa) International organizations
         bbb) Bilateral coordination
         ccc) Domestic legislature
         ddd) Domestic administrative agencies
         eee) Operating companies
      cc) Judicial review or other legal recourse
   c) Terms of usage of the national networks
      aa) Contents of the terms
         aaa) Tariffs, accounting between networks
            (1) International framework (including transformation into domestic law)
            (2) Domestic law unaffected by international law
         bbb) Technical standards
            (1) International framework (including transformation into domestic law)
            (2) Domestic law unaffected by international law
         ccc) Liability (for errors, malfunction, etc.)
      bb) Power to regulate tariffs and technical standards
         aaa) International organizations
         bbb) Bilateral coordination
         ccc) Domestic legislature
         ddd) Domestic administrative agencies
         eee) Operating companies
      cc) Judicial review or other legal recourse

B. Legal regulation of the terminal and network equipment markets

I. Demand side (procurement)

1. Impact of the regulation of telephone services on the terminal and network equipment market
   a) Who procures the equipment?
      aa) To what extent does the domestic telecommunications law allow the network owners/operators and the users to purchase equipment according to their own choice?
      bb) Competitive situation of network owners/operators in purchasing network and terminal equipment
   b) Conditions of the procurement of equipment
      aa) Power to set the conditions
         aaa) International framework
         bbb) Domestic legislature and administrative agencies
         ccc) Operating companies
      bb) Contents of the conditions
         aaa) Technical standards and research/development of equipment
         bbb) Pricing, contractual terms
         ccc) Who maintains the equipment; under what conditions?
         ddd) Criteria for choice among several suppliers
2. Impact of further regulations (besides telecommunications law) on the terminal and network equipment markets
   a) Impact of the regulation of foreign trade on the domestic procurement of terminal and network equipment
      aa) General rules for foreign trade in goods
      bb) Particular rules for foreign trade in terminal and network equipment
   b) Impact of other regulations (e.g., antitrust law; general regulation of economic activities)

II. Supply side

1. Effect of demand-side situation on the access to the market of network and terminal equipment for suppliers
2. Impact of economic dependencies and other relations between demand and supply sides on the market for network and terminal equipment

1. This part calls for a survey of the regulations. Details should be given at parts II and III.
2. It should also be described to what extent the relevant institutions have actually exercised their regulatory powers.
3. The notion »public networks« means common carriers that offer their telephone services to all interested parties. The notion includes operators being owners of the networks as well as companies that offer telephone services by means of leased lines.
4. The »users« of public networks may be:
   - customers, who use telephone services for their own needs
   - lessees, who offer telephone services to third parties by means of leased lines
5. In the following parts, the international regulations and their transformation into domestic law should also be considered even if this may not be particularly mentioned in the outline.
6. General regulations other than telecommunications law should also be considered (e.g., antitrust law)
7. As far as private networks are operated by means of lines leased from common carriers, the conditions for access and usage, as stated at Part II.1.a) dd), should be referred to.
8. The different kinds of telephone networks have to be taken into account (see Part II.1.a)–c) above).
9. In this part, regulations regarding terminal equipment should only be dealt with, insofar as the admission of the equipment to the network is concerned. The impact of these regulations on the market for terminal equipment is to be treated in Part B of the outline.
10. The notion »international network« embraces all networks used for transborder telephone services except domestic networks.
11. »Requirements of access« means the criteria for determining which domestic carrier has access to foreign networks.
12. The conditions for access to and usage of networks used for transborder services can only be described comprehensively if the respective foreign telecommunications law is taken into account. This would go beyond the scope of a purely national report. However, information on bilateral relations should be added if available.

Part 2: Remote data processing (also: Videotex and remote sensing)

A. Legal regulation of transborder data processing

I. General legal rules that may be applicable to transborder data processing

1. Export of data
   a) General laws for the protection of national security and public safety (e.g., protection of secrets related to national security)
   b) Rules for the protection of domestic economic interests (e.g., regulations imposing tariffs on exports of data, disquettes, cassettes, hardware and software)
   c) General laws for the protection of private and individual interests
   d) Privacy protection

2) Import of data
   a) General laws for the protection of national security and public safety
   b) Rules for the protection of domestic economic interests (e.g., regulations imposing tariffs on the import of data, disquettes, cassettes, hard- and software)
   c) General laws for the protection of private and individual interests
   d) Privacy protection

II. Regulations relating to transborder data processing as a service

1. Import of data processing services
   a) Commercial data processing services (data processing services offered to third parties that are not members of closed-user-group networks)
      aa) Principles of international business transactions law of the reporting country for transborder business in services in general (especially import regulations)
      bb) Particular rules for data processing services

aaa) Data processing
bbb) Data storage and retrieval
b) Intra-company communication
aa) Data processing
bb) Data storage and retrieval
c) Closed-user-group networks
aa) Data processing
bb) Data storage and retrieval
2. Export of data processing services
a) Commercial data processing services (data processing services offered to third parties that are not members of closed-user-group networks)
aa) Principles of international business transactions law of the reporting country for transborder business in services in general (especially export regulations)
bb) Particular rules for data processing services
aaa) Data processing
bbb) Data storage and retrieval
b) Intra-company communication
aa) Data processing
bb) Data storage and retrieval
c) Closed-user-group networks
aa) Data processing
bb) Data storage and retrieval

III. Regulations applicable specifically to transborder data processing survey of international law

1. Basic legal principles of domestic telecommunications law for the transborder transmission of data[1]
a) Transformation of legal requirements set up by international law into domestic law and practice
aa) Survey of the relevant international law
aaa) Multilateral agreements (e.g., ITU, regional organizations)
bbb) Bilateral agreements
bb) Scope of the issues of telecommunications reserved for domestic regulation
cc) Domestic regulatory power to transform international requirements into domestic law and practice

aaa) Power to issue regulations affecting the domestic sphere and regulations issued[2]
(1) Legislature
(2) Administrative agencies
(3) Operating companies providing data transmission services

bbb) Power to issue regulations affecting the international or foreign sphere
(1) Legislature
(2) Administrative agencies
(3) Operating companies providing data transmission services

dd) Content of the international rules as transformed into domestic law (including application and construction of the rules)

b) Domestic law unaffected by international law
aa) Regulating Power
aaa) Legislature
bbb) Administrative agencies
ccc) Operating companies
bb) Survey of the contents of the domestic law (including application and construction)

2. Rules of domestic law regulating the relations between domestic operating companies providing international data transmission services and domestic users of those services
a) Use of data transmission services
aa) Public networks (common carriers)[3]
aaa) Who in fact operates public networks?
bbb) Legal requirements for installation and operation of public networks
(1) Content of requirements
(2) Jurisdiction (for making the regulations and granting licenses, etc.)
(3) Judicial review or other legal recourse against regulatory decisions
ccc) What services legally may be offered via the public network?
(1) Transmission services alone
(2) Enhanced services (i.e., transmission *and* data

processing services)

ddd) Requirements for access to and use of public networks[4,5]

(1) Jurisdiction to regulate access and use of networks – who actually regulates?

(2) Who has access to the networks?[6]

(2.1) Users (ultimate consumers) of data processing services

(2.2) Offerors of data processing services (who offer data processing services to other parties.

(2.3) Lessees of networks, who offer either transmission services alone or enhanced services

(2) Setting of tariffs

(1.1) Regulatory jurisdiction (or market pricing)

(2.3) Principles of setting tariffs

(3) Liability for errors in data processing

(4) Technical standards (especially for terminal equipment and its usage)

(4.1) Source of regulation: international or national; governmental or private

(4.2) Contents

(5) Judicial review or other legal recourse

bb) Private networks

aaa) Who operates private networks?

bbb) Legal requirements for installation and operation of private networks[6]

(1) Regulatory power[7]

(2) Judicial review or other legal recourse

(3) Contents of requirements[7]

ccc) Which services are offered through private networks?

(1) Data transmission for the network operator only

(2) Data transmission also for third parties

ddd) Are private network operators allowed to sublet the networks? If so, under which conditions is a sublease allowed?

cc) Networks operated by closed user groups[6]

aaa) Who operates closed-user-group networks (e.g., Swift, Sita)?

bbb) Legal requirements for installation and operation of closed-user-group networks[6]

(1) Contents of requirements[7]

(2) Regulatory power[7]

(3) Judicial review and other legal recourse

ccc) What services are offered?

(1) Data transmission for the network operating company only

(2) Data transmission also for third parties

ddd) Conditions for access to and usage of the networks

(1) Who can become a member of the »user group« and thus gain access to the network?

(2) Setting of tariffs

(2.1) Principles

(2.2) Who determines the tariffs?

(3) Liability for errors in data processing

(4) Technical standards

(5) Judicial review or other legal recourse

(6) Government supervision of private networks

b) Admission of terminal equipment[8,9]

aa) Who regulates the admission of terminal equipment to the network?

aaa) Public authorities

bbb) Operating companies

bb) What terminal equipment is part of the network according to domestic telecommunications law and is therefore subject to the respective regulatory powers?

cc) Criteria for admission (e.g., technical standards for compatibility; non-discriminatory competition for foreign suppliers of terminal equipment)

dd) Judicial review or other legal recourse

3. Rules regulating the relations between domestic and international or foreign network operators

a) Access to and modes of usage of international networks[10,11] by domestic carriers

aa) Requirements of domestic telecommunications law for access to international networks[12]

aaa) Contents of requirements
  (1) International preconditions (multilateral or bilateral agreements)
  (2) domestic telecommunications law
bbb) Regulatory powers
  (1) International organizations
  (2) Bilateral agreements
  (3) Domestic legislation
  (4) Domestic administrative agencies
  (5) Operating companies

bb) Requirements of domestic telecommunications law for the use of international networks (to what extent are these conditions influenced by domestic law?)[14]
  aaa) Contents of conditions
    (1) Tariffs, accounting
      (1.1) The international framework (bilateral and multilateral agreements and their transformation into domestic rules)
      (1.2) Domestic law unaffected by international law
    (2) Technical standards
      (2.1) International framework
      (2.2) Domestic Law
    (3) Liability for errors in data transmission
  bbb) Regulatory powers for setting tariffs and technical standards
    (1) International institutions
    (2) Bilateral agreements
    (3) Domestic legislation
    (4) Domestic administrative agencies
    (5) Operating companies
  ccc) Judicial review and other legal recourse

b) Access to and modes of usage of domestic networks by foreign network operators
  aa) How many domestic networks are accessible from abroad?
  bb) Requirements set by domestic telecommunications law[6] for access to domestic networks
    aaa) Contents of requirements
      (1) International framework

(2) Domestic law

bbb) Regulatory powers

(1) International organizations

(2) Bilateral agreements

(3) Domestic legislation

(4) Domestic administrative agencies

(5) Operating companies

ccc) Judicial review or other legal recourse

cc) Conditions for the use of domestic networks

aaa) Contents of conditions

(1) Tariffs, accounting between domestic and international networks

(1.1) International framework and transformation into domestic law

(1.2) Domestic law

(2) Technical standards

(2.1) International framework and transformation into domestic law

(2.2) Domestic law

(3) Liability for errors in data transmission

bbb) Regulatory powers over tariffs and technical standards

(1) International institutions

(2) Bilateral agreements

(3) Domestic legislation

(4) Domestic administrative agencies

(5) Operating companies

ccc) Judicial review or other legal recourse

B. Regulation of the markets for network and terminal equipment

I. Demand side

1. Impacts of the regulation of data transmission services on the markets for network and terminal equipment

a) Demand

aa) To what extent does the domestic telecommunications law allow the operating companies or the users to purchase network and terminal equipment according to their own choice?

bb) Competition among the network operators in purchasing network and terminal equipment

b) Conditions of procurement of network and terminal equipment

aa) Regulatory powers to set conditions

aaa) International framework

bbb) Domestic legislature and administrative agencies

ccc) Conditions set by operating companies themselves

bb) Contents of the conditions

aaa) Technical standards and development of equipment

bbb) Pricing, contractual conditions

ccc) Maintenance of equipment; conditions

ddd) Criteria for choice among several suppliers

2. Impact of other regulations (besides the rules for data transmission services) on the market for network and terminal equipment

a) Effects of the rules regulating international business transactions upon the market for network and terminal equipment

aa) General provisions for the trade in goods

bb) Particular rules for network and terminal equipment within the law relating to international business transactions

b) Impact of other regulations, e.g., antitrust law, especially regulations against misuse of demand power; general regulation of economic activities

II. Supply side

1. Effect of the demand-side situation on access to the market for network and terminal equipment

2. Impacts of economic dependencies and other relations between the supply and demand sides on competition in the market for network and terminal equipment

1. This part of the outline calls for a survey of the regulations. Details should be given at parts III 2 and 3.
2. The constitutional framework of the legislative activities as well as the content of the provisions should be explained.
3. »Public networks« means common carriers, which offer their data transmission services to any interested parties. »Operating companies« includes the owners of the networks and also companies that use leased lines to offer data transmission services.
4. »Users« of public networks may be:
   - customers, who use the data transmission services for the remote processing for their own needs
   - lessees, who use leased lines to offer third parties remote data processing capacities.
5. Also the international regulations and their transformation into domestic law are to be considered, even if this may not be particularly mentioned in the outline.
6. Also legal rules other than telecommunications law should be taken into account here (e.g., antitrust law)
7. If the private networks are operated with lines leased from common carriers, the conditions for access and usage of the networks are to be treated, as stated at part III 2a, aa, ddd, dd above.
8. At this point, the different kinds of data transmission methods have to be taken into account (see part III 2a above)
9. Regulations relating to terminal equipment should be dealt with here only insofar as the admission of the equipment to the network is concerned. The impact of these regulations on the market for terminal equipment is to be treated in part B of the outline
10. Account should be taken of whether the regulation of access to international networks distinguishes
    a) between different kinds of data to be transmitted or different kinds of data transmission services
    b) between »pure« data transmission services and enhanced services.
11. If special rules exist for the transit of data on the way to third countries, they should be mentioned separately.
12. The notion of »international networks« encompasses all networks that are used for transborder data transmissions, except domestic networks.
13. »Requirements of access« means the criteria for determining which

domestic carrier has access to foreign networks.

14. The conditions under which networks for transborder data transmissions may be accessed and used can only be covered comprehensively if the respective foreign telecommunications law is taken into account. Although this goes beyond the scope of a national report, information on bilateral relations should be added if available.

Part 3: Audiovisual media programmes

A. Regulation of the flow of media programmes from abroad to the reporting state (RS)
(Admission of programmes to the domestic territory; principles and conditions of access)

I. Legal relations between foreign states and programme and transmitting companies on the one hand and the reporting state on the other

1. The international framework and its transformation into national law
(Extent of international obligations of RS to give access to its territory for foreign programmes)

a) Multilateral agreements and international organizations subscribed to by RS

aa) ITU convention and rules arising from it

aaa) Relation of RS to ITU

bbb) Audiovisual broadcast programmes

(1) Jamming

(2) Prohibition of reception

(3) Technical standards and import regulations for receiver equipment

(4) Different treatment according to origin and/or domicile of foreign programme/transmitting company

ccc) Direct-Broadcast Satellites (DBS)

(1) Jamming

(2) Prohibition of reception

(3) Technical standards and import regulations for receiver equipment

(4) Different treatment according to origin and/or domicile of foreign programme/ transmitter company

(5) Different treatment of intended/unintended overspill

ddd) Cable TV (CATV)

(1) Ability of foreign cable operators to link their

systems with domestic cable networks
(1.1) General conditions of access
(1.2) Setting of tariffs
(1.3) Technical standards
(1.4) Programme standards
(2) Access to networks for foreign programmes
(1.1) General conditions of access
(1.2) Setting of tariffs
(1.3) Technical standards
(1.4) Programme standards

bb) Transformation of ITU rules into national law (for broadcast, DBS and CATV programmes)
aaa) Power to transform ITU rules into national law
bbb) Form and extent of transformation
ccc) Jurisdiction for application of transformed rules to foreign programmes of companies
ddd) Practice of application
eee) Judicial review or other legal recourse against regulatory decisions

cc) Human Rights Conventions and rules arising from them
aaa) Extent of adoption by RS
bbb) Audiovisual broadcast programmes
(1) Jamming
(2) Prohibition of reception
(3) Technical standards and import regulations for receiver equipment
(4) Preferential treatment of states of programme companies
ccc) Direct-Broadcast Satellites
– subdivided as above bbb)
ddd) Cable television
– subdivided as above bbb)

dd) Transformation of Human Rights Convention into national law (for broadcast, DBS and CATV)
aaa) Power for transformation of Human Rights Conventions into international law
bbb) Form and extent of transformation
ccc) Jurisdiction for application of transformed

rules to foreign programmes of companies

ddd) Practice of application

eee) Judical review or other legal recourse against regulatory decisions

ee) Other multilateral agreements subscribed to by RS

aaa) Audiovisual broadcast programmes

bbb) Direct-Broadcast Satellites

ccc) Cable Television (CATV)

ff) Transformation of other multilateral agreements into national law (broadcast, DBS and CATV) – subdivided as above dd) –

b) Bilateral agreements

aaa) Scope left for bilateral agreements under ITU rules

(1) Audiovisual broadcast programmes

(2) Direct-Broadcast Satellites

(3) Cable television (CATV)

bbb) Noteworthy bilateral agreements to which RS subscribes

ccc) Special rules provided by bilateral agreements to which RS subscribes

(1) Audiovisual broadcast programmes

(1.1) Jamming

(1.2) Technical standards and import regulations for receiver equipment

(1.3) Preferential treatment for certain states/programme companies

(1.4) Bilateral monopolies

(2) Direct-Broadcast Satellites
– subdivided as above (1)

(3) Cable television
– subdivided as above (1)

c) Summary: Scope of action left to reporting state under international law or international law as transformed into national law for regulation of access of audiovisual broadcast programmes to its territory.

2. National law independent of international framework (Regulations generally governing the emission of audiovisual broadcast, satellite and cable programmes)

a) Structure of the domestic media and their regulation

aa) Constitutional bases of the national media organization
  - aaa) Newspapers, magazines and other print media
  - bbb) Audiovisual broadcast programmes
  - ccc) Direct-Broadcast Satellites
  - ddd) Cable television

bb) Power to regulate, legal technique or regulation
  – subdivided as above aa)

cc) Essentials of the national media regulation
  – subdivided as above aa)

b) General laws applicable to media programmes (classified according to legal spheres or objects of legal protection, e.g.:
- General laws
- Penal laws
- Law against obscenity
- Law of advertising
- Antitrust law
- Other telecommunications laws)

c) Specific applicability of national law, actually or potentially, to incoming foreign programmes
  - aa) Audiovisual broadcast programmes
  - bb) Direct-Broadcast Satellites
  - cc) Cable television

II. Legal relations between reporting state and receivers (Regulations governing the *reception* of broadcast/cable transmitted programmes and legal recourse of receivers to enforce rights of reception)

1. The international framework and its transformation into national law

a) Multilateral agreements

aa) ITU convention and rules arising from it

aaa) Audiovisual broadcast programmes
  - (1) Prohibition of reception
  - (2) Technical standards and import/operating regulations for receiver equipment
  - (3) Tariffs for reception

bbb) Direct-Broadcast Satellites
  – subdivided as above aaa)

ccc) Cable television
 (1) Principles of access to networks
 (2) Technical standards and import/operating regulations for receiver equipment
 (3) Tariffs for access

bb) Human rights convention and rules arising from them
 aaa) Audiovisual broadcast programmes
 (1) Prohibition of reception
 (2) Technical standards and import regulations for receiver equipment
 (3) Tariffs for reception
 bbb) Direct-Broadcast Satellites
 – subdivided as above aaa)
 ccc) Cable television
 – subdivided as above aaa)

b) Bilateral agreements
 aa) Frame for bilateral agreements under multilateral rules
 aaa) Audiovisual broadcast programmes
 bbb) Direct-Broadcast Satellites
 ccc) Cable television
 bb) Rules provided by bilateral programmes
 aaa) Audiovisual broadcast programmes
 (1) Technical standards and import regulations for receiver equipment
 (2) Tariffs
 bbb) Direct-Broadcast Satellites
 – subdivided as above aaa)
 ccc) Cable television
 – subdivided as above aaa)

c) Transformation of international agreements on receiver's rights into national law (for broadcast, DBS and CATV programmes)
 aa) Power for transformation of rules into national law
 bb) Form and content of transformation
 cc) Jurisdiction for application of transformed rules
 dd) Practice of application
 ee) Judicial review or other legal recourse against regulatory decisions

d) Summary: Scope of action left to reporting state under international law for regulation of relations between state and receivers of broadcast/cable-transmitted programmes from abroad

2. National law independent of international framework (Regulations governing the *reception* of broadcast/cable transmitted programmes for reasons of public interest)
   a) Constitutional framework of audivisual media reception (Civil rights of receivers and their judicial review)
      aa) Audiovisual broadcast programmes
      bb) Direct-Broadcast Satellites
      cc) Cable television
   b) Power to regulate, legal technique of regulation
      – subdivided as above a)
   c) Content of regulations (Audiovisual broadcast, DBS and CATV)
      aa) Prohibition of reception/principles of access to networks
      bb) Technical standards, manufacturing and operating interdictions for receiver equipment
      cc) Reception tariffs

III. Legal relations between media companies and individuals, including personal claims against companies (Audiovisual broadcast, DBS and CATV)

1. International agreements and their transformation into national law
   a) Protection of privacy law; protection of honour; right to have a counter-statement published
   b) Copyright law
   c) Illicit advertising (individual claims)

2. Conflict law of the reporting state
   – subdivided as above 1.

3. National rules providing individual claims against programme companies and thus potential barriers to free transborder flow of media programmes
   – subdivided as above 1.

B. Establishment and activities of foreign programme companies/programme transmitting companies *on the territory of the RS*

I. International framework

1. Establishment and operation of transmitter stations and cable networks
   a) Audiovisual broadcast programmes
   b) Direct-Broadcast Satellites (including participation in national satellite operating companies, operations of national satellite systems)
   c) Cable television (establishment and operation of cable networks)

2. Establishment and activities of programme companies
   a) Multilateral agreements (e.g., EEC-treaty)
      aaa) Audiovisual broadcast programmes
      bbb) Direct-Broadcast Satellites
      ccc) Cable television
   b) Bilateral agreements (e.g., AFN, RFE)
      – subdivided as above a)

II. National framework
– subdivided as above I.

C. Regulation of the flow of media programmes transmitted from reporting state to other countries (legal relations between RS and programme companies transmitting to other countries)

I. International framework and its transformation into national law

1. ITU convention and rules arising from it
   a) Audiovisual broadcast programmes
      (rights of RS to transmit abroad)
   b) Direct-Broadcast Satellites
      (Orbital positions of RS)
   c) Cable television
      Access of domestic programmes to foreign cable systems)

2. Other multilateral agreements
   – subdivided as above 1.

3. Bilateral agreements
   – subdivided as above 1.

II. National law independent of international framework

1. Regulations governing the establishment and operation of transmitting facilities
   a) Constitutional framework
      aa) Audiovisual broadcast programmes
      bb) Direct-Broadcast Satellites
      cc) Cable networks
   b) Power to regulate, legal technique of regulation
      – subdivided as above a)
   c) Content of regulations
      aa) Principles of authorization
         aaa) Audiovisual broadcast programmes
         bbb) Direct-Broadcast Satellites
         ccc) Cable television
      bb) Rules governing the content of programmes
         – subdivided as above aa)
      cc) Other conditions of authorization, including tariffs
         – subdivided as above aa)

2. Regulations governing the production of programmes for abroad
   – subdivided as above 1.